BLUE GUIDE

D0808967

EMILIA ROMAGNA

ALTA MACADAM

WITH ANNABEL BARBER AND ELLEN GRADY

EMILIA ROMAGNA
Updated chapter from *Blue Guide Northern Italy*
2nd edition 2017

Published by Blue Guides Limited, a Somerset Books Company
Winchester House, Deane Gate Avenue, Taunton, Somerset TA1 2UH
www.blueguides.com
'Blue Guide' is a registered trademark.

ISBN 978-1-905131-80-8

The first ever Blue Guide, *London and its Environs*, was published in 1918
by two Scottish brothers, James and Findlay Muirhead. The first edition of
Blue Guide Northern Italy was compiled by them and L.V. Bertarelli in 1924.
Subsequent editions were revised by the Muirhead brothers (1927, 1937);
Stuart Rossiter (1971); Alta Macadam (1978, 1984, 1991, 1998) and Paul Blanchard
(2001, 2005). The chapter on Emilia Romagna was updated by Alta Macadam in
2014 and Alta Macadam with Annabel Barber and Ellen Grady in 2017.

Series editor: Annabel Barber
Town plans © Blue Guides
Site plans: Imre Bába © Blue Guides
Maps: Dimap Bt. © Blue Guides
Prepared for press by Anikó Kuzmich.

Cover image: Detail of the dome mosaic in the Arian Baptistery, Ravenna.
Photo by James Howells © Blue Guides.

www.blueguides.com
'Blue Guide' is a registered trademark.
We welcome reader comments, questions and feedback:
editorial@blueguides.com.

About the author

ALTA MACADAM is the author of over 40 Blue Guides to Italy. She lives in the hills above Florence with her husband, the painter Francesco Colacicchi. She has worked for the Photo Library of Alinari and for Harvard University's Villa I Tatti. She is at present external consultant for New York University at the photo archive of Villa La Pietra in Florence, and is author of the Blue Guides to Florence, Rome, Tuscany, Venice, Central Italy, Umbria and Lazio (the last two being e-chapters from *Central Italy*), as well as two further chapters on North Italian regions, the Veneto and Friuli-Venezia Giulia. She travels extensively every year to revise new editions of the books.

Contributors

ELLEN GRADY is the author of *Blue Guide Sicily* and *Blue Guide the Marche and San Marino*, from which the section on the towns of the Montefeltro is extracted. In 2009 seven towns (Pennabilli, San Leo, Talamello, Novefeltria, Sant'Agata Feltria, Maiolo and Casteldelci) voted by plebiscite to secede from the Marche and to join Emilia Romagna. ANNABEL BARBER is series editor of the Blue Guides and co-author of *Blue Guide Rome*. For this volume she updated the sections on Bologna, Ravenna and Comacchio.

CONTENTS

Bologna

Bologna (*map B, C2*), the capital of Emilia, is one of the oldest cities in Italy, large and bustling, with a population of around 400,000. It has a somewhat faded, scruffy air in many parts but is well stocked with excellent museums of art and architecture as well as numerous important churches, and the great Bolognese school of painting is extremely well represented. Its university has been famous since the 12th century and today the town is full of students, who give it a particularly lively atmosphere. Numerous cafés and restaurants of all types and categories abound, the best of them always crowded. On Sundays, when the entire centre is closed to traffic, the town is at its best. Its streets are memorable for their brick buildings, often with terracotta decorations and windows shaded by red Roman blinds, but above all for their porticoes, which line a great number of streets on both sides. Because of these, pedestrians are well protected both from the rain and from the traffic, which makes Bologna an easy place to get around on foot.

HISTORY OF BOLOGNA

Felsina, an important Etruscan city on the site of Bologna, was overrun by the Gauls in the 4th century BC. They named their settlement Bononia, and the name was retained by the Romans when they conquered the plain of the Po in 225–191 BC. After the fall of the Western Empire, Bologna became subject to the exarchs of Ravenna and later formed part of the Lombard and Frankish dominions. It was recognised as an independent commune by Emperor Henry V in 1116; its university first became prominent at about this time. One of the foremost cities of the Lombard League (1167), Bologna reached the height of its power after the peace of Constance (1183) and sided with the Guelphs. Taddeo Pepoli founded a lordship here c. 1337, which was held in turn by the Visconti, the Pepoli and the Bentivoglio, under the last of whom (Giovanni II Bentivoglio; 1463–1506) Bologna enjoyed its greatest period of fame and prosperity. Pope Julius II reconquered the city in 1506, and for three centuries Bologna was incorporated into the Papal States, except for a brief interval (1796–1814) when it was part of Napoleon's Cisalpine Republic. In 1814 Bologna was occupied by the British, in support of the Austrians against Napoleon. Unsuccessful insurrections broke out in 1831 and 1848, and the town was held by an Austrian garrison from 1849 until the formation of the Kingdom of Italy in 1860. For months Bologna was the focal point of German resistance in the Second World War, but its artistic treasures escaped serious damage.

BOLOGNESE ART AND ARCHITECTURE

The predominant material in the architecture of Bologna has always been brick, for both structural and decorative purposes, and the late-Gothic buildings of the 14th century show the height attained by local skill in brick designing. Sculptors from Tuscany who left important works in the city include Nicola Pisano, Jacopo della Quercia and Giambologna. Art in the early 14th century was dominated by the expressive love of ornament of Giovanni da Modena. The wealthy court of the Bentivoglio attracted Lorenzo Costa from Ferrara (c. 1490). Francesco Francia, a goldsmith by training, formed a partnership with Costa and can be said to have founded the Bolognese school of painting. One of its greatest pupils was Amico Aspertini (*see p. 19*). At the end of the 16th century the Bolognese school entered an important revival period with the Carracci and Bartolomeo Passarotti, master of the genre scene, who probably trained under Annibale Carracci. The Flemish-born artist Denys Calvaert was also active in Bologna at this time (he died in the city in 1619). Though not a great painter in his own right, his influence was important: Francesco Albani and Guido Reni both trained in his academy (Albani also studied under Lodovico Carracci). Another artist to feel the Carracci's influence was Guercino (1591–1666), who dominated Bolognese painting for a quarter of a century with his exuberant brushwork and dramatic colour and light effects.

PIAZZA MAGGIORE

In the heart of the city the spacious Piazza Maggiore (*map Bologna West, 11*), known simply as *la piazza* to the Bolognese, is surrounded by public buildings and has always been the town's political centre. It has a slightly raised pavement in the centre with lovely large paving stones and numerous public events are held here.

Opposite the huge church of San Petronio (*described on p. 15*) is **Palazzo del Podestà**, begun at the beginning of the 13th century but remodelled in 1484. At the centre of the building is the tall tower (Arengo) of 1212: a cruciform passageway runs beneath it, and in the spandrels of the vault are very worn statues of the patron saints of the city by Alfonso Lombardi (1525). There are cafés beneath the tall arcades.

To the right as you face Palazzo del Podestà is the handsome long façade of **Palazzo dei Banchi** (1412, remodelled by Vignola in 1565–8), once occupied by moneylenders. At street level are the Portico del Pavaglione and two tall arches that give access to side streets. You can see the dome of Santa Maria della Vita and the top of the Torre degli Asinelli above the roof of the palace.

The fourth side of the piazza is closed by the long façade of the huge **Palazzo Comunale** (*map Bologna West, 10*), which incorporates **Palazzo d'Accursio** and also fronts Piazza Nettuno with its fountain. It is made up of several buildings of different dates, modified and restored over the centuries. Taddeo Pepoli began to

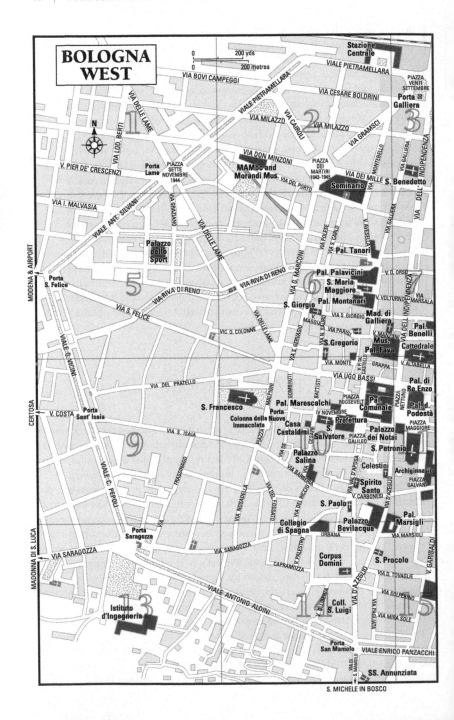

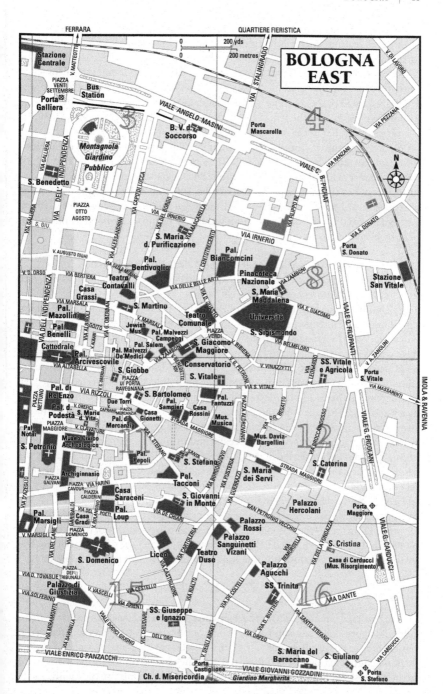

QUARTIERE FIERISTICA

200 yds
200 metres

BOLOGNA EAST

Stazione Centrale

PIAZZA VENTI SETTEMBRE

Porta Galliera

Bus Station

VIALE ANGELO MASINI

Porta Mascarella

VIA MATTEOTTI

VIA STALINGRADO

VIA DI LAVORO

VIA PEZZANA

B. V. d. Soccorso

Montagnola Giardino Pubblico

VIALE C. B. PICHAT

N

VIA FILIPPO RE

S. Benedetto

VIA CAPODILUCCA

VIA DEL BORGO

VIA S. DONATO

Porta S. Donato

PIAZZA OTTO AGOSTO

VIA DELL'INDIPENDENZA

VIA GALLIERA

VIA S. GIU

VIA IRNERIO

S. Maria d. Purificazione

Pal. Biancomcini

Pinacoteca Nazionale

Stazione San Vitale

V. AUGUSTO RIGHI

Pal. Bentivoglio

VIA DELLE MOLINE

VIA CENTOTRECENTO

S. Maria Maddalena

VIA ZAMBONI

Teatro Contavalli

VIA DELLE BELLE ARTI

Universitá

VIA S. GIACOMO

VIA Q. FILOPANTI

Stazione San Vitale

V. D. ORSO

VIA BERTIERA

Casa Grassi

Pal. Mazzollini

S. Martino

S. Sigismondo

Pal. Benelli

Jewish Mus.

Teatro Comunale

Pal. Malvezzi Campeggi

PIAZZA VERDI

VIA BELMELORO

Cattedrale

Pal. Salem

S. Giacomo Maggiore

SS. Vitale e Agricola

Porta S. Vitale

Pal. Arcivescovile

Pal. Malvezzi De'Medici

S. Giobbe

Conservatorio

VIA S. VITALE

VIA MASSARENTI

VIA ALTABELLA

PIAZZA DI PORTA RAVEGNANA

S. Vitale

IMOLA & RAVENNA

Pal. di Re Enzo

VIA RIZZOLI

Due Torri

S. Bartolomeo

Pal. Sampieri

Pal. Fantuzzi

VIA BROCCAINDOSSO

VIALE G. ERCOLANI

Pal. d. Podestá

S. Maria d. Vita

Casa Rossini

Casa Gionetti

Mus. Musica

Pal. Notai

PIAZZA MAGGIORE

Pal. di Mercanzia

STRADA MAGGIORE

Mus. Davia-Bargellini

S. Caterina

Museo Civico Archeologico

S. Petronio

Pal. Pepoli

S. Santa

S. Stefano

S. Maria dei Servi

STRADA MAGGIORE

Archiginnasio

PIAZZA GALVANI

PIAZZA CAVOUR

VIA FARINI

Pal. Tacconi

S. Giovanni in Monte

Palazzo Hercolani

Porta Maggiore

VIALE G. CARDUCCI

Casa Saraceni

Pal. Loup

Teatro Duse

Palazzo Rossi

S. Cristina

Pal. Marsigli

Casa Gradi

PIAZZA DOMENICO

VIA DE CHIARI

Palazzo Sanguinetti Vizani

Casa di Carducci (Mus. Risorgimento)

V. MARSIGLI

S. Domenico

Liceo

Palazzo Agucchi

SS. Trinita

MA DANTE

Palazzo di Giustizia

V. VASCELLI

SS. Giuseppe e Ignazio

VIA D. BUTTIERI

S. Maria del Baraccano

S. Giuliano

VIALE ENRICO PANZACCHI

Porta Castiglione

Ch. d. Misericordia

VIALE GIOVANNI GOZZADINI

Giardino Margherita

Porta S. Stefano

VIA CARDUCCI

unite various palaces on this site as a Town Hall in 1336, and in 1425–8 the military engineer Fieravante Fieravanti rebuilt part of the palace and the whole edifice was fortified in the 16th century and used by the papal legates as their residence (the battlemented rear façade is particularly impressive). The monumental entrance to the courtyard is by Galeazzo Alessi (c. 1555): it is surmounted by a bronze statue of Pope Gregory XIII, the reformer of the calendar, who was born Ugo Buoncompagni in Bologna in 1502. To the left of the pope, slightly higher between two windows, is a terracotta relief of the *Madonna and Child* by Niccolò dell'Arca, with the date (1478) and signature ('Nicolaus'). The original building, at the left end, with its clock tower, was acquired by the *comune* in 1287 from Francesco d'Accursio on his return from the court of King Edward I of England. The loggia was used as a public granary. At the corner of the *piazza* here is the smaller **Palazzo dei Notai**, the old College of Notaries, which is the best-preserved medieval building in the square, with its battlements and Gothic two-light windows. It was begun in 1381 and completed in 1422 by Bartolomeo Fieravanti.

COLLEZIONI COMUNALI D'ARTE (PALAZZO D'ACCURSIO)

Entrance under the statue of Pope Gregory XIII from the courtyard. Open Tues–Sun 8–6.30. Handlists are lent to visitors in each room.

The grand staircase, a ramp ascribed to Bramante, leads up to the first floor, where the Chamber of Hercules contains a colossal terracotta statue by Alfonso Lombardi and a *Madonna* by Francesco Francia (1505). On the second floor the Sala Farnese has a good view of the piazza. Here is the entrance to the large collection of paintings and furniture (of relative interest): the rooms were used by the cardinal legates of the city from 1506 up to the 19th century. The long gallery was decorated in the 17th century by the papal legate Pietro Vidoni. One wing is arranged chronologically as a Pinacoteca (Rooms 5–9) and includes works by Vitale da Bologna, Simone de' Crocifissi, Francesco Francia (*Crucifixion*), Amico Aspertini (*Madonna and Child*), Lodovico Carracci, Giuseppe Maria Crespi, and 18th-century miniatures. The 18th- and early 19th-century period décor of the Sale Rusconi (Rooms 11–16) is largely the product of the paintings and furniture left to the museum by the Rusconi family. The end room (Room 16) is the prettiest, entirely painted to imitate a garden arbour with a statue of *Apollino* by Canova in the centre (1797). Another group of rooms (17–20) exhibit lace, drawings, a very fine painting of *Ruth* by one of Italy's best 19th-century painters, Francesco Hayez (Room 18), and an unfinished painting of the Isom family by Pelagio Palagi (Room 19). The large chapel has fragmentary frescoes of 1562 by Prospero Fontana, and the adjoining room detached frescoes by Bartolomeo Cesi.

PIAZZA NETTUNO

The piazza takes its name from the **Neptune Fountain** (1566), decorated with a splendid figure of Neptune and other bronze sculptures by Giambologna (his name has nothing to do with Bologna: born in Douai, then in Flanders, he was called Jean de Boulogne but his name was italianised when he came to work in Italy). He was one of the greatest Mannerist sculptors and served as court sculptor to the Medici for 40 years. This is the most important work by him outside Florence. The exquisite small bronze model that he made for the statue is preserved in the Museo Medioevale.

The wing of Palazzo Comunale here, known as the **Sala Borsa**, has some coats of arms and an unusual war memorial consisting of photographs of people from Bologna who died during the Resistance movement from 8th September 1943 (when Italy signed the Armistice) to 25th April 1945 (the country's final liberation by the Allies). This part of the building has been excellently restored as a public library. Inside, in the basement, you can see remains of the Roman city (*follow signs to the Scavi Archeologici; free admission*).

Opposite is the battlemented **Palazzo di Re Enzo**, built in 1246, which was the prison of Enzo (1225–72), King of Sardinia and illegitimate son of Emperor Frederick II, from his capture at Fossalta in 1249 until his death in 1272.

SAN PETRONIO

Map Bologna East, 11. Usually open all day until 6pm or later. For up-to-date opening times, see basilicadisanpetronio.org. The panoramic terrace (entrance on Piazza Galvani; entry fee) closes for a couple of hours around lunchtime. Some of the side chapels have coin-operated lights.

Medieval houses and churches were demolished so that the immense church of San Petronio could be erected here, in Bologna's principal piazza and political centre, as a symbol of civic pride and independence. Although it never became Bologna's cathedral (the cathedral is on Via dell'Indipendenza; *described on p. 44*), San Petronio has always been the city's most important religious building. Significantly enough, even the orientation, north to south, disregards the normal Christian practice of having the altar at the East end.

It is one of the most remarkable brick buildings in existence: it was begun in 1390 under the direction of a certain Antonio di Vincenzo, a local builder-architect who was apparently also responsible for the basically simple design of a long nave with uniform side chapels and no transepts (he is only known for this work and just a few other buildings in Bologna). He oversaw the construction until his death in 1401. In around 1500 the little-known architect called Arduino Arriguzzi proposed that the design be altered to a Latin-cross plan and enlarged to about twice its present size, but as construction continued this proved unrealistic. Work lasted right up until the mid-17th century, when finally the magnificent nave vault was completed.

The church is dedicated to the otherwise obscure Petronius, who became a saint after he had served as bishop of Bologna in 431–50 and was buried in Santo Stefano (*map Bologna East, 11*). Very little is known with certainty about him and many legends are associated with his name: it is thought he travelled to the Holy Land. But for all that he has always been Bologna's much-loved patron saint and there are numerous paintings and sculptures of him all over the town.

EXTERIOR OF SAN PETRONIO

Only the lower part of the huge brick front (restored in 2013) was ever covered: the beautiful pink-and-white marble decoration between the three doorways was begun in 1538. The **central doorway** has magnificent sculptures by the famous Sienese sculptor Jacopo della Quercia. Begun in 1425 it is considered amongst his masterpieces although it was left unfinished at his death in 1438. The carving has echoes of Gothic, Classical and Renaissance art. The ten large bas-reliefs in Istrian stone illustrate the story of Genesis, and smaller inner pilasters are decorated with half-figures of prophets. The architrave has five reliefs of the childhood of Christ. In the lunette is a beautiful statue of the *Madonna and Child* also by Jacopo, and he also sculpted the standing figure of *St Petronius* (holding a model of the church) beside her, but the *St Ambrose* on the other side was added later in 1510 (when the arch above was also carved). Jacopo produced beautiful works also in Tuscany (especially in Siena and in Lucca), but he had few followers, although he clearly influenced the young Michelangelo.

The two flanking portals date from 1518–30, with bas-reliefs on the pilasters by Amico Aspertini, the Florentine sculptor Nicolò Tribolo, Alfonso Lombardi and others. The lunette in the one to the left of the *Risen Christ* with soldiers is also by Lombardi, whereas the dramatic scene of the *Deposition* (with Joseph of Arimathea) in the lunette on the right is the work of Amico Aspertini, flanked by the figures of the Madonna and St John the Evangelist.

On the base of the pillars are quadrilobes with reliefs of saints carved around 1393 by Paolo di Bonaiuto and others, and the basement of the building is also beautifully designed (by its first architect Antonio di Vincenzo).

The magnificent Gothic side walls of the church in white marble and red brick with traceried windows also survive from the time of Antonio di Vincenzo.

The **terrace** at the top of the façade can sometimes be visited (*11–1 & 4–6.30*), from where there is a magnificent view.

INTERIOR OF SAN PETRONIO

The great pink and white **nave**, 41m high, is lit by round windows and is separated from the aisles by ten massive compound piers. Because it faces north the church is unusually light. The splendid Gothic **vaulting** dates from 1648; it is a masterpiece by Girolamo Rainaldi, who adapted the 16th-century designs of the local architect Francesco Morandi (known for some reason as 'Terribilia'). The huge wooden **pulpit** on the left-hand side, of very eccentric design (there are others like it in Bologna), was built in the 15th century when there was presumably a ladder up to the inconspicuous little door. Against a pier also on the left is a fine late 14th-century **processional statue of St Petronius** in gilded wood with a model of the church at his feet.

The uniform side chapels are all closed by beautiful screens, many of them in marble dating from the late 15th century, others in wrought ironwork. The four 11th–12th-century **crosses** placed outside four of them were set up by St Petronius, it is said, to mark the limits of the late medieval city, and they were moved here in 1798. Important works of art are preserved in all 22 chapels.

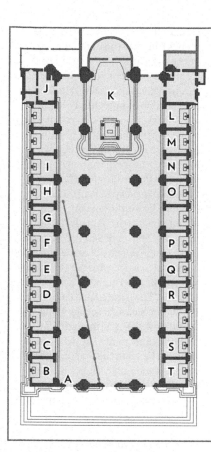

SAN PETRONIO

A *Adam and Eve*
B Frescoes by Giovanni da Modena
C Chapel of St Petronius
D Bolognini Chapel (frescoes by
   Giovanni da Modena
E Works by Francesco Francia and
   Lorenzo Costa
F Altarpiece by Scarsellino
G Altarpiece by Lorenzo Costa;
   tomb of Elisa Bonaparte
H Altarpiece by Parmagianino
I Altarpiece by Denys Calvaert
J Museum
K Sanctuary
L Chapel of the Relics
M 15th-century marble screen
N Frescoes by Girolamo da Treviso
O 16th-century inlaid stalls
P Lorenzo Costa: *St Jerome*
Q Amico Aspertini: Pietà
R 15th-century stained glass
S Polyptych by Garelli
T Madonna della Pace

(A) Above the right door on the inside façade are *Adam and Eve*, attributed to the Ferrarese sculptor Alfonso Lombardi.

(B) Chapel of St Abbondio: The (framed) allegorical frescoes, by Giovanni da Modena, are extremely unusual for their iconography. They represent theological issues of redemption and sacrifice and the triumph of the Church over the Synagogue (where the arms of Christ's Cross have human hands).

(C) Chapel of St Petronius: The chapel (reserved for prayer) is a Baroque work by Alfonso Torreggiani (c. 1742). Above the altar, borne by cherubs, is the reliquary casket of the patron saint, whose head was brought here by order of Pope Benedict XIV, a native of Bologna.

(D) Cappella Bolognini/Chapel of the Magi (*open daily 9.15–1 & 3–6; entrance fee*): The chapel has a huge frescoed *St Christopher* on the left-hand entrance pier and is preceded by a lovely red marble balustrade. It was one of the first chapels to be built in the church. The remarkable frescoes on all three walls, dating from 1408–20 (they were restored in 2013 a year after the earthquake) are the best-known works by Giovanni da Modena and one of the most important late Gothic fresco cycles in Emilia Romagna. It is for his works in San Petronio that this obscure painter Giovanni (born in Modena) is best remembered. Nothing known to be by him survives anywhere outside Bologna (where there is also a Crucifix by him in the Pinacoteca). The frescoes were commissioned by the wealthy silk merchant Bartolomeo Bolognini, whose tomb is in the middle of the pavement. The chapel is dedicated to the Three Kings and on the right wall are eight very interesting scenes, unusual for their iconography, showing the kings preparing for their trip to Bethlehem and on their journey accompanied by camels and horsemen, stopping at various towns where the inhabitants are shown indicating the way ahead. The appearance of the great star to encourage them, as well as their arrival at the stable itself, are all illustrated. The last scene shows them returning home, this time by sea, with the entire entourage tucked into a variety of splendid boats while long-beaked ducks observe them from the shore. On the opposite wall is a huge scene of the *Last Judgement* based on Dante's vision, with a monstrous black devil eating the damned and 'digesting' them. Sinners hang by their feet and are caught in trees and all around chaos reigns. Above, the scene changes totally with the well-behaved 'saved' sitting patiently in pews in serried ranks below Christ crowning the Madonna, surrounded by the blessed and angels.

On the altar wall Giovanni frescoed scenes from the (invented) life of St Petronius, showing him setting out from Constantinople and, having received his bishop's hat, performing a succession of miracles. The stained glass dating from the same period is by Jacopo di Paolo, the very skilled Bolognese artist who we know was at work in the town from 1378–1426: it depicts the Twelve Apostles (with Judas replaced by St Paul). The magnificent Gothic altarpiece by an unknown artist named after this work the 'Master of San Petronio' is a polychrome polyptych carved in gilded and painted wood with the *Coronation of the Virgin* and numerous statuettes of saints. The painted predella, also by Jacopo, has eight scenes which again show the Magi on their way to Bethlehem; their visit to Herod; kneeling beneath the Star; and their arrival at the stable where the Holy Family greet them in a particularly homely scene. Outside the chapel is an 18th-century clock.

(E) Chapel of St Sebastian: This chapel preserves its decorations intact from 1487–97. The lovely huge altarpiece of the *Martyrdom of St Sebastian* is by an unknown artist. It is flanked by an *Annunciatory Angel* by Francesco Francia and a *Virgin Annunciate* by Lorenzo Costa, who also painted the *Twelve Apostles* around the walls. The stalls and pavement in enamelled tiles (a rare survival) are by Pietro Andrea da Faenza.

(F) Chapel of St Vincent Ferrer: The sixth north chapel has a *Madonna in Glory* by Scarsellino (c. 1600), who worked with the Carracci.

(G) Chapel of St James: The seventh chapel has a particularly fine marble screen attributed to Pagno di Lapo, and a lovely altarpiece of the *Madonna and Child with Saints* signed by Lorenzo Costa (1492), one of his most important works. The Neoclassical funerary monument of Elisa Bonaparte, Napoleon I's sister who became granduchess of Tuscany, and her husband Felice Baciocchi, is by Cincinnato Baruzzi (1845; with two charming putti and a bust by the much better-known Tuscan sculptor Lorenzo Bartolini). Their three children (who predeceased them) had already been buried here in 1813.

(H) Chapel of St Roch and meridian line: The eighth north chapel has a Mannerist painting of *St Roch* by **Parmigianino.** In front of the marble and terracotta monument to Bishop Cesare Nacci, by Vincenzo Onofri (1479), begins the **meridian line**, nearly 67m long, traced in 1655 by the astronomer Gian Domenico Cassini. It has since been several times adjusted; a hole in the roof admits the sun's ray.

(I) Chapel of St Michael: The altarpiece of *St Michael Archangel* (1582) is by the Flemish painter Denys Calvaert, born in Antwerp but who came to live in and work Bologna.

(J) Museum: At the end of the aisle, on either side of the museum entrance, are two doors painted by Amico Aspertini in 1531 for the organ now in the sanctuary. They illustrate the life of St Petronius.

AMICO ASPERTINI

When Charles V was crowned emperor at the high altar of San Petronio in 1530 by Pope Clement VII, the artist chosen to design the (ephemeral) triumphal arch for Charles and the Pope's entry into Bologna and the scenery for the festivities was Amico Aspertini (c. 1470–1552). Vasari describes him as an eccentric and mentions what a fast worker he was: he tells us that sometimes he even resorted to the use of his fingers. Certainly a prodigy, Aspertini's frescoes and altarpieces depart entirely from the gentle restraint of Francia, his master, and display a quick-witted, extemporised style that foreshadows Mannerism. He often favoured crowded scenes. Apart from his works in San Petronio examples of his skill can be admired in numerous other churches all over Bologna, as well as in the Pinacoteca and Museo Civico Medioevale.

The museum (*open 10–5; closed all day Mon and Sun morning*) is arranged in three rooms. It displays 16th- and 17th-century plans of the church and a wood model showing the early 16th-century project for a Latin-cross building by Arduino Arriguzzi. The drawings made for the completion of the façade, submitted over the centuries by some of the leading architects of the day, include proposals by Baldassare Peruzzi, Domenico Tibaldi—brother of Pellegrino— and even Palladio. The latest ones date from 1933, but none of them (thankfully) were ever carried out. There is a collection of illuminated choir books (some by Taddeo Crivelli), as well as 17th–18th-century Church vestments, silver and reliquaries.

(K) Sanctuary: The domed tabernacle dates from 1673 (by Gian Giacomo Monti). The fine organ constructed by Lorenzo da Prato in 1471–5 on the right was given its Baroque casing at the same time.

(L) Chapel of the Relics: There is a very fine framed high relief (left wall) of the *Assumption* by Nicolò Tribolo (with 18th-century additions). Beneath the organ, opposite, is a lovely *Lamentation* group by Vincenzo Onofri (1480): the open-mouthed Mary Magdalene is particularly striking (and has echoes of Niccolò dell'Arca's more famous figure in Santa Maria della Vita; *see p. 34*).

(M) Chapel of St Peter: The marble screen fronting this chapel is particularly beautiful (c. 1460).

(N) Chapel of St Anthony: The chapel preserves a statue of St Anthony of Padua and monochrome frescoes of the saint's life, all by Girolamo da Treviso (1525). Girolamo worked at the court of Henry VIII of England from 1538 and died on the battlefield in France (where he had gone in the capacity of military engineer). The design of the stained

glass here is attributed to Pellegrino Tibaldi.

(O) Chapel of the Holy Sacrament: The very beautiful carved and inlaid stalls are by the Olivetan monk Fra' Raffaele da Brescia (1521).

(P) Chapel of St Jerome: Lorenzo Costa's *St Jerome* (1484) is a very lovely painting.

(Q) Chapel of St Lawrence: The *Pietà* by Amico Aspertini (1519) caused consternation when it was painted, for its blunt, unsentimental style.

(R) Chapel of the Holy Cross: The lovely stained glass was made by the Dominican friar Jacob Griesinger (known as Jacob of Ulm) in 1466. Jacob died in Bologna and is buried in the church of San Domenico.

(S) Chapel of St Bridget: The polyptych is by the little-known Tommaso Garelli (1477). On the side walls are early 15th-century frescoes.

(T) Chapel of the Madonna: A little sculpture of the *Madonna della Pace* by a German artist of 1394 (the Istrian stone was later painted) is framed by a later painting by Giacomo Raibolini (son of Francesco Francia).

THE DUE TORRI

Bologna's famous **Due Torri** (*map Bologna East, 11*) are often taken as a symbol of the city. These two medieval leaning towers are a remarkable survival in the central Piazza di Porta Ravegnana, a few steps away from Piazza Maggiore. At one time some 180 such towers existed in the city. As in the rest of central Italy, wealthy merchants built them as symbols of their prestige, each vying to build higher than the other. The exceptionally tall **Torre degli Asinelli**, thought to have been built by the Asinelli family or by the *comune* (1109–19), is 97.5m high and leans 1.23m out of the perpendicular. The masonry at the base was added in 1488. A flight of 500 steps takes you up to the top (*open daily 9–5 or 6*).

The **Torre Garisenda**, also named after the family who built it around the same time as the other, was left unfinished owing to the subsidence of the soil and was shortened for safety in 1351–60. It is now only 48m high and but leans dramatically 3.22m out of the perpendicular. It was higher when Dante wrote the descriptive verses about the 'tilted tower', with clouds scudding past its top, making it appear to be falling (*Inferno*, XXXI, 136). The lines are inscribed at the base of the tower.

At the foot of the towers (and with its green dome visible between them) is the church of **San Bartolomeo**, where the rich decoration of the portico (1515), by Formigine (the architect Andrea Marchesi, from Modena), has been worn away, although a 16th-century portal is in better condition. The ornate interior, with small domes over the side aisles, is largely the work of Giovanni Battista Natali (1653–84). In the fourth chapel of the south aisle is an *Annunciation* by Francesco Albani (1632), and the tondo of the *Madonna* in the north transept is by Guido Reni.

Adjoining Piazza di Porta Ravegnana is Piazza Mercanzia, where Via Santo Stefano and Via Castiglione begin. As can be seen from the map of Bologna, five long straight streets fan out from near the foot of the Due Torri to end at gates in the city walls: Via Castiglione, Via Santo Stefano, the Strada Maggiore, Via San Vitale and Via Zamboni.

STRADA MAGGIORE

The Strada Maggiore (*map Bologna East, 11–12*) is an attractive old street running due southeast from the Due Torri on the line of the Via Emilia: you can see all the way to its end at the city walls. It is lined with a series of characteristic mansions of all periods from the 13th–19th centuries. **Casa Gelmi** (no. 26) was built in 1827 for the composer Gioacchino Rossini, who studied at Bologna's Conservatorio. The **Casa Isolani** (no. 19) has a tiny upper storey supported on very tall wooden brackets, characteristic of 13th-century dwellings in Bologna.

MUSEO INTERNAZIONALE DELLA MUSICA
Map Bologna East, 12. Entrance at no. 34 Strada Maggiore (Palazzo Sanguinetti). Open Tues–Fri 9.30–6, Sat–Sun 10–6.30. Excellent labelling also in English. museibologna.it/musica.

This museum, dedicated to music, is housed in **Palazzo Aldini Sanguinetti**, which has a Neoclassical cornice carved in the 18th century on the façade inspired by a Roman temple. A wall in the second courtyard, with a garden of banana trees, has a prettily frescoed landscape dating from the early 19th century. The splendid staircase (with an oval balcony around the lantern in the ceiling) leads up to the museum (and library) on the **first floor**, first opened in 2004. The first room retains its delightful 18th -century painted decorations by Vincenzo Martinelli and Pelagio Palagi which imitate a garden arbour with views out to the landscape beyond *trompe l'oeil* busts and statues. Room 2 has Etruscan-style decorations with scenes in large framed ovals against a black ground, also by Palagi. Other rooms have delicate Oriental-style decorations with rose bushes (and one room of the library retains Egyptian motifs on the walls and ceiling carried out in the 1880s by Gaetano Lodi, who had worked in Egypt in the previous decade).

The nine rooms contain a small part of the extraordinary collection of musical scores and manuscripts, some 17,000 books, and portraits of composers, put together by Giambattista Martini (1706–84), an erudite Franciscan friar. Martini's *History of Music*, which he published from 1757 onwards, is famous, although he never finished the last two tomes which were to be dedicated to the period from the Etruscans through Christian chant up to the birth of polyphony. He was also a theorist and even a composer. Martini met the young Mozart when he came to Bologna in 1770 and was elected (at the age of 14) to the Accademia Filarmonica, founded in 1666 (it is at no. 13 Via Guerrazzi), and the friar corresponded with him toward the end of his life. The exhibits are shown on a rotating basis, and some are kept in drawers which visitors are invited to open.

One of the highlights (in Room 3) is a portrait of Bach's youngest son Johann Christian (who had been a student of Martini's), commissioned from Gainsborough c. 1776 for Martini's collection (before sending it to the friar, Gainsborough made a replica of it which now hangs in the National Portrait Gallery in London). In 1770 the famous historian of music Charles Burney visited Martini in his convent at San Francesco in Bologna. The delightful cupboard, with its doors painted with books on music by Giuseppe Maria Crespi in the early 18th century, came from that convent. Musical instruments (harps, harpsichords, pianos, lutes etc) of various provenance are also exhibited in each room.

The last rooms document the history of opera, with particular attention paid to Rossini, who had studied at the Liceo Musicale in Bologna from 1806–10 and in 1839, as the greatest Italian opera composer of his time, was appointed its director (in 1942 the Liceo, in Piazza Rossini off Via Zamboni, became the Conservatorio named after Martini). There is an early 20th-century gramophone player which belonged to the composer Ottorino Respighi and a portrait of the violinist Arrigo Serato by Felice Casorati (who studied music before becoming a painter).

SANTA MARIA DEI SERVI

The wide arcades of the Strada Maggiore open out to form four porticoes around the harmonious Piazza dei Servi, built in a consistent style at various periods from the 14th century to 1855. The attractive Gothic church of Santa Maria dei Servi (*map Bologna East, 12*) was begun in 1346 and enlarged after 1386.

The interior is dark and cool. The fourth south chapel has a painting, by Denys Calvaert, of *Paradise* (1602). The finely-carved main altar is the work of Giovanni Angelo Montorsoli (1561). Outside the door into the sacristy (end of the south aisle) are fragments of frescoes by Vitale da Bologna, which survive from the Gothic church. But the most interesting works are in the **ambulatory**: a polyptch by

Lippo di Dalmasio (in very poor condition) and a delightful high relief in terracotta of the *Virgin Enthroned with Sts Lawrence and Eustace* by Vincenzo Onofri. Here in the chapel to the left of the east chapel is a beautiful *Madonna Enthroned* (*Maestà*), one of the few works by the great artist **Cimabue**, active in the last years of the 13th century, celebrated by Dante (two other *Maestà* by him are now in the Uffizi in Florence and in the Louvre). It is not certain who commissioned it nor how it came to be here. The standing Child reaching up to his Mother is particularly charming. Unfortunately the panel appears to be in poor condition.

The sixth north chapel has a pretty *Annunciation* by Innocenzo da Imola.

MUSEO DAVIA BARGELLINI

Map Bologna East, 12. Entrance at no. 44 Strada Maggiore (Piazza Santa Maria dei Servi). Open Tues–Sat 9–2, Sun 9–1.
Two grand atlantes flank the entrance to the palace, built in 1638. The fine staircase dates from 1730. Arranged in seven rooms on the ground floor, this eclectic **museum**, founded in 1924 by Malguzzi Valeri, retains its crowded old-fashioned arrangement from that time. The gloomy rooms are full of a great miscellany of objects from door handles to paintings, from ceramics to woodcarvings, from furniture to puppets, from Church vestments to glass (*there are handlists available in each room*).

Piazza Aldovrandi, with chestnut trees and a street market, leads north to Via San Vitale. Here on the left, beyond an old city gate (11th–12th-century), is the church of **Santi Vitale e Agricola**, rebuilt in 1824 except for its 12th-century crypt. It is dedicated to two saints martyred under Diocletian in the arena, thought to have been in this area. Inside are frescoes attributed to Giacomo Francia and Il Bagnacavallo.

The Strada Maggiore ends at Porta Maggiore and on the right beyond the gate, at Viale Carducci 5, is the **Casa di Carducci** and **Museo del Risorgimento** (*map Bologna East, 16; open Tues–Sun 9–1*), where the poet Giosuè Carducci lived from 1890 to 1907. In the same area is the church of **Santa Cristina** (*open for concerts*), which has sculptures of *St Peter* and *St Paul* by Guido Reni (rarities by an artist otherwise known as a painter) and a high altarpiece by Lodovico Carracci.

SAN GIACOMO MAGGIORE & VIA ZAMBONI

This Romanesque church (*map Bologna East, 7*) was begun in 1267 (but altered over the centuries). Its aisleless nave is surmounted by a bold vault of unusually wide span. The chapels are crowned by a terracotta frieze of statues of Christ and the Apostles and urns, added in 1727. On the altar in the sanctuary is a polyptych with the *Coronation of the Virgin and Saints* **(1)** by Jacopo di Paolo (c. 1420), above which hangs a large painted Crucifix, also by him. The huge altarpiece of the *Resurrection* on the east wall **(2)** is by Tommaso Laureti (1574).

The most interesting works are in the ambulatory chapels. Starting from the right, the second chapel has a beautiful **polyptych by Paolo Veneziano (3)** from

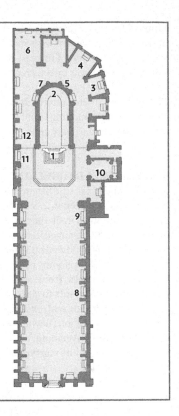

SAN GIACOMO MAGGIORE

1 Jacopo di Paolo: *Coronation of the Virgin*
2 Laureti: *Resurrection*
3 Polyptych by Paolo Veneziano
4 Crucifix by Simone dei Crocifissi
5 Fava monument
6 Cappella Bentivoglio: works by Lorenzo Costa and Francesco Francia
7 Jacopo della Quercia: Bentivoglio tomb
8 B. Passarotti: *Madonna and Saints*
9 Lodovico Carracci: *St Roch*
10 Chapel by Pellegrino Tibaldi
11 T. Passarotti: *Martyrdom of St Catherine*
12 Bartolomeo Cesi:*Madonna in Glory*

before 1344, incorporating Byzantine and Gothic elements. The elegant paintings of saints surround a plain golden cross-shaped reliquary (where there may formerly have been another painting). It includes representations of Sts Martin and George on horseback and three scenes from the life of St Nicholas of Tolentino. The damaged frescoes of the life of St Mary of Egypt, by Cristoforo da Bologna, are also 14th century. In the third chapel is a **Crucifix (4)** signed and dated 1370 by Simone dei Crocifissi. Opposite, on the choir wall, is the **funerary monument (5)** of a philosopher and a doctor, both called Nicolò Fava, by a follower of Jacopo della Quercia.

The **Cappella Bentivoglio (6)** (*coin-operated light, but sadly the gate is kept locked*) is the loveliest chapel in the church, added at the east end by Annibale Bentivoglio when in power in the city government in 1451 and enlarged by Giovanni II, who ruled Bologna from 1463 until 1506, when the Bentivoglio were deposed by Julius II. On a domed centrally-planned design, inspired by Brunelleschi, the architect was Pagno di Lapo Portigiani. It has superb decorations dating from the 1480s and '90s: an altarpiece by Francesco Francia and frescoes by Lorenzo Costa (these two painters often collaborated and are considered the founders of the Bolognese school). Costa's frescoes on the left wall depict the Apocalypse in two extraordinary scenes (the 'celestial' activity taking place in huge circular compositions) and those on the right wall show the Madonna enthroned with charming portraits of Giovanni II Bentivoglio and his family standing in a large group below. The relief of Annibale on horseback dating from 1458 was inserted next to it. The original majolica floor tiles, now very worn, survive. There are three more frescoed lunettes on the walls above by a pupil of Costa's.

Against the sanctuary wall, opposite the chapel, is the **tomb of Anton Galeazzo Bentivoglio (7)** Annibale's father, showing him sitting at his desk surrounded by pupils (he had a degree in Law and was prior of the College of Lawyers) below his effigy. This is one of the last works of Jacopo della Quercia (1435; with the help of assistants).

Some of the most interesting works of art in the long nave include (on the south side): in the fifth chapel the large altarpiece of the *Madonna and Saints* **(8)**, painted in 1565 by Bartolomeo Passarotti, in a lovely frame by the workshop of Formigine (and a scagliola altar frontal dating from 1674); and, in the ninth chapel, a painting of *St Roch* by Lodovico Carracci **(9)**. The largest chapel on this side **(10)**, at the entrance to the ambulatory, is a splendid Mannerist work designed by Pellegrino Tibaldi, who also carried out the frescoes in 1552. Opposite, on the north side, a chapel near the high altar steps has a Mannerist *Martyrdom of St Catherine* **(11)** by Tiburzio Passarotti (1577), and in the chapel next to it is a *Madonna in Glory* **(12)** by Bartolomeo Cesi.

VIA ZAMBONI

The entrance beneath the lovely long Renaissance portico along the side of the church of San Giacomo Maggiore, which was added in 1477 by Giovanni II Bentivoglio, is also that of the Augustinian monastery and you can see the little irregular courtyard beyond. The **Oratory** (*map Bologna East, 7; entrance at Via Zamboni 15; open daily 10–1 & 2–6; 3–7 in summer. Concerts are held here every weekend and on Mon*) is the former church of Santa Cecilia (it shares a common wall with the Cappella Bentivoglio in San Giacomo). It was decorated for Giovanni from 1504 to 1506 with frescoes by the leading artists of the day: Francesco Francia, Lorenzo Costa and their pupils, including Amico Aspertini. The ten scenes, beginning on the left-hand wall nearest the altar, show episodes from the life of the virgin martyr St Cecilia: her (forced) marriage to the pagan Valerian; the conversion of Valerian by Pope St Urban; the baptism of Valerian by Urban; an angel crowning Cecilia and Valerian with martyrdom; the martyrdom of Valerian and his brother Tiburtius; their burial; the trial of Cecilia in which she is condemned to death; the attempted martyrdom of Cecilia by scalding in her bath (the executioner is shown kneeling to fan the flames); Cecilia dispensing charity; and the burial of Cecilia. The altarpiece of the *Crucifixion and five Saints* is by Francia.

At Via Zamboni 20 is **Palazzo Magnani Salem** by Domenico Tibaldi (1577–87). The *Salone* (*open to visitors by appointment, T: 051 23183*) has a beautiful frescoed frieze of the *Founding of Rome* by the Carracci (1588–91), and there is a collection of paintings.

Via Zamboni runs through **Piazza Verdi**, the centre of student life in Bologna (the main University building is just out of the square). There are numerous places to sit (including a much-frequented café; no table service) and this is one of the liveliest spots in town. The Teatro Comunale, by Antonio Bibiena (1756; façade 1933), occupies the site of the great palace of the Bentivoglio, which was destroyed in a riot in 1507 when their power came to an end: it was left in ruins until 1763 and was always known to the Bolognese as *Il Guasto*—the Ruin. Via Petroni, which runs into the square, has an extraordinary variety of cheap eating places crowded with students on weekdays.

THE UNIVERSITY

The university of Bologna (*map Bologna East, 8*) is the oldest in Italy, founded in the second half of the 11th century and already famous just a century later. Its former seat in the Archiginnasio can be visited (*see p. 35*). Since 1803 its headquarters has been in Palazzo Poggi (*Via Zamboni 33*), built by Pellegrino Tibaldi (1549), and containing his frescoes of the story of Ulysses. The University Library (*Via Zamboni 35*), with a huge number of books and manuscripts, has a fine 18th-century reading-room. Here Cardinal Mezzofanti (1774–1849), who spoke 50 languages and was called by Byron 'the universal interpreter', was librarian, and his own library is added to the collection.

DISTINGUISHED ALUMNI

Irnerius, the celebrated jurist who revived the study of the Roman system of jurisprudence, later became an almost legendary figure. He is considered the founder of the law school of Bologna, where he taught probably between 1070 and 1100. It was due to him that the study of law became an autonomous science. The excellence of the *glosse* he produced gave the name to the School of Glossators (*see p. 39*), and his disciples spread over Europe—in 1144 Vacarius went to England, perhaps summoned by Thomas Becket. His *Liber pauperum* became the core law text book at Oxford University. In return, many Englishmen and Scotsmen served as rectors at Bologna.

Here Petrarch was taught and Copernicus embarked on his studies of astronomy. In 1789 the university became renowned for the discoveries of Luigi Galvani (1737–98). His experiments in applying an electric charge to severed frogs' legs and making them twitch in response was in fact the foundation stone of electro-technology and neuroscience. The term galvanism is derived from his name. Bologna is also remarkable for the number of its female professors, among them the learned Novella d'Andrea (14th century), Laura Bassi (1711–88), mathematician, scientist and mother of twelve, and Clotilde Tambroni, professor of Greek in 1794–1817.

Today the university is known particularly for its School of Medicine and for its faculty of Art, Music and Drama (DAMS). Umberto Eco, author of *The Name of the Rose*, taught semiotics here. There are four external campuses in Romagna: at Cesena, Forlì, Ravenna and Rimini.

PINACOTECA NAZIONALE

Map Bologna East, 8. Via delle Belle Arti 56. Open Tues–Sun 8.30–7.30. Closed Mon. Last tickets 30mins before closing. www.pinacotecabologna.beniculturali.it.

Just out of Via Zamboni, in an old Jesuit college with a handsome courtyard, the Pinacoteca houses one of the great collections of paintings in northern Italy. The gallery is especially important for its many works of the Bolognese school from the 14th century (Vitale da Bologna) up to the wonderful era of the Carracci, all born in the mid-16th century, and Guido Reni, who was at work in Bologna in the first years of the 17th century. Here, too, is a masterpiece by Raphael, painted for one of the city's churches. The paintings are arranged chronologically by period and school.

Room 1: The huge Crucifix is attributed to the 'Master of Franciscan Crucifixes' and Jacopo di Paolo, who was at work in Bologna in the late 14th century (there is another Crucifix by him in San Giacomo Maggiore). Vitale da Bologna is represented by a lovely (if damaged) *St George and the Dragon* (with a terrified horse). This, together with the frescoes he carried out at Mezzaratta (now in Rooms 7–8), are considered his masterpiece: he was one of the protagonists of 14th-century Gothic art in Italy and his production is best seen in Bologna, where he was active from around 1330–59. Also by him are the four intriguing scenes from the life of St Anthony Abbot exhibited here.

The panel with the *Crucifixion, Burial of Christ* and *Descent into Limbo* is a delicate work by Giovanni Baronzio (or a close follower), of the Riminese school. Paintings by a master known as 'Pseudo Jacopino', active in Bologna in the first half of the 14th century, include two fine polyptychs. A *Madonna and Child* is a good work by Simone dei Crocifissi.

Room 2 displays a crowded *Crucifixion with Four Saints* by Jacopo di Paolo, a polyptych by Lippo di Dalmasio of c. 1390 and works by Simone dei Crocifissi. In **Room 3** a painted Crucifix by Rinaldo di Ranuccio (1265) hangs opposite a polyptych by the great painter Giotto (c. 1333), in rather poor condition (and probably with the intervention of his workshop). The lovely large *Madonna and Child with four Angels* displayed close by is the work of the well-known Florentine painter Lorenzo Monaco.

Steps lead up to **Room 4**, where Zanobi Strozzi's two panels showing the *Triumph of Fame* and the *Triumph of Time* are interesting for their iconography. In **Room 5** is a painting of St Ursula and her companions by Lorenzo di Venezia (c. 1444). **Room 6** has damaged 14th-century frescoes by Simone dei Crocifissi, Jacopo da Bologna and Pseudo Jacopino, including a memorable *St James the Great*, on his horse at a gallop, out to defeat the infidels in battle.

Rooms 7 and 8 (*the two halls on the right*) exhibit the sinopie and frescoes detached in the 1960s from the small church of Sant'Apollonia of Mezzaratta on the hills on the outskirts of Bologna. Begun in 1338, some ten artists were involved and the decorative scheme was only completed at the end of the 14th century. They include the frescoes from the west wall of the church depicting the *Nativity* (with the unusual scene of the Bathing of the Child), considered the best works of Vitale da Bologna (1330s). Other scenes illustrate the childhood of Christ, and Old Testament stories (Jacob and Joseph, Moses).

The long gallery exhibits the most important works of the 15th–16th centuries. It is divided into sections:

9: Venetian works by Antonio Vivarini (*Risen Christ* and a magnificent polyptych), Cima da Conegliano (*Madonna and Child*) and L'Alunno (*Annunciation*).

10: Ferrarese school: Francesco del Cossa, a beautiful *Madonna Enthroned with Saints*; Ercole de' Roberti, the weeping *Mary Magdalene* (a fresco fragment; the tears are particularly well rendered).

11: Less well-known painters, but with particularly interesting works: the so-called 'Maestro della Pala dei Muratori' (*Madonna and Saints*); Michele Coltellini (*Death of the Virgin*); and Giovanni Francesco Maineri (portrait of Alessandro Faruffino).

12–14: The Bolognese school, with fine works by its first protagonists: Francesco Francia, Lorenzo Costa and Amico Aspertini (*Adoration of the Magi*).

15: At the end of the gallery is displayed **Raphael's** *Ecstasy of St Cecilia*, one of his most famous works. It was commissioned by the Blessed Elena Duglioli dall'Olio for San Giovanni in Monte around 1515. After the suppression of her convent it was seized by Napoleon and taken to Paris

(where it was transferred to canvas): when it returned to Bologna after the downfall of Napoleon (along with many other art treasures which had left the country for France) it became part of this collection and was substituted in the church by a copy. Its innovative iconography shows St Cecilia standing in a group of four saints, all in very different attitudes and poses, with a wonderful still life of musical instruments on the ground at their feet. St Cecilia, in a magnificent golden robe, is listening in rapture to a holy choir of angels in the sky above, but it is the striking, almost profane, Mary Magdalene, dressed in muted colours with a veil lightly covering her head, who is the most memorable figure in the group as she looks straight at us out of the painting. Opposite hangs a typical *Madonna and Saints* by another famous painter from Umbria, Perugino. Also here is *St John the Baptist* by Bugiardini and a tondo by Franciabigio.

16–17: Works by Innocenzo da Imola and Giacomo and Giulio Raibolini, the sons of Francesco Francia.

18: The *Madonna and Child with Saints* is one of a group of paintings carried out by Parmigianino when he came to Bologna after the Sack of Rome in 1527 (before returning north to his

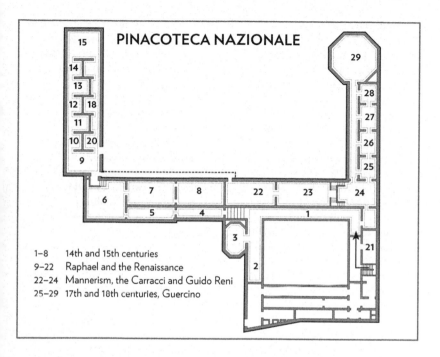

PINACOTECA NAZIONALE

15
14
13
12 18
11
10 20
9
29
28
27
26
25
7 8 22 23 24
6
5 4 1
3
21
2

1–8   14th and 15th centuries
9–22   Raphael and the Renaissance
22–24   Mannerism, the Carracci and Guido Reni
25–29   17th and 18th centuries, Guercino

birthplace, Parma, for the rest of his life). Even though he was not a prolific painter, he is recognised as one of the most influential of his time, his work characterised by a marked formal elegance, instantly recognisable, which led the way to the Baroque and the dramatic Bolognese canvases of the Carracci.

19: Il Bagnacavallo the Younger (Giovanni Battista Ramenghi).

20: The fragment from a *Crucifixion* (with Christ and the Good Thief) is by Titian.

It is now necessary to return all the way back to the entrance, from which you can visit the little **Room 21**, which has frescoes illustrating *Orlando Furioso* (detached from Palazzo Torfanini in Via Galliera) by Niccolò dell'Abate, dating from around 1550. Outside is an exquisite small painting by Guido Reni of *St Francis consoled by an Angel*, which is on loan from Sir Denis Mahon's collection. Mahon, an art historian, did much to re-evaluate the late 16th-century Bolognese school and he curated the first exhibition on the Carracci here in 1956. His contribution to the formation of this gallery was recognised in 2002, when he was given an honorary degree from Bologna University.

Next are three large halls with a spectacular display of Mannerist (late 16th- and early 17th-century) paintings: the chronological display begins in Room 22, at the far end.

Room 22: On the end wall, Denys Calvaert, *Flagellation*. Viewed from the top of the steps is a charming painting of a child in a crib (c. 1583) by Lavinia Fontana, one of the few women painters represented in the gallery. Close by hangs her portrait of the Gozzadini family, painted around the same time. There are also huge paintings here by Vasari (*Supper of St Gregory the Great*, who has been given the features of the Medici pope Clement VII, Vasari's patron) and Passarotti.

Room 23 has a superb collection of **paintings by Lodovico Carracci**, who worked almost exclusively in Bologna where he was born in 1555, a cousin of the more famous Annibale and his brother Agostino, both of whom are also well represented here. Lodovico's works from the 1580s and 1590s range from his simple *Annunciation* (with exceptionally young protagonists) to a small landscape, a huge *Transfiguration*, a *Madonna and Child with Saints* (with Bologna prominent in the background), the *Conversion of Saul* and the *Preaching of the Baptist*.

At the bottom of the circular steps, **Room 24** has a very fine group of early 17th-century **works by Guido Reni**: *Crucifixion* (with St John in a superb red cloak); *Sibyl*; *Samson*; portrait of his mother, Ginevra Pucci; *Massacre of the Innocents*; and a huge *Pietà* with the Madonna and Saints and Bologna portrayed beneath. His *Christ crowned with Thorns* was donated to the gallery by Denis Mahon.

The last group of rooms (25–29) houses paintings from the late 17th century and the 18th century, typified in the end (circular) hall (**Room 29**) by seven huge altarpieces, notably the *Martyrdom of Lionello Spada* by Domenichino; *Baptism of Christ* by Francesco Albani, and the *Birth of the Baptist* by Lodovico Carracci. Other artists represented in this group of rooms include Guercino, Giuseppe Maria Crespi, the Gandolfi and Donato Creti.

THE AREA OF THE GHETTO & SAN MARTINO

From the Due Torri (*map Bologna East, 11*), Via de' Giudei ('of the Jews') leads past a lane called Via San Giobbe (St Job; the deconsecrated church of **San Giobbe** now forms part of a covered precinct with shops and cafés) and then left into the narrow Via dell'Inferno, on the site of the **ghetto of Bologna** (the synagogue was at no. 16). Jews were confined here from 1556 until their expulsion from the city in 1593. The **Jewish Museum** (Museo Ebraico) at Via Valdonica 1 (*map Bologna East, 7; open Sun–Thur 10–6, Fri 10–4*) documents the history of Jewish life in Bologna and Emilia Romagna from the Middle Ages to the present day. The present synagogue, rebuilt in 1954 after a bomb destroyed the 19th-century synagogue on the same site, is in Via dei Gombruti (*map Bologna West, 10*), where the parallel Via Mario Finzi is named after a famous Jewish anti-Fascist who was deported in 1944 and died in Auschwitz.

At the end of Via dell'Inferno is a little piazza named after Marco Biagi, a government consultant on economics, who was assassinated outside his house here in 2002. Bologna, for long famous for its left-wing administration, had been the scene of another atrocity: in August 1980 a bomb placed by right-wing terrorists in the waiting room of the railway station killed 85 people and wounded 200 others.

An archway leads out into Piazza San Martino, enlivened by a number of cheap eating places including *pizzerie* with tables outside in warm weather.

SAN MARTINO

Founded in 1217, the basilica of San Martino (*map Bologna East, 7*) was remodelled in the mid-15th century and the façade was rebuilt in 1879. The most interesting works of art are in the chapels and over the altars on the north side.

The first chapel, built in 1506, has a lovely altarpiece of the *Madonna and Child with Saints* by Francesco Francia, who also painted the *Dead Christ* supported by angels above. The grisaille altar frontal of the *Deposition* is by Amico Aspertini. Unfortunately the gate is kept locked so it is very difficult to see the **fresco fragment by Paolo Uccello** on the right wall, discovered in 1980 in the sacristy. Probably dating from 1437 and commissioned from the famous Florentine artist by a wealthy family (the donors are included in the scene), it shows the ass and the ox in perfect foreshortening bending low over the Child, beautifully painted, lying outstretched on the ground beneath their noses. The statue of the *Madonna and Child* is by the famous Sienese artist Jacopo della Quercia, best known for his sculptures on the façade of San Petronio.

In the second chapel is a typical devotional image of *St Francis* by Guercino. On the third altar is a painted Crucifix with three saints, a good work by Bartolomeo Cesi. The fourth altarpiece of *St Jerome* is by Lodovico Carracci. The fifth altarpiece is a lovely *Assumption* by Lorenzo Costa. On the aisle wall here is a (framed) fresco of the *Madonna and Child* by Simone dei Crocifissi. In the chapel to the left of the sanctuary there is a triptych of the *Crucifixion and Saints,* complete with its predella dated 1469, by an unknown master of the Bolognese school. The splendid high altarpiece in an elaborate frame on the east wall of the sanctuary is by Girolamo Sicciolante. The organ was built in 1556 by Giovanni Cipri from Ferrara and is considered his most important work (he made organs for a number of churches in Emilia and the Veneto).

The chapel to the right of the sanctuary is a pretty Baroque work (1750). The last altarpiece on the south side is an interesting painting by Amico Aspertini showing three young girls kneeling to receive dowries from St Nicholas of Bari while the Madonna and Child look on from above. On the aisle wall here is a fresco fragment with the head of Christ by Vitale da Bologna. The first south chapel has an elaborately framed *Adoration of the Magi* by Girolamo da Carpi.

Behind the votive column crowned by a Madonna, erected in 1705, it is worth crossing over Via Oberdan into the narrow **Via Marsala**, where there are two medieval houses with tall wooden porticoes (Casa Grassi was built in the 13th century but rather over restored in 1913). This area is an interesting survival of medieval Bologna, with many old houses and remains of the towers erected by patrician families. Via Marsala ends in Via Galliera with its grand palaces, described on p. 42.

VIA SANTO STEFANO & VIA CASTIGLIONE

These two old streets begin just a few steps away from the Due Torri on either side of **Palazzo della Mercanzia** (*map Bologna East, 11*), the best-preserved example of ornamented Italian Gothic architecture in the city. It was built in 1382–4 from the plans of Antonio di Vincenzo (architect of San Petronio) and the little-known Lorenzo da Bagnomarino.

Via Santo Stefano has a series of lovely 15th–16th-century mansions including (nos 16–18) Palazzo Isolani by Pagno di Lapo Portigiani (1455). **Corte Isolani**, a precinct of shops and cafés occupying old town houses, links Via Santo Stefano with the Strada Maggiore. Via Santo Stefano opens out into a peaceful triangular **piazza** (the paving recently redesigned), with bars and cafés with outdoor seating in front of the picturesque group of ancient buildings belonging to the former abbey of Santo Stefano.

SANTO STEFANO

These monastic buildings (*map Bologna East, 11; open daily 9–6*), mentioned as early as 887, are dedicated as a whole to St Stephen the Martyr. In the piazza you can see the three churches in a row. From left to right they are Santi Vitale e Agricola, the oldest ecclesiastical building in the city; San Sepolcro, with cypresses in the little garden; and the Crocifisso, the largest church, with a 12th-century pulpit on its front, which now provides the entrance to all three buildings.

The **Crocifisso** has a painted crucifix by Simone dei Crocifissi (c. 1380) hanging in the choir raised high above the crypt. The life-size *Pietà* was made in the 18th century by Angelo Piò.

On the left (by the Aldovrandi tomb dating from 1438) is a door into the venerable polygonal church of **San Sepolcro**, perhaps founded as early as the 5th century to serve as a baptistery but dating in its present form from the 11th century. On a central plan with an ambulatory and brick cupola, it is a remarkable architectural work. In the centre is an imagined imitation of the Holy Sepulchre at Jerusalem, but this was partly hidden by the Romanesque pulpit which has very interesting reliefs (the stair and altar were placed against it in the 19th century). Behind a grille here is the **tomb of Petronius**, Bologna's greatly venerated patron saint. A little ceremony re-enacting the Entombment, with an effigy of the Crucified Christ, is held here on Good Friday.

A door leads out to the charming little **Cortile di Pilato** (12th century): in the middle of this open pebbled court is a stoup known as Pilate's Bowl (8th century) bearing an obscure inscription relating to the Lombard kings Liutprand and Ilprand. On a pillar in a little window of the Cappella della Consolazione is a delightful cockerel, sculpted in the 14th century. One end of the courtyard is closed by the beautifully patterned brickwork of the exterior of San Sepolcro, and opposite is the façade (reconstructed in 1911), again with lovely patterned brick, of the **Martyrium**. This chapel has a central line of columns with good capitals and a lovely old pavement. Here is a charming group of wooden statues of the *Adoration of the Magi* painted by Simone dei Crocifissi (c. 1370), as well as a damaged stone statue of St Peter. Also off the courtyard is the chapel of Santa Giuliana, with a very worn 14th-century fresco and a beautiful sarcophagus complete with its lid. Close by is another chapel which is an Air Force War Memorial, with photographs of all those who lost their lives in service in the last War.

Adjoining the Corte del Pilato is the **cloister**, which has two beautiful colonnades, the lower one dating from the 11th century and the upper from the 12th century, with fine capitals. The walls are covered with plaques to the war dead. Here you can see the Romanesque campanile. Off it is a small, ill-kept **museum** (*closed 12–3.30*), with a few late Gothic paintings (and some charming wood panels from a ceiling painted with birds and animals). There is also a detached fresco by Michele di Matteo and a collection of Church silver. A chapel has a detached 13th-century fresco of the *Massacre of the Innocents* and reliquaries, including that of St Petronius by Jacopo di Roseto (1370).

Santi Vitale e Agricola, a venerable building perhaps of the 5th century, with massive columns and capitals, incorporates many fragments of Roman buildings. The three apses (rebuilt in the 8th and 11th centuries) are lit by tiny alabaster windows. The altars in the side apses are 8th- or 9th-century Frankish sarcophagi enclosing the relics of St Vitalis and St Agricola, martyred in Bologna under the emperor Diocletian.

Continue up Via Santo Stefano and on the right (off Via Farini), on a little hill, beside its former convent building now animated by its use as a faculty of the University, stands the church of San Giovanni in Monte.

SAN GIOVANNI IN MONTE

Map Bologna East, 11. There are inconspicuous lights outside each chapel.
Of ancient foundation, in its present form this church is a 13th-century Gothic building with extensive 15th-century additions. The **façade** has a projecting porch of 1474, with St John the Evangelist's symbol of an eagle in painted terracotta by Niccolò dell'Arca filling the lunette above.

In the **interior**, the lovely stained-glass **tondo on the west wall** showing St John writing the Book of Revelation was designed by Ercole de' Roberti or Lorenzo Costa. The Romanesque Cross on an inverted Roman pillar capital bears a dramatic figure of Christ, carved in the 16th century from the trunk of a fig tree, attributed to two brothers called Gian Giacomo and Giovanni del Maino from Lombardy (it has been repainted several times). Over the altar in the sanctuary hangs a small 14th-century painted Crucifix by the native artist Jacopino di Francesco and on the east wall, in a huge frame, is the *Madonna in Glory* by Lorenzo Costa (1501), but a finer work by him can be seen in the large chapel at the end of the south aisle (*Madonna and Child,* above four Saints and two angel musicians), with golden highlights and in a lovely frame.

The **north transept** is a good architectural work of 1514 built by Arduino Arriguzzi for the blessed Elena Duglioli Dall'Oglio (1472–1520), who is buried here (the gilded angels were made by the workshop of Francia on a design by Raphael). Elena's sarcophagus is opened on her festival. This holy lady is also remembered for having commissioned the famous St Cecilia altarpiece (*see p. 28*) for this chapel from Raphael: now in the Pinacoteca. It was substituted here by a poor copy in 1861, but still enclosed in the original frame by Formigine. In the chapel on the left of the sanctuary there is a pretty relief in enamelled ceramic by the local 19th-century Minghetti workshop.

In the chapel in the **south transept** is a tondo of the *Madonna della Sanità*, frescoed by Giovanni da Modena in the early 15th century and surrounded by much later paintings. In the **south aisle** is a 14th-century fresco of the *Madonna della Pace* by Lippo di Dalmasio, and two very unusual paintings by Pietro Faccini (*Martyrdom of St Lawrence*) and Girolamo da Treviso (*Noli me Tangere*).

The **second north chapel**, well lit with windows high up, has lovely woodwork carried out in 1640; the paintings are by Guercino.

PALAZZO PEPOLI (HISTORY MUSEUM)
Vicolo Monticelli descends to Via Castiglione (*map Bologna East, 15*), a handsome old street which leads to the city gate of the same name. Palazzo Pepoli (no. 8; *map Bologna East, 11*), a huge Gothic building begun in 1344 by Taddeo Pepoli and restored in 1925, houses the **Museo della Storia di Bologna**, illustrating the history of the city with interractive supports (*open Tues–Sun 10–7, Thur 10–10; genusbononiae.it*).

SANTA MARIA DELLA VITA
Via Clavature, which connects Via Castiglione with Piazza Maggiore, is a particularly attractive old street with numerous shops and cafés. On it stands the little church of **Santa Maria della Vita**, part of the Genus Bononiae group of museums and exhibition spaces (*map Bologna East, 11; open Tues–Sun 10 or 10.30– 6.30 or 7; for up-to-date opening times, see genusbononiae.it*). The church was rebuilt by Bergonzoni in 1692 and its tall cupola was added by Antonio Bibiena in the following century. The name of the church ('St Mary of Life') records the hospital attached to it which was founded in the 13th century and which over the centuries became renowned for its excellence: it remained the main hospital of the city right up until the 18th century.

The church contains a dramatic evocation of grief, the terracotta *Lamentation over the Dead Christ* (*entry fee*), a superb work by Niccolò dell'Arca dating from the late 15th century. The life-size figures of this *tableau* are extraordinarily expressive; the women have their mouths wide open in screaming anguish. The figure of St John stands gripped by speechless pain. Joseph of Arimathea, in splendid 15th-century dress, holds the tools used to hew out the tomb. Once polychrome, this is arguably the greatest work produced in terracotta in the Renaissance. Niccolò may have taken as his model the grief he witnessed in the relations of those in this hospital, and it is known that his work became well known at once and an object of great devotion.

TERRACOTTA IN BOLOGNA

Emilia Romagna has few good stone quarries, but it is blessed with wonderful clays. Hence all the brick rather than stone architecture in the region, and hence, too, the pre-eminence of Faenza for ceramics. Whether Emilian terracotta sculpture would have developed as highly without what had gone before in Florence with Desiderio da Settignano, Sansovino and others is perhaps debatable; but certainly the area has a grand tradition in churches and on public buildings of terracotta figures and groups (much of it polychrome). And, of course, with terracotta an artist can be much bolder with gesture and movement than is ever possible with stone. Possibly the finest example of the genre is Niccolò dell'Arca's *Lamentation* here in Santa Maria della Vita: six free-standing figures grouped in moving, almost Baroque, poses around the dead body of Christ—a wonderfully dramatic piece. Other masters working in Bologna include Vincenzo Onofri (fl. 1479–1506) and Sperandio da Mantova (c. 1425–1504), who was also a very skilled medallist.

The **Oratory** (*open Tues–Sun 10–12 & 3–7; approached by a monumental staircase off the left side of the church or from inside the church itself*) belonged to a confraternity connected to the hospital and the 17th-century rooms are now used as a little museum dedicated to the history of the hospital and charitable confraternity. The Oratory itself dates from the early 17th century and has a pretty gilded ceiling with paintings and stuccowork and statues in niches round the walls (the two on the window wall representing St Francis and St Petronius are attributed to Alessandro Algardi). The extraordinary group of 15 over-life-size terracotta statues are the work of Alfonso Lombardi (1519–22). They illustrate the legend that at the funeral of the Virgin, as the twelve Apostles accompanied the bier, a Jewish high priest, as a sign of contempt and with a deeply profane gesture, attempted to overturn it but was thrown to the ground by an angel (seen here descending from above, brandishing a sword). The drama of the scene takes precedence whereas the Virgin is practically invisible. In a little room there is a collection of majolica jars which belonged to the hospital.

MUSEO CIVICO ARCHEOLOGICO & THE ARCHIGINNASIO

Via dell'Archiginnasio skirts the east flank of San Petronio. Beneath the marble-paved Portico del Pavaglione, with elegant uniform shopfronts, the windows enclosed in tall wooden frames, is the entrance to the Archaeological Museum.

SAN DOMENICO

The peaceful cobbled Piazza San Domenico (*map Bologna East, 15*), with a few benches, has two tall columns erected in the early 17th century bearing statues of St Dominic and the Madonna. The monumental canopied tombs commemorate two distinguished members of the School of Glossators at Bologna University (*see p. 41*): Rolandino de' Passeggeri, a famous notary who died in 1300 (and who was also involved in the Guelph government of Bologna), and Egidio Foscherari (or Foscarari) who died in 1289 and was probably the first lay teacher of canon law. Both these tombs had to be reconstructed after damage from bombing in 1943.

The church (*open 9–12 & 3.30–6; Sun 3.30–5*) was dedicated by Innocent IV in 1251 to St Dominic, founder (in 1216) of the order of Preaching Friars, who died here in 1221, two years after establishing the monastery on this site. He was canonised in the following decade. It is still one of the principal Dominican convents in Italy, with about 35 monks, and is celebrated as the burial place of St Dominic.

Interior of San Domenico

The white interior, hung with chandeliers, survives intact from its remodelling by Carlo Francesco Dotti (1728–31).

The **Chapel of St Dominic**, off the right side, rebuilt in 1597–1605 (and restored in the 19th century), with a splendid *Glory of St Dominic*, by Guido Reni in the apse, provides an over-elaborate setting for the famous monumental sarcophagus, a masterpiece of sculpture, where the saint is buried (*the gate is opened and lit on request*). The sarcophagus itself has exquisite high reliefs of scenes from the saint's life, carved in 1267 to a design by Nicola Pisano, mostly by his pupils, including Fra' Guglielmo and the much more famous Arnolfo di Cambio. On the front are two episodes on either side of a statuette of the *Madonna and Child*: one showing the fall of a young man from his horse brought back to life by the saint, and the other St Dominic with a holy text written by him which has survived the flames of the fire below (where instead pagan texts have been consumed): unable to solve a dispute between Dominic and an erudite pagan, judges had ordered that both texts be burnt. The lid of the sarcophagus and crowning sculpture was designed by Niccolò dell'Arca, who took his name from this tomb ('*arca*' in Italian). It has eight statuettes of the protectors of Bologna: three years after Niccolò's death in 1492, the 20-year-old Michelangelo—who was staying for a year with Gianfrancesco Aldovrandi—carved two of these statuettes: St Petronius holding a model of Bologna (with his right leg shown in pronounced movement), and (behind) St Proculus, with a cloak over his left shoulder (next to St John the Baptist, which was the last sculpture to be made for the monument in 1539). Michelangelo also carved the right-hand angel kneeling and bearing a candelabrum, flanking the smaller sculptural panel on the front (below the sarcophagus proper), as a pair to the left-hand angel by Niccolò dell'Arca. It is interesting to note how the petite and sweet angel on the left contrasts in spirit to that by Michelangelo, which appears to have an almost disturbing expression and is much more 'muscular'. The tiny scenes in relief between the two angels are by Alfonso Lombardi (1532). They illustrate (on either side of a central *Adoration of the Magi*) the birth of St Dominic, the penitent Dominic asleep on the floor (instead of in his more comfortable bed), selling his books in order to help the poor, and climbing to heaven by a ladder held up by the Redeemer and the Madonna. The altar beneath dates from the 18th century. A niche in the tomb behind contains an exquisite reliquary signed by Jacopo Roseto da Bologna (1383), decorated with enamels, made to preserve the saint's skull. The sarcophagus is crowned by a figure of the Redeemer holding the World, standing on a terrestial globe. Below are festoons of fruit (the Earth) held up by putti, with eight dolphins below representing the sea. Two angels kneel on either side of Christ in *Pietà* and at the four corners there are statuettes of the Evangelists, in exotic head-dresses. This upper part of the monument is also ascribed to the hand of Niccolò dell'Arca.

The little chapel to the right of the choir contains a ***Marriage of St Catherine*** signed by the Florentine painter Filippino Lippi (1501), with wonderful colours.

To see the choir, museum and cloister there is a very small entrance fee. The well-lit **choir** has beautiful stalls and a lectern (1541–51) all in marquetry by Fra' Damiano. The huge painting here in a gilded frame of the *Magi* is by Bartolomeo Cesi. The **museum**, arranged in just one room, is interesting in particular for a marble bust of St Dominic by Nicola Pisano (easy to miss, it is on top of the reliquary display case) and a polychrome terracotta half-length figure of the saint reading, a typically realistic figure by Niccolò dell'Arca (also inconspicuous, in a niche on the wall). There are some paintings and frescoes by Lippo di Dalmasio, Lodovico Carracci and Bernardino Luini, as well as intarsia panels by Fra' Damiano, and books of anthems. The church treasury and vestments are in a room above (*at present kept closed*). Beyond the sacristy, a marquetry door (1538) leads into the little **cloister of the Dead**, its fourth side closed by the exterior of the apse and cupola of the Chapel of St Dominic. This is where foreigners who died in Bologna were buried, including students and professors from the University. A simple tomb slab opposite the apse of the Chapel of St Dominic marks the burial place of those from the British Isles.

Inside the convent (*willingly shown by a monk on request*) is **St Dominic's cell**, where the bull of 1234 which proclaimed his canonisation is preserved, together with other relics (behind curtains); and the **chapter house**, where there is a fresco of the red-headed St Dominic dating from 1230, so presumably painted by a monk who knew him.

In the **south transept** is a painting by Guercino of *St Thomas Aquinas*. In the **north transept**, an inscription of 1731 marks the tomb of King Enzo (*see p. 15*). The adjoining chapel has a very fine painted Crucifix signed by Giunta Pisano (mid-13th century). In the **north aisle**, the chapel opposite that of St Dominic has an altarpiece incorporating small dark paintings of the *Mysteries of the Rosary* by Lodovico Carracci, Bartolomeo Cesi, Denys Calvaert, Guido Reni and Francesco Albani. There is a legend that the Virgin gave a rosary to St Dominic as protection against Albigensianism, and for much of the Middle Ages Confraternities of the Rosary were under Dominican control. On the second altar is *St Raimondo* by Lodovico Carracci. Guido Reni is buried here.

THE DISTRICT TO THE SOUTH AROUND THE COLLEGIO DI SPAGNA
To the south of San Domenico, at the end of Via Garibaldi, is Palazzo Ruini, with an imposing Palladian façade and courtyard (1584). Via delle Tovaglie leads to the attractive and peaceful Via d'Azeglio, one of the few old main streets in Bologna without arcading. Here is **San Procolo**, a church of ancient foundation, with a Romanesque façade decorated in terracotta. In the choir is an interesting Roman sarcophagus, probably reworked in the late 15th century. Opposite is a good building with a tall arcade, used by the University. At no. 54 is **Palazzo Bevilacqua**, built in 1474–82, clearly modelled on a Florentine palace with rustication and a bench at the foot of the façade, and a pretty courtyard, but all on a very small scale (and now in very poor condition). The Council of Trent held two sessions in this building in 1547, having moved from Trento to Bologna to escape an epidemic. Palazzo Marsigli opposite dates from 1735.

Via Tagliapietra, parallel to Via d'Azeglio, skirts a pretty wall next to the church of **Corpus Domini**, built in 1478–80, with a good façade and terracotta portal by Sperandio da Mantova. In a 17th-century chapel (*ring Tues, Thur Sat, Sun 9.30– 11.30 & 4–5.45, closed order of nuns*) are preserved the relics of St Catherine de' Vigri (d. 1463), an erudite ascetic of Bologna, greatly venerated.

Via Urbana and Via Belfiore lead to the **Collegio di Spagna** (*not open to the public*). Founded in 1365 for Spanish students, it is the last survivor of the many colleges, resembling those at Oxford and Cambridge, which existed in Bologna in the Middle Ages. Ignatius Loyola and Cervantes were among its famous students. Now an institute for Italo-Spanish American studies, it still has a high academic reputation. At an entrance on the corner at no. 4 Via Collegio di Spagna, the large carved coat of arms of Ferdinand VI, King of Spain, survives from 1751. From Via Urbana, which follows the garden wall, you can see part of the external painted decoration on the building. In Via Val d'Aposa, which leads back towards Piazza Maggiore, is the charming little façade of **Spirito Santo** (*map Bologna West, 10*), a gem of terracotta ornament, in very good condition. Close by, on Via d'Azeglio, is the church of the **Celestini**, where Niccolò dell'Arca was buried in 1494, with an epitaph (according to the exterior plaque on the church wall) commemorating 'him who gave life to stones' and whom 'Praxiteles, Phidias et Polyclitus now adore, marvelling at thy hands, O Nicholas.'

FROM PIAZZA MAGGIORE TO SAN FRANCESCO

On the left of Palazzo d'Accursio (Palazzo Comunale) the pleasant Via Quattro Novembre skirts the interesting exterior of the huge building and there are some attractive old shops and a clock outside the pleasant little hotel named after it. In Piazza Roosevelt there is a magnificent view of the castellated exterior of Palazzo Comunale, and here, too, is Palazzo della Prefettura dating from 1561–1603, perhaps by Terribilia. In Via IV Novembre Palazzo Marescalchi built in 1613 adjoins no. 7, where Guglielmo Marconi was born in 1874.

MARCONI AND THE TELEGRAPH

Aged only twenty-two, through his British mother Annie Jameson, Marconi first received encouragement for his experiments in London where it was recognised that the telegraph he had discovered would be an extremely useful method of communication. By the end of his life he had crossed the Atlantic no fewer than 87 times and received honours from all over the world in recognition for his services to humanity. Some of his experiments are illustrated in the Museo della Comunicazione in Via Col di Lana 7 (*only open by appointment: T: 051 6491008, museopelagalli.com*). Pontecchio (*map B, C3*), on the Pistoia road south of Bologna, is where Marconi made his first experiments in the transmission of signals by Hertzian waves at his father's Villa Griffone above the town. The great scientist is buried there in a mausoleum designed by the prominent early Modernist architect Marcello Piacentini. In the park is a relic of the boat *Elettra* (named after his daughter) from which, while at anchor in the port of Genoa in 1930, Marconi lit up the lights of Sydney.

SAN SALVATORE

This church (*map Bologna West, 10*) was rebuilt in 1605–23 by Giovanni Ambrogio Magenta, a Barnabite and architect from Milan. In the pleasant bright interior in the apse is a painting of the *Redeemer* by Guido Reni (1620). In the first north chapel, *St Zaccaria with Saints* by Garofalo. In the south transept is a lovely polyptych by Vitale da Bologna (1353) and the altarpiece here is by Jacopo Coppi (also called Jacopo del Meglio, 1579).

Via Porta Nuova, with its pretty arcade, leads west, passing a clockmaker's laboratory (*closed Sat*) and a picturesque butcher's shop and a bakery. It crosses Via dei Gombruti, where at no. 23 the 'Old Pretender', son of King James II of England and Mary of Modena, stayed during several visits to Bologna. The Synagogue is in this street (*for more on Jewish Bologna, see p. 30*).

Outside Porta Nuova, one of the old city gates, is the long **Piazza Malpighi**, really just the widening of a busy road, beside the Colonna dell'Immacolata, crowned by a copper statue designed by Guido Reni.

SAN FRANCESCO

The church (*map Bologna West, 10*) is in a more or less French Gothic style, begun in 1236, completed early in 1263, but considerably altered since. The churchyard has a little lawn and cypresses beside the east end of the building with its Gothic buttresses and lovely campanile. The three quaint tombs here, raised on columns and protected by green pyramidal roofs, date from the 13th century (well restored in 1891) and they belong to Glossators.

THE SCHOOL OF GLOSSATORS

Founded by Irnerius at the University of Bologna, this school of jurists was extremely famous in its time and for many centuries afterwards. The commentaries (or glosses) of these law professors sowed the seeds of modern civil law. When the most eminent amongst them died they were commemorated with handsome canopied tombs born on columns which can still be seen outside the churches of San Francesco and San Domenico. Here outside San Francesco is the tomb of Accursio, the last and most famous glossator, who died around 1259. His authoritative *Glossa perpetua* contained 96,260 glosses and his studies were diffused throughout Europe. Also here lie Odofredo (d. 1265), extremely famous in his day, and Rolandino de' Romanzi (d. 1284). Even though these names are forgotten by most of us today, the name of the school survives in academic circles, where glosses and glossaries are still essential tools of learning.

The church façade (c. 1250), on Piazza San Francesco, has two lovely 8th-century plutei carved with animals and birds, including peacocks, on either side of the door, and 13th–14th-century majolica plaques in the pitch of the roof.

Interior of San Francesco

The magnificent vaulting with brick ribs stands out against the white walls, and the splendid marble reredos by Jacobello and Pier Paolo dalle Masegne (1388–92) dominates the view of the sanctuary. The dalle Masegne carried out important works in Venice on the exterior of Palazzo Ducale and in San Marco, but this dossal is unique for its amazingly tall crockets, pinnacles and finials. It had a strong influence on the Bolognese school of sculpture. On the sanctuary walls are frescoes by Francesco da Rimini. There is a coronet of chapels in the ambulatory: in the central (east) one is a 14th-century painted Crucifix attributed to Pietro Lianori. In a chapel to the left there is a blue majolica *arca* by the local 19th-century ceramists Minghetti (in imitation of 15th-century Faenza ware) and, in the adjoining chapel, a gold-ground painting of the *Madonna and Saints* by Jacopo Forti (1485). The north aisle was cordoned off at the time of writing after slight damage in the earthquake of May 2012: it has the polychrome terracotta tomb of Pope Alexander V, with an effigy by Niccolò di Pietro Lamberti (1423): the lower part with angels, added in 1482, is the best sculptural work by Sperandio da Mantova. In the south aisle, opposite the side door, is the well-carved tomb of Pietro Fieschi (d. 1492), also with an effigy.

VIA GALLIERA, MUSEO MEDIOEVALE & THE CATTEDRALE

Via Galliera (*map Bologna West, 6*) was the main north–south artery of the city before (the parallel) Via dell'Indipendenza was built in 1888. It begins at the junction with Via Manzoni. It used to be famous for the splendour of its palaces but is now rather neglected. It descends slightly from the crossroads and is well worth exploring, lined as it is with buildings which used to be the grandest residences in the city. The first palace on the left is **Palazzo Torfanini**, with finely-carved capitals in its early 16th-century portico. The frescoes by Niccolò dell'Abate illustrating

Orlando Furioso, which used to decorate its early 16th-century interior, can now be seen in the Pinacoteca. On the same side, a smaller 16th-century palace (no. 6) has a relief (on the corner of Via San Giorgio) with a head in profile in a tondo, thought to be a portrait of Giovanni II Bentivoglio, and next to it a marble capital decorated with eagles. Both of these may once have decorated the Bentivoglio palace, destroyed in 1507.

Opposite is **Palazzo Dal Monte**, an elegant building attributed to Andrea da Formigine (1529). The huge **Palazzo Aldovrandi Montanari** (no. 8) was built for Cardinal Pompeo Aldovrandi; the pink and white Baroque façade (without a portico) was added by Alfonso Torreggiani in the early 18th century. It has been turned into flats and offices. The palace on the corner of Via Volturno (no. 13–15) has good terracotta windows above its portico. Opposite is the church of **Santa Maria Maggiore** (*closed since the earthquake of 2012*), with two 18th–19th-century statues on its façade. Palazzo Bonasoni, on the right (no. 21), with a portico, was built by Antonio Morandi (Terribilia) in the mid 16th century. Opposite, at no. 14, is the lovely brick **Palazzo Felicini** (Fibbia), with a handsome portico and portal and terracotta decorations dating from 1497 (well restored in 1906). The name of Via Riva di Reno records the Reno canal which once flowed here.

MUSEO CIVICO MEDIOEVALE

Map Bologna West, 6. Open Tues–Fri 9–3; Sat, Sun and holidays 10–6.30. Entrance at Via Manzoni 4.

Housed in Palazzo Ghisilardi-Fava, begun in 1483, with a pretty brick courtyard, this museum was founded in 1881 and has an important collection of medieval and Renaissance sculpture and decorative arts, beautifully arranged.

Ground floor: Rooms 1–2 illustrate the history of the private collections in the 17th and 18th centuries which were the origins of the civic museum. On the other side of the courtyard, which has 16th-century Jewish tombstones, **Room 4** has 14th-century tombs by the dalle Masegne and seven sculptures from Palazzo della Mercanzia: *Justice Enthroned* by Pier Paolo dalle Masegne (unfortunately damaged) between the half-figures of Bologna's patron saints (all carved by different sculptors in 1382–91 but all clearly influenced by the Dalle Masegne workshop).

Room 5 has remains of the Roman imperial palace in the first city walls, destroyed in 1116, and displays medieval metalwork and ivories.

The collection continues in **Room 6**, where there is a very fine bronze 13th-century Mosen ewer in the shape of a horse and rider. **Room 7** is dominated by the splendid over-life-size bronze and beaten-copper statue of Pope Boniface VIII by Manno Bandini (1301), formerly on the façade of Palazzo Pubblico. The 14th-century cope displayed here is one of the finest works ever produced in *opus anglicanum* (English medieval embroidery). It includes scenes showing the martyrdom of St Thomas Becket.

Lower ground floor: Room 9 contains a statuette of St Peter Martyr by Giovanni di Balduccio and **Room**

10 has remains of a Roman building on this site, and charming 14th-century tombs of university lecturers surrounded by their (mostly attentive) students. In **Room 11** is the red-marble tomb slab of Bartolomeo da Vernazza (d. 1348). **Room 12** has a triptych of the *Madonna and Child with Saints*, carved in bas-relief by Jacopo della Quercia and assistants, and a terracotta *Madonna* in high relief, also by Jacopo. The interesting recumbent image of a saint (with his pillow) in stuccoed and painted wood is by Antonio Federighi. In **Room 13** are several 15th-century floor tombs and the tomb of Pietro Canonici (d. 1502), attributed to Vincenzo Onofri.

First floor: Room 15 has three cases of small bronzes, which include Giambologna's model for the Neptune Fountain in Piazza Nettuno, the first version of the famous *Mercury* by the same artist, *St Michael and the Devil*, by Alessandro Algardi, and a bronze bust of Gregory XV by Gian Lorenzo Bernini. **Rooms 17–22** display the collection of decorative arts. Don't miss the ceremonial sword and sheath given to Lodovico Bentivoglio by Pope Nicholas V (Room 17); the European armour in Room 18; the ivory parade saddle (German, 15th century) in Room 19; and the collection of very fine bronzes and armour dating from the 13th–15th centuries made in Turkey (Room 20).

Rooms 21–22 display Northern European ivories and Venetian and German glass, including a rare blue glass cup with a gilt enamelled frieze, perhaps from the Barovier workshop in Murano (mid-15th century) and two vessels probably made for the wedding of Giovanni Bentivoglio and Ginevra Sforza in 1464. Another room downstairs has a fine display of 15th-century choirbooks, including one illustrated by Sano di Pietro.

Palazzo Fava next door, with rooms frescoed by the Carracci, is now an exhibition venue run by Genus Bononiae (*open Tues–Sun 10–7; genusbononiae.it*). Opposite is the church of the Filippini (known as the **Madonna di Galliera**), remodelled in 1479 with a Renaissance façade decorated with worn sculptures (statues and half-figures) in niches.

THE CATTEDRALE

On the busy Via dell'Indipendenza is the cattedrale (*map Bologna West, 7*), Bologna's cathedral (*open all day*), dedicated to St Peter, which, despite its status, is one of the least interesting churches in the city. Probably founded before the 10th century, it was rebuilt several times after 1605 and is now essentially a 17th-century Baroque building with an elaborate west front by Alfonso Torreggiani (18th century; its proportions difficult to appreciate because of the dimensions of the street). Just inside the door are two delightful red marble lions which survive from the Romanesque building. In the first south chapel is a terracotta group of figures in a *tableau* portraying the moment between the Deposition and Burial of Christ. It is the work of Alfonso Lombardi (1522–6) and has been restored (the polychrome was destroyed in the Neoclassical era, when the figures were painted white). The second south chapel preserves the skull of St Anne, presented in 1435 by Henry VI of England to Nicolò Albergati (the decoration of the altar in unusual perspective dates from 1906). There is a 12th-century polychrome *Crucifixion* group carved in cedar wood in the sanctuary (but it is difficult to see). The Treasury (*only open at weekends 2–5.30*) is arranged in five rooms and contains vestments, Church silver, processional Crosses and reliquaries, as well as a damaged *Madonna and Child* by Lorenzo Monaco.

MUSEO D'ARTE MODERNA (MAMbo)

Via Don Minzoni 14. Map Bologna West, 2. Open Tues, Wed, Sun and holidays 10–6; Thur, Fri and Sat 10–7. Closed Mon. Café and bookshop. www.mambo-bologna.org.

This modern art museum, with a permanent collection and the Morandi Museum, as well as temporary exhibition halls, was opened in 2007 in a huge building built in 1915 (and enlarged in 1929) as a flour mill and bakery. It has been imaginatively restored; the halls where temporary exhibitions are held were once the capacious bread ovens. The simple stark halls, spacious and light, provide excellent exhibition space. Renato Guttuso's *Funeral of Togliatti* (featuring the bright red flags of his Communist supporters) is one of the earliest works in the permanent collection. Palmiro Togliatti, a founder of the Italian Communist Party in 1921, died in 1964. Guttuso, who had joined the Communist Party in 1940, painted this in 1972, 15 years before his own death. The painting is well displayed, with beside it a captioned outline version showing who is who. Portraits of Pablo Neruda, Jean-Paul Sartre, Ho Chi Minh, Leonid Brezhnev, Stalin, Dimitrov and five likenesses of Lenin are included in the crowd, as well as a self-portrait of the artist.

The **Morandi Museum** on the upper floor (*well signposted*) contains the most representative collection in existence of works by Giorgio Morandi (1890–1964), born in Bologna. It was donated to the city by his family and includes oil paintings (including some of his characteristic still-lifes of bottles, but also landscapes and particularly interesting Metaphysical works) interspersed with watercolours, drawings and etchings. He was one of the most famous painters of the Italian *Novecento* movement and one of the few who is well-known outside Italy.

The **Casa Morandi** at Via Fondazza 36, where Morandi lived and worked, also run by MAMbo, is open by appointment (*map Bologna East, 16; T: 051 6496611, casamorandi@comune.bologna.it or check the MAMbo website*).

A public garden below the MAMbo, **Parco del Cavaticcio**, has been designed around a canal: this was once the port area of Bologna. The city used to be connected by waterways to Ferrara and as far as Venice. Also here can be seen an 18th-century salt warehouse.

THE OUTSKIRTS OF BOLOGNA

On a hill to the southwest of the city (bus 30 from the railway station) stands the former Olivetan convent of **San Michele in Bosco** (*beyond Map Bologna West, 14*), with a splendid view of Bologna. Here, on 1st May 1860, Camillo Cavour and Vittorio Emanuele II met to approve the sailing of the 'Thousand' to Sicily. The church, rebuilt since 1437 and completed in the early 16th century, has a façade ascribed to Baldassare Peruzzi (1523). In the cloister are the remains of an important fresco cycle by Lodovico Carracci, Guido Reni and others.

The sanctuary of the **Madonna di San Luca** (*map B, C2*) is a famous viewpoint, reached by bus 20 from Via Indipendenza to the public park of Villa Spada in Via Saragozza, at the foot of the hill of San Luca. From here a minibus (roughly every 30mins) ascends the hill. The church is connected with Porta Saragozza (*map Bologna West, 13*), just over 3km away, by a portico of 666 arches (1674–1793). Where the portico begins the ascent of the hill is the Arco del Meloncello, by Carlo Francesco Dotti (1718). The sanctuary, built by Dotti in 1725–49, contains a *Noli me Tangere* by Guercino, and paintings by Calvaert.

There is a **British Military Cemetery** off the Via Emilia, 5km southeast of Bologna. For details, see www.cwgc.org.

BOLOGNA PRACTICAL TIPS

INFORMATION OFFICES

Bologna Welcome in Piazza Maggiore (*T: 051 2239660, bolognawelcome. com; open Mon–Sat 9–7, and Sun and holidays 10–5; map Bologna East, 11*). The website has useful information and up-to-date opening times. There is also an office at the airport.

The **Bologna Welcome Card** gives a variety of discounts, free entrance to certain museums and free use of public transport including an airport transfer. Two tiers of card are available. See *bolognawelcome.com* for details.

GETTING AROUND

• **By air:** International airport (Marconi) at Borgo Panigale, 7km northwest. *Aerobus* every 15mins between the airport and Bologna railway station in 20mins with stops in Via Ugo Bassi and Via dell'Indipendenza. Taxis are available outside the arrivals hall. At the time of writing a shuttle rail service ('People Mover') was being constructed between the airport and railway station.

• **By car:** The large free car park outside the historic centre in Via Tanari has a minibus service (A) every 15mins to the station and Piazza Maggiore; also served by bus 29B which goes direct to Piazza Maggiore. Underground car park in Piazza 8 Agosto (*map Bologna East, 7*).

• **By rail:** Bologna is Italy's most important rail junction. A huge new underground station reserved for the fastest (and most expensive) trains (Alta Velocità, AV) has recently been opened, adjoining the old Stazione Centrale (*map Bologna West, 2*). Allow time if you are changing trains here since there is a lot of walking to do. To exit it is best to follow the signs for Piazzale Medaglia d'Oro which bring you through the old station concourse (closest to the centre of Bologna).

The *freccia rossa* services follow a tunnel beneath the Apennines (journey time between Florence and Bologna is less than 30mins); and they continue north from Bologna non-stop to Milan (journey time just over 1hr).

Intercity trains (IC), much less frequent than the AV trains, are slower (but much cheaper) and they stop at Modena, Reggio Emilia, Parma and Piacenza on the main north–south line which closely follows the Via Emilia from Bologna to Milan. There are also services to Ancona (2hrs, stopping at Rimini, Forlì and/or Faenza), Venice (via Ferrara and Padua, 1hr 50mins) and Verona (1hr 20mins). Commuter trains (Regionali and Interregionali) serve Ravenna and other centres in the region.

• **By bus:** Nos 25, 30, 37 or 90 from the railway station to Via Ugo Bassi (for Piazza Maggiore). Bus 30 continues to San Michele in Bosco. Bus 20 from Via Indipendenza to Villa Spada (and from there minibuses every 30mins to the Madonna di San Luca). The bus station at Piazza XX Settembre (*map Bologna West, 3*) has excellent services run by Tper (*T: 051 242150; tper.it*) to nearly all places of interest in the region.

• **By taxi:** Radio Taxi, T: 051 372727.

WHERE TO STAY

€€€ **Grand Hotel Majestic**. Successor to the historic Hotel Baglioni, this is an elegant and refined hotel with ample space and a good restaurant. A member of The Leading Hotels of the World group. *Via dell'Indipendenza 8, T: 051 225445, grandhotelmajestic. duetorrihotels.com. Map Bologna East, 7.*

€€ **Corona d'Oro** 1890. Central and comfortable. *Via Oberdan 12, T: 051 7457611, hco.it. Map Bologna East, 11.*

€€ **Art Hotel Orologio**. A small hotel in an ancient building in a quiet little lane just out of Piazza Maggiore. Slightly tired décor but an excellent location. Part of the Bologna Art Hotels group (*www.bolognarthotels.it*). *Via IV Novembre 10, T: 051 7457411, art-hotel-orologio.it. Map Bologna West, 10.*

€€ **Touring**. Peaceful, cosy and friendly, with good views from the rooftop terrace. *Via de' Mattuiani 1/2, T: 051 584305, hoteltouring.it. Off Piazza Tribunali, map Bologna East, 15.*

RESTAURANTS & WINE BARS

Bologna is full of excellent restaurants, and only a small selection is given here.

€€€ **Al Pappagallo**. Good ambience and excellent food in the heart of the old city. Closed Sat and Sun. *Piazza della Mercanzia 3c, T: 051 232807, alpappagallo.it. Map Bologna East, 11.*

€€€ **Cesari**. ■ Family-run restaurant in business since 1955. The present owner's uncle runs the large Cesari vineyards. Lively atmosphere and a warm welcome. The pasta speciality is *gramignone verde*, stout spaghetti served in a slow-cooked sausage sauce. Best to book. Closed Sun. *Via Carbonesi 8, T: 051 237710, www.da-cesari.it. Map Bologna West, 10.*

€€€ **Franco Rossi**. Popular and much-lauded restaurant, where tradition meets innovation. Also particularly good for fish. Excellent wines. Closed Sun. *Via Goito 3, T: 051 238818, ristorantefrancorossi.it. Map Bologna East, 7.*

€€ **Diana**. Old-fashioned Italian city *ristorante*, where waiters in white coats bring your meal on a trolley under a chafing dish. A slight feeling of time-warp lingers in the air (and characterises the kitchen) but the food and wines are respectable and the place is patronised by Bolognese at lunchtime. No loose wine but you can order a half-bottle. Closed Mon. *Via Indipendenza 24, T: 051 231302, ristorante-diana.it. Map Bologna East, 7.*

€€ **Trattoria La Corte Galluzzi**. Seasonally based traditional fare in a secluded courtyard, overlooking a medieval tower. Closed Mon. *Corte de' Galluzzi 7b, T: 051 226481. Off Piazza Galvani, map Bologna East, 11.*

€ **Bottega del Vino Olindo Faccioli**. Wine bar offering good cold dishes and a limited selection of hot dishes. Closed Sun. *Via Altabella 15b, T: 3493002939, enotecastoricafaccioli.it. Map Bologna East, 11.*

€ **Cantina Bentivoglio**. A good wine bar; open evenings only, with live jazz. Closed Mon. *Via Mascarella 4b, T: 051 265416, cantinabentivoglio.it. Map Bologna East, 7.*

€ **Divinis**. Good selection of wines, matched by interesting selections of cheeses and cold meats. Closed Sun. *Via Battibecco 4c, T: 051 2961502,* *divinis.it. Off Piazza Galileo, map Bologna West, 10.*

CAFÉS & PASTRY SHOPS

Zanarini. Always crowded with the Bolognese. Taken over in 2013 by Anoniazzi of Mantua, renowned for their excellent chocolates, pastries and cakes. A good place to stop for a snack. Tables outside in the peaceful piazza in warm weather. *Piazza Galvani. Map Bologna East, 11.*

Gelateria delle Moline. For Bologna's best ice-cream. *Via delle Moline 13d. Map Bologna East, 7.*

Pasticceria Impero. For coffee and pastries. *Via Caprarie 4. Map Bologna East, 11.*

SPECIALITY FOOD SHOPS

Antica Drogheria Calzolari. A good selection of Bolognese food and wines. *Via G. Petroni 9. Map Bologna East, 12.*

Boutique del Formaggio. For local and Italian cheeses. *Viale Oriani 16 (near Santo Stefano). Map Bologna East, 11.*

Casa Dolciaria Giuseppe Majani. A historic confectioner (no seating; you come here to buy sweetmeats to take away). *Via Carbonesi 5. Map Bologna West, 10.*

Paolo Atti. Historic baker and confectioner known for their bread, cakes and pastas. This is the place to come for *certosino*, the traditional candied-fruit confection of Bologna. *Via Caprarie 7. Map Bologna East, 11.*

ENTERTAINMENT

Bologna probably has more theatres per square metre than any other

Italian city. There are opera, ballet and concert programmes at the Teatro Comunale (*map Bologna East, 7; www. comunalebologna.it*), late Oct–May, as well as numerous other classical music series. Concerts also at the EuropAuditorium in the Quartiere Fieristica (*Piazza della Costituzione; beyond map Bologna East, 4; www. teatroeuropa.it*) and at the Auditorium Manzoni behind the Madonna di Galliera (*map Bologna West, 6; www. auditoriumanzoni.it*). Concerts are regularly held in the Oratory of Santa Cecilia next to San Giacomo in Via Zamboni (*map Bologna East, 7*). The Bologna Festival (*www.bolognafestival. it*) organises a wide range of musical events in spring and autumn. Live Jazz is played in the evenings at numerous wine bars. All up-to-date details of performances in the city from the *Bologna Welcome* office in Piazza Maggiore (*T: 051 231454, bolognawelcome.it*). English-language listings can be found in the free booklet *L'Ospite di Bologna*.

For art exhibitions, check what is on at GAM (*Via d'Azeglio 15, maggioregam.com*).

LOCAL SPECIALITIES

The central shopping district is known as the Quadrilatero, the area bounded by Via Rizzoli, Via dell'Archiginnasio, Via Farini and Via Castiglione, where the medieval guilds had their headquarters. Today you will still find plenty of historic shops offering jewellery, crafts and food. In fact some of the best things to buy in Bologna are eatables: *tortellini, raviole, mortadella, passatelli*, etc. Markets are held on Fri and Sat in Piazza 8 Agosto (*map Bologna East, 7*). At Easter time the *pasticcerie* sell special dove-shaped cakes called *colombe*. *Certosino* is a traditional cake made from almonds, pine nuts, chocolate, candied fruit and spices.

RAGÙ ALLA BOLOGNESE

Ragù is a meat sauce for pasta used in numerous regions of Italy, including Naples, but Bologna has always been the place where it is most popular. In England, in the days when pasta was virtually unknown (up until the 1960s), 'spaghetti bolognaise' was a favourite institutional meal: overcooked spaghetti, often conveniently cut up and tinned in a glutinous mince and tomato sauce—a far cry from any pasta available then or now in Italy itself. To make a true *ragù*, the Bolognese simmer minced veal in butter and then add a little bacon and/or Parma ham or *mortadella*, an onion, a stick of celery, a carrot, a clove, with chopped chicken livers. When this is cooked they add a glass of good hot broth and a glass of tepid milk. Then a little tomato paste diluted in a spoon of broth, and seasoning (salt, pepper, a pinch of marjoram, and nutmeg). No more tomato than that. The sauce has to cook over a very low heat for two or even three hours. Nowadays many Italians substitute the butter with olive oil, and cut down the cooking time, but it remains an excellent condiment for pasta of any shape or size. It is now invariably found on restaurant menus all over the country, not just in Emilia Romagna.

East end
The exterior of the triple apse is a wonderful sight, continuing the architecture of the rest of the exterior with tall blind arcades ending in pretty loggias above. Another inscription here, dating from the early 13th century, records the foundation of the church by Lanfranco.

North side
On the north side, with more very fine capitals, the Porta della Pescheria has delightful carvings by the school of Wiligelmus, showing in the lunette an assault by six mounted knights on a castle; beasts on the architrave and Labours of the Months on the inner jambs (*the Cathedral Museum in the lane here is described below*).

Two Gothic arches link the duomo to its beautiful detached campanile, the **Torre Ghirlandina**, 86m high and slightly inclined. It was begun at the same time as the duomo, the octagonal storey being added in 1319; the spire was rebuilt in the 16th century. The interior can sometimes be visited (*open April–Oct Sun 10–1 & 3–7; closed Aug*).

INTERIOR OF THE DUOMO
The Romanesque arcades, in pale red brick, have alternate slender columns and composite piers that support an early 15th-century vault. The capitals are by Wiligelmus and his school. The pavement is made up of stripes of beautiful pink and white marble. The two huge stoups are carved out of Roman capitals.

The most conspicuous sculptures are in front of the raised choir on the **roodscreen** or parapet and pulpit, which are supported by columns resting on lions and crouching figures, and with intricately carved capitals. The polychrome scenes of the Passion were splendidly carved by Anselmo da Campione in 1200–25. The largest and most striking is the *Last Supper* in the centre, with the Disciples sitting at a very long table covered with a white tablecloth; this panel is preceded on the left by the *Washing of the Feet* and followed on the right by the *Kiss of Judas, Christ before Pilate* and *Christ carrying the Cross*. The reliefs on the pulpit represent Christ enthroned in majesty in the centre flanked by two panels each with a pair of symbols of the Evangelists. The two last scenes on the left depict St Jerome and St Ambrose together, and St Augustine and St Gregory, while the last on the right, by the parapet, shows Jesus rousing St Peter from his slumbers. Above hangs a wooden crucifix in painted high relief (1270–1300).

In the raised **choir**, a screen of slender pink-and-white marble coupled columns in two tiers, by Campionese artists, surrounds the beautiful altar table. The inlaid stalls are the masterpiece of the brothers Cristoforo and Lorenzo da Lendinara (1460s), famed for their illusionistic intarsia work (four inlaid portraits of the Evangelists by Cristoforo can be seen at closer range on the wall here). The decoration in imitation of mosaic in the central and right apse dates from the early 20th century. In an elaborate frame in the left apse is a beautiful polyptych with the *Coronation of the Virgin,* the *Crucifixion,* and saints and donors, the best work by Serafino de' Serafini, born in Modena (signed and dated 1385).

The lovely **crypt** has more remarkable capitals, some attributed to Wiligelmus himself. Here, protected by glass, is a stone slab which covers the simple 4th-century sarcophagus where St Geminian is buried. The expressive group of five polychrome terracotta life-size statues is by Guido Mazzoni (1480). This is known as the *Madonna della Pappa*, since it includes a servant girl who is offering a little bowl of food (*pappa*) to the Baby Jesus. The tiny organ here by Domenico Traeri dates from 1719.

At the beginning of the **south aisle**, behind the font and within a terracotta arch, are (damaged) frescoes attributed to Cristoforo da Lendinara, apparently painted a few years after he carved the stalls for the choir, with the *Last Judgement* and a frescoed triptych. The terracotta group of small statues illustrating the *Adoration of the Shepherds*, also in this aisle, is a beautiful work by Antonio Begarelli (1527), who produced a number of other such groups, mostly life-size, for the churches of Modena, where he was born c. 1499.

Near the beginning of the **north aisle**, the elaborately carved terracotta ancona is attributed to Michele da Firenze (c. 1440), and above a silver altar frontal is an altarpiece by Dosso Dossi, with a central figure of St Sebastian. On the steps up to the choir is a wall monument to Claudio Rangoni (d. 1537), to a design by Giulio Romano. The pulpit is by a Campionese master called Enrico (1322).

MUSEI DEL DUOMO (LAPIDARY MUSEUM AND CATHEDRAL MUSEUM)
Via Lanfranco 4. Open daily except Mon 9.30–12.30 & 3.30–6.30.

In the little garden court is the entrance to the **Museo Lapidario**, arranged in just two rooms, with Roman and medieval epigraphs (transcribed) and some Roman fragments found in the foundations of the duomo, as well as early Christian carvings from the earlier church (8th–11th centuries). The most important sculptures here are the eight so-called 'metopes' from the exterior of the duomo (brought under cover in 1948 and replaced *in situ* by copies). These weird carved monsters, with an Archaic Greek look about them, are by an unknown master named from these works the 'Maestro delle Metope', who was probably active in the workshop of Wiligelmus in the early 12th century.

Upstairs is the **Museo del Duomo**, opened in 2000. Beyond the first room (with Church silver, mostly 17th-century), Room II has a precious small portable altar made in northern Europe at the end of the 11th or beginning of the 12th century. It is a very unusual piece, with green serpentine marble decorated with a border of silver and gilded reliefs on all four sides, and the base is also decorated (seen reflected in the mirror). The Evangelistery cover in silver and ivory dates from the 12th century. The restored statue in bronze and copper of Bishop St Geminian was made by Geminiano Paruolo in 1376 (it used to stand in the loggia of the duomo, on the south side above the Porta Regia, where it has been replaced by a copy). There is more Church silver in Room III, from all periods, including a silver and gilded processional Cross dating from the 14th century. Room IV has vestments and in Room V there are two tapestries made in Brussels in the mid-16th century. The last room has precious codices and antiphonals (some of them in facsimile) which belong to the Cathedral Chapter and a painting of *St Vincent Ferrer* by Angelo and Bartolomeo degli Erri, dating from the 1480s.

PIAZZA GRANDE

This lovely cobbled piazza (*map Modena 5*) is closed on its north side by the splendid flank of the duomo. In the corner outside Palazzo Comunale is a massive red stone block raised off the ground, known as the '*pietra ringadora*', which was used in medieval times for public announcements and later as a 'punishment block'.

PALAZZO COMUNALE

This palace, with an arcaded ground floor and a grand clock tower, was first erected in the 12th century but dates in its present form from a reconstruction of 1624. The historic rooms are open to visitors (*Mon–Sat 8–7, Sun 9–1 & 3–6*), approached directly from the piazza by a broad staircase. The Sala del Fuoco has the most interesting frescoes (1546) by Niccolò dell'Abate, born in Modena around 1509. They show episodes in a battle which took place here in 43 BC and beneath the scenes is a lovely frieze of fruit and flowers. In the little adjoining room is the '*secchia rapita*', a trophy traditionally identified as a bucket stolen by the Modenese from Bologna in a battle in 1325 and described in a satirical epic poem of the same name, the best-known work of Alessandro Tassoni (1622). The Sala del Vecchio Consiglio has a good vault decorated with paintings (1608) by Ercole dell'Abate, a descendant of Niccolò. The Sala degli Arazzi is so called because the walls were painted with tapestries in 1769. The corner room has paintings by Adeodato Malatesta, Modena's most important 19th-century painter.

Just out of Piazza Grande is **Piazza XX Settembre**, with pretty houses and a side entrance to the busy covered **market** (*open daily except Sun until 2.30*), with excellent food stalls and places selling snacks. Nearby is the **University** (*map Modena 6*), founded c. 1178, in a building of 1773.

Off the other side of Piazza Grande is the little Piazza della Torre beside the splendid **Torre Ghirlandina** (*see p. 54*), fronting the Via Emilia which runs through the centre of the town, and where a statue (1859) by a local sculptor Alessandro Cavazza celebrates the Modenese writer Alessandro Tassoni.

PALAZZO DEI MUSEI

The huge Palazzo dei Musei (*map Modena 3; www.palazzodeimuseimodena.it*) was built in 1771 as a poorhouse. It now houses a number of museums.

GALLERIA ESTENSE

Open Tues–Sat 8.30–7.30; Sun and holidays 2–7.30, except 1st Sun of the month when it opens at 8.30am and entrance is free. www.gallerie-estensi.beniculturali.it.

The gallery is situated on the top floor of the huge palace. It has a fine collection of pictures put together by the Este family and notable especially for its works by the 15th–17th-century Emilian schools. The most important part of the collection was dispersed during the Napoleonic era and ended up in Dresden. The highlights of the surviving holdings are as follows:

Paintings

The collection of paintings gives a broad representation of Northern Italian painting from the 14th–16th centuries. The earliest works include paintings by Tommaso da Modena and Barnaba da Modena. There are also representative works by Cristoforo Lendinara, Bartolomeo Bonascia and Francesco Bianchi Ferrari along with works by Francesco Botticini (*Adoration of the Child*), Giuliano Bugiardini and Andrea del Sarto (*Madonna and Child with St Elizabeth and St John*). The *Deposition* by Cima da Conegliano is one of the finest paintings in the collection. Also represented are Vincenzo Catena, Giovanni Cariani, Francesco Maineri and Filippo Mazzola (father of Parmigianino). Another masterpiece is the *Madonna Campori* by Correggio. Works by the Ferrara school include a *St Anthony of Padua* by Cosmè Tura and the *Madonna and Child between Sts and George and Michael Archangel* by Dosso Dossi. Sixteenth-century Emilian paintings include works by Garofalo (d. 1559), who helped establish the High Renaissance style (with Raphael as his model) in this region of Italy. Notable among the portraits is a likeness of Francesco I d'Este by Velázquez.

The later paintings (16th–17th-century) include works by the Venetian school, including Tintoretto (notably the octagons with scenes from Ovid's *Metamorphoses* for the villa of Vittore Pisani), Il Padovanino, Veronese (*Saints*), Palma il Giovane, Pietro Liberi and Jacopo Bassano. The Emilian school is represented by Guercino (*Martyrdom of St Peter*), Guido Reni (*St Roch in Prison*), Lodovico Carracci, Prospero Fontana (*Holy Family*), Scarsellino, Pier Francesco Cittadini (still lifes) and Carlo Cignani (*Flora*). There are also works by Camillo and Giulio Cesare Procaccini, Pomarancio, Il Cerano, Rosa da Tivoli, Salvator Rosa and Daniele Crespi and twelve panels from the ceiling of Palazzo dei Diamanti in Ferrara by the Carracci and others.

The non-Italian paintings include Flemish works by Albrecht Bouts, *Madonnas* by Joos van Cleve and Mabuse, a portable altar painted by El Greco and the *Marriage of Moses and Zipporah* by Charles Le Brun.

Sculpture, antiquities and artefacts

There is a marble bust of *Francesco I d'Este*, founder of the collection, by Gian Lorenzo Bernini (1652). Also on display are bronzes by L'Antico (including the Gonzaga Vase) and terracotta statues by 16th-century Emilian artists. The collection of medals includes some by Caradosso, Pisanello, Moderno, Bonacolsi and Giovan Cristoforo Romano. There is a marble head of a veiled lady by François Duquesnoy and a carving by Grinling Gibbons. Egyptian and Italic antiquities also form part of the collection. There is also a beautiful 16th-century portable writing desk and the Estense harp, beautifully decorated at the end of the 16th century.

MUSEO D'ARTE MEDIEVALE E MODERNA AND
MUSEO ARCHEOLOGICO ETNOLOGICO

Open Tues–Sat 9–12 & 3–6, Sun and holidays 10–1 & 3–7.

Both collections are housed on the floor below the Galleria Estense. The medieval and 'modern' holdings include the terracotta *Madonna di Piazza*, commissioned from Begarelli in 1523 for the façade of the Palazzo Comunale; reliquary crosses; musical instruments including a harpischord by Pietro Termanini (1741) and flutes made by Thomas Stanesby (1692–1754) in London; scientific instruments including the microscope of Giovanni Battista Amici; ceramics; and arms. Room 8 preserves its furnishings of 1886, when it was opened to display the Gandini collection of ancient fabrics, textiles and embroidered silks (with about 2,000 fragments dating from the 11th–19th centuries).

The large hall (10) displays the archaeological holdings, arranged chronologically from the Palaeolithic era onwards. There is an important section devoted to Mutina, Roman Modena. The ethnological material is arranged in rooms 11, 12 and 13, with exhibits from New Guinea, pre-Columbian Peru, Asia, South America and Africa. The last room (14) displays the Matteo Campori (1857–1933) collection of paintings with 17th- and 18th-century works, and a collection of cameos.

Also on the first floor is the city archive and the **Biblioteca Estense** (*open daily except Sun and holidays 9–1*), with illuminated manuscripts, notably the Bible of Borso d'Este, illuminated by Taddeo Crivelli and Franco Russi; a 14th-century edition of Dante; and the missal of Renée of France by Jean Bourdichon (16th century). Renée was the wife of Ercole II of Modena and was noted for her Calvinist sympathies.

Beside the palace is the church of **Sant'Agostino** (*map Modena 3; closed since the earthquake*), with a sumptuous interior designed by Giovanni Giacomo Monti in 1664. The *Deposition* (1524–6), with stucco figures bearing traces of colour, is the masterpiece of Antonio Begarelli. The detached 14th-century fresco of the *Madonna and Child* is by Tommaso da Modena.

PALAZZO DUCALE

Map Modena 4. Open for guided visits on some weekends by appointment. Contact Modenatur (T: 059 220022) or IAT (T: 059 203 2660).

Preceded by the spacious Piazza Roma (*map Modena 4*), the huge Palazzo Ducale was begun in 1634 by the Roman architect Bartolomeo Avanzini for Francesco I, on the site of the old Este castle. On the façade are sculptures (1565) in niches by the local sculptor Prospero Sogari (called Clemente). Since 1798 it has been used as a barracks and it has been the seat of the Italian Military Academy since the early 20th century. The interior has a fine courtyard and a monumental 17th-century staircase. In the state apartments, with portraits and frescoes by Francesco Stringa, the Salone d'Onore has a ceiling fresco by Marcantonio Franceschini, and the Salottino d'Oro has elaborate decorations dating from 1751. There is a museum (inaugurated in 1905) illustrating the history of the Military Academy, founded in Turin in 1669.

Beside the palace is the church of **San Domenico**, rebuilt in 1708–31. In the baptistery is a colossal terracotta statuary group by Begarelli, thought to represent Christ in the House of Martha.

OTHER CHURCHES OF MODENA

SOUTH OF VIA EMILIA
Reached from the duomo by the arcaded Corso Canal Chiaro, is the church of **San Francesco** (1244; altered in the 19th century; *map Modena 5*), which contains a terracotta *Descent from the Cross* (1530–1) by Begarelli. The Baroque church of **San Bartolomeo** (*map Modena 5*) has paintings by Giuseppe Maria Crespi and others. The 15th-century church of **San Pietro** (*map Modena 8*), with an ornamented brick front, contains more sculptures by Antonio Begarelli, an organ with 16th-century paintings, and a good painting by Francesco Bianchi Ferrari. Beyond the church is a pleasant park with a war memorial of 1926.

NORTH OF VIA EMILIA
The domed **Chiesa del Voto** (*map Modena 3*) was built in 1634 and has 17th-century works by Francesco Stringa and Lodovico Lana. The 17th-century church of **San Vincenzo** (*map Modena 6–4*) has Estense tombs and paintings by Matteo Rosselli and Guercino. The Baroque church of **San Giorgio** (*map Modena 4*) is by Gaspare Vigarani. Nearby in Piazza Mazzini is the **synagogue**, built in 1869–73 (*open by appointment; T: 059 223978*).

Santa Maria Pomposa (*map Modena 3*) is the burial place of Lodovico Antonio Muratori (1672–1750), provost of the church from 1716 and an eminent historian (nicknamed the 'Father of Italian History'). He lived and died in the adjacent house, now a museum (*open Mon–Fri 5.30pm–7.30pm*), which preserves his autograph works and other mementoes.

THE GIARDINO PUBBLICO

Map Modena 4. Entrances on Corso Cavour and Corso Vittorio Emanuele II.

These pleasant public gardens were laid out in 1602. The Palazzina dei Giardini, a garden pavilion begun in 1634 by Gaspare Vigarani (and altered in the 18th century), is used for exhibitions by the Galleria Civica. It adjoins the Botanical Gardens (*opened on request at the Istituto Botanico of the University*), founded by Francesco III in 1758. Beyond the other end of the gardens is the huge **Tempio Monumentale** (*map Modena 2*), a war memorial built in an eclectic style by Achille Casanova and Domenico Barbanti in 1929.

MODENA AND SPORTS CARS

In 2012 the **Museo Casa Enzo Ferrari** was opened in Via Paolo Ferrari 85 (*map Modena 2*). It consists of the house where Enzo Ferrari was born in 1898, and a modern building next to it, which has a roof in the favourite 'Modena yellow', in imitation of the louvred bonnet of the famous racing cars produced by the firm which he founded and which bears his name. The museum (*open every day 9.30–6; 7 in summer; combined ticket available with the Maranello Museum, to which you can book a shuttle bus service; museocasaenzoferrari.it*) is close to the railway station and Tempio Monumentale. It has a section on the history of motoring and an exhibition centre and café. In Ferrari's birthplace there is a multimedia exhibition illustrating his life and including a reconstruction of his office. Ferrari's first victory was at the Rome Grand Prix in 1947. The racing cars and sports cars he built soon became world famous and his single-seaters and prototypes won the most important championship races. He managed to maintain the firm's leading position despite fierce competition. He is remembered for his complex Machiavellian character, a self-styled 'agitator of men', though by the time of his death in 1988 he was also greatly revered as one of the most successful industrialists in Italy. The **Ferrari works** which he founded are at **Maranello**, about 16km south of town (*map B, A2*). Here some 7,000 cars are still manufactured every year for wealthy clients all over the world. Close to the factory is a much visited museum (*Via Dino Ferrari 43; open as for the Museo Casa Enzo Ferrari; museo.ferrari.com*), which preserves more mementoes of Enzo Ferrari and examples of racing and sports cars, both vintage and modern. Important exhibitions are held here regularly. (A good place to have a meal in suitable surroundings, which has for long been favoured by motoring enthusiasts, is the €€ Ristorante Cavallino in Maranello.) Near the musuem at Fiorano is the Ferrari test track.

The Fiat group also produces another world-famous brand of sports and racing car in Modena, the **Maserati** (the factory is in Viale Ciro Menotti; *map Modena 6*). The works moved from Bologna in 1940 and in 1997 the brand was acquired by the Ferrari group.

About 19km east of the Modena (beyond Nonantola; *map B, B2*) is Sant'Agata Bolognese, where the **Lamborghini works** are located. This company at first produced tractors but entered the world of racing cars in the 1960s and managed to withstand the competition from Ferrari with considerable success. Now owned by the Volkswagen group, outrageously imaginative models of sports cars are still produced by Lamborghini and a museum was opened here in 2001 (*open Mon–Fri 10–12.30 & 3.30–5; Via Modena 12*).

MODENA PRACTICAL TIPS

INFORMATION OFFICE

IAT. *14 Piazza Grande, T: 059 203 2660, visitmodena.it.*

GETTING AROUND

• **By air:** The nearest airport is Bologna, 36km from Modena.
• **By rail:** Modena is on Italy's main north–south line from Milan via Bologna and Florence to Rome. Some fast trains and most Intercity trains stop at Modena (1hr 30mins from Milan, 30mins from Bologna), and there are through trains also from Rome/Florence. Commuter trains (Regionali and Interregionali) connect Modena with Mantua and Verona.

Modena has two railway stations: Piazza Dante (close to the historic centre; *map Modena 2*) for all main line services and for Sassuolo; Piazza Manzoni for local trains to Fiorano and Sassuolo.
• **By car:** Car parks at Parco Novi Sad (*map Modena 1*), Viale Vittorio Veneto (*map Modena 5*), Viale Berengario (*map Modena 3*), Viale Fontanelli, (*map Modena 1*) Viale Sigonio (*map Modena 7*) and Piazza Roma (*map Modena 4*). Free parking in Piazza Giovani di Tienanmen (*map Modena 1*).
• **Trolleybuses** provide all town transport: no. 7 from the station to the museums and Via Emilia (for the duomo). SETA (setaweb.it) run services to localities in the province from the bus station in Via Molza (*map Modena 1*).

WHERE TO STAY

€€ **Canalgrande**. Elegant and refined, in an 18th-century palace with luxuriant garden and excellent restaurant. *Corso Canal Grande 6, T: 059 217160, canalgrandehotel.it. Map Modena 6.*
€ **Libertà**. Central, in an ancient townhouse. *Via Blasia 10, T: 059 222365, hotelliberta.it. Map Modena 4.*
€ **Cervetta5**. In a short side street off Via Selmi which runs south from Piazza Grande. Perhaps a little pretentious but good value. Garage parking for small extra charge. The **Antica Trattoria Cervetta** is next door. *Via Cervetta 5, T: 059 238447, hotelcervetta5.com. Map Modena 5.*
€ **Ostello San Filippo Neri**. A very simple hostel. *Via Sant'Orsola 48–52, T: 059 234598, ostellomodena.it. Map Modena 2.*

RESTAURANTS

€€€ **Hosteria Giusti**. Specialising in traditional and old recipes, good cheeses, selection of wines and spirits. Closed Sun–Mon. *Via Farini 75, T: 059 222533, hosteriagiusti.it. Map Modena 4.*
€€ **Bianca**. Good, upmarket *trattoria*. Closed midday Sat and Sun. *Via Spaccini 24, T: 059 311524, trattoriabianca.it. Beyond map Modena 1.*
€€ **Francescana**. Elegant *osteria* specialising in traditional recipes, good selection of wines. Closed Sat midday–

Sun. *Via Stella 22, T: 059 210118, osteriafrancescana.it. Map Modena 5.*
€€ **Oreste**. Delicious Modenese specialities. Closed Sun evening and Wed. *Piazza Roma 31, T: 059 243324. Map Modena 4.*
€€ **Ristorante l'Erba del Re**. With a rather grand atmosphere, this restaurant concentrates on local products. For vegetarians there is a set menu of four dishes. Not far from the museums in the little piazza in front of Santa Maria Pomposa. Closed Sun and Mon at midday. *45 Via Castelmaraldo, T: 059 218188, lerbadelre.it. Map Modena 3.*
€€ **Stallo del Pomodoro**. Good wine selection, regional food. Closed Sat midday, Sun. *Largo Hannover 63, T: 059 214664, stallodelpomodoro.it. Map Modena 6.*
€ **Trattoria Aldina**. A simple but good place to eat in the centre of town beside the covered market. Closed Sun. *Via Albinelli 40, T: 059 236106. Map Modena 5.*
€€ **Vinicio**. Personal interpretations of traditional recipes, with garden seating in summer. Closed Sun–Mon. *Località Fossalta (outside the historic centre), Via Emilia Est 1526, T: 059 280313, ristorantevinicio.it.*

FESTIVALS & EVENTS

San Geminiano (patron saint), 31 Jan with a fair. Carnival celebrations on the Thur preceding Shrove Tuesday. Pavarotti & Friends, benefit concert, June (Pavarotti was born in Modena). Biennial International Military Band Festival, July (even years). Philosophy festival in September. The prose season at the Teatro Storchi (1886; *map Modena 6*) has a high reputation.

ACETO BALSAMICO TRADIZIONALE DI MODENA

The traditional balsamic vinegar of Modena is made exclusively in Modena province. The best vinegar is obtained from crushed Trebbiano and Lambrusco grape must, which is heated and reduced over an open flame, naturally fermented, then aged in wooden casks. The ageing process darkens and concentrates the liquid so that the finished product is rich and glossy, smooth and syrupy, with a complex, penetrating bouquet and an agreeable, balanced acidity. Its inimitable flavour, a delicate balance between sweet and sour, comes out entirely in the ageing: despite what one might think, no aromatic substances are added at any time. Production follows simple yet precise steps that must be performed with care and in the proper order. Nevertheless, each master vinegar-maker brings a personal touch to his or her own small output. These secrets are passed down, usually by word of mouth, from generation to generation, giving a distinct personality to each brand of balsamic vinegar.

Reggio Emilia

Reggio Emilia (or Reggio nell'Emilia; *map B, A2*) is the large, flourishing centre of an important agricultural area. Excellent Parmesan cheese (*Parmigiano-Reggiano* or *Grana*) is produced here. It was the Roman *Regium Lepidi* and is still divided in two by the Via Emilia: the southern part of the town retains a medieval pattern, whereas broad streets and open squares predominate to the north. The most settled period of Reggio's turbulent history was under the Este domination (1409–1796).

EXPLORING REGGIO EMILIA

ON AND AROUND PIAZZA DEL MONTE

The long **Via Emilia**, with pretty arcades along one side in front of shops and a medley of buildings lining its northern side (including at no. 27 the handsome Palazzo Sacrati, with a late 15th-century paved courtyard) passes straight through the little **Piazza del Monte**, which marks the centre of the town. Here is the altered 14th-century **Palazzo del Capitano del Popolo**, part of which is the Palazzo dell'Albergo Posta, transformed in the 16th century into a hospice and restored in an eclectic style in 1910. It adjoins the central Piazza Prampolini. The Romanesque **cathedral** has one of the oddest façades in Italy, added in 1555 by Prospero Sogari (who also carved the statues of Adam and Eve above the central door), but left unfinished. The unusual tower bears a group of the Madonna and donors, in copper, by Bartolomeo Spani (1522), who also carved the tomb of Valerio Malaguzzi, uncle of Ariosto, in the interior. The tomb of Bishop Rangone and the marble ciborium are also by Sogari.

It was here, in the **Palazzo Comunale**, that the green, white and red tricolour was proclaimed the national flag of Italy in 1797. The Sala del Tricolore has a small museum (*open Tues–Fri 9–12, weekends 10–1 & 4–7*). A passageway leads into the piazza in front of the church of **San Prospero**, guarded by six red marble lions. Rebuilt in 1514–27, it has a choir frescoed by Camillo Procaccini and fine inlaid stalls.

PIAZZA MARTIRI DEL 7 LUGLIO

On the other side of Via Emilia, Via Crispi leads north from Piazza del Monte to the huge **Piazza Martiri del 7 Luglio**, which adjoins the even larger Piazza della Vittoria. There is an ingenious fountain basin here as well as a harrowing bronze monument (1958) to Italian Resistance heroes. The elegant **Teatro Municipale** (1852–7), with statues on the roof, has a high reputation. Behind it are extensive public gardens, with another War memorial and a Roman family tomb of c. AD 50.

The large Palazzo San Francesco on the east side of the square, once a convent, has housed since 1830 the **Musei Civici** (*entered at Via Spallanzani 1; open Tues–Fri 9–12, weekends 10–1 & 4–7; numerous activities for children are organised*). At the time of writing these civic museums were undergoing rearrangement while the building is being radically restored, but some of them still have their charming, old-fashioned displays including, on the ground floor, the Collezione Spallanzani, founded in 1772 and bought by the city in 1799, which has a natural history collection (including fossils), an extensive zoological section, and botanical specimens. The Galleria dei Marmi, first opened in 1875, has Roman epigraphs, architectural fragments, and medieval sculptures. At the end is a modern hall with Roman portrait heads, glass, jewellery and bronzes, and an interesting numismatic collection with examples from the Reggio mint. Upstairs are the Galleria Fontanesi, founded in 1893, with 14th–15th-century frescoes and works by Emilian painters from the 15th–19th centuries (including Antonio Fontanesi and Prospero Minghetti, and Giovanni Costetti). The prehistory collection here, which has finds from the locality, includes a 5th-century treasure (with a fine gold fibula) and has been given a modern arrangement. The Museo Chierici has archaeological material (including Etruscan finds).

PIAZZA DELLA VITTORIA AND GALLERIA PARMEGGIANI

In **Piazza della Vittoria**, beside the Teatro Ariosto, designed in 1741 by Antonio Cugini (and rebuilt after a fire in 1851), is the Gothic-revival spire of the building built specially to house the **Galleria Parmeggiani** (*open Tues–Fri 9–12, weekends 10–1 & 4–7*), entered through a fine 16th-century Hispano-Moresque doorway brought from Valencia. This extraordinary collection retains its *fin-de-siècle* atmosphere, but the rooms are now a little shabby. It was put together by Luigi Parmeggiani, born near Reggio in 1860, who became an Anarchist and after being involved in an assassination attempt on two Socialist politicians. He escaped to London where he met Ignazio Leon y Escosura and the two of them became associates in an art gallery in Paris, named Louis Marcy Maison (Marcy was the maiden name of Escosura's wife). They dealt in fakes, inspired by medieval and Renaissance pieces, produced for them by skilled artisans. On Escosura's death Parmeggiani took up with his widow and even lived under the assumed name of Louis Marcy. His commerce thrived and he was able to sell numerous fakes to public art galleries as well as to private collectors. In 1924 he returned to his birthplace bringing with him this collection, for which he had this building built by Ascanio Ferrari (in 1932 he sold the gallery and its contents to the town of Reggio Emilia). Many of the works await a scientific study.

Handlists in the shape of fans are provided in each room, but in the first two, filled with arms and armour, jewellery and medieval metalwork, the fact that most of the objects are turn-of-the-century fakes is played down. Beyond a small room with Spanish 16th-century costumes, the central *Salone* is arranged as a commercial art gallery, with a great miscellany of objects from ceramics to sculpture, furniture and decorative arts. Amongst the most interesting pieces are a 15th-century *cassone* frontal painted with a Triumph; a painting by El Greco (on an easel in front of the fireplace); a Chinese screen of the Edo period; a triptych by a painter from Bruges and a statue of the pregnant Virgin by a 15th-century Flemish master. Paintings by Parmeggiani's father-in-law Cesare Detti (1847–1914) fill one room, and another has genre paintings by his erstwhile business partner, Escosura. Other rooms are devoted to Flemish and Dutch works and, more importantly 15th–16th-century Spanish works. In the last room are velvet embroideries dating from the 16th and 17th centuries.

MADONNA DELLA GHIARA

Off the south side of the Via Emilia (reached from the broad Corso Garibaldi) is the splendid Baroque church of the **Madonna della Ghiara** (*entered through the door on the right of the main portal*), built in 1597–1610 on a domed central plan by an architect from Ferrara, Alessandro Balbo. It has a very well-preserved interior, with its vaults and domes entirely decorated from 1615–40 with splendid Mannerist frescoes and stuccoes by Emilian artists including Alessandro Tiarini, Lionello Spada and Camillo Gavasseti. The main altarpiece on the north side is a dark *Crucifixion* (with St Prospero) by Guercino. On either side of the door into the sacristy, *St Philip Benizi* beneath a *Deposition*, by Orazio Talami, and *St George and St Catherine on their way to Martyrdom*, by Lodovico Carracci. The main south altar was designed in 1618 to contain the fresco of the *Madonna and Child* by the local painter Giovanni Bianchi (known as Bertone) of 1573, a copy of a miraculous image for whom the church was built and after whom it is named. A museum (*open Sun 3.30–6.30*) displays the church treasury.

REGGIO EMILIA PRACTICAL TIPS

INFORMATION OFFICE

Via Farini 1/a. *T: 0522 451152, turismo.comune.re.it*. For opening times of museums, see *www.musei.re.it*.

GETTING AROUND

• **By rail:** Reggio Emilia is on Italy's main north–south line from Milan via Bologna and Florence to Rome. Some fast trains stop at Reggio, and there are through trains also from Rome/ Florence. A new station for the fast *Alta Velocità–TAV* trains was under construction at the time of writing, designed by Santiago Calatrava.
Car parking in the former Caserma Zucchi (Viale Isonzo); underground car park in Piazzale Marconi in front of the railway station.
Bus station Piazzale Europa behind the railway station (services for the province operated by Agenzia Mobilità Reggio Emilia; *am.re.it*).

WHERE TO STAY

€€ **Hotel Posta**. Pleasant and comfortable, in the heart of town. *Piazza del Monte 2, T: 0522 432944, hotelposta.re.it.*

€€ **Delle Notarie**. A classic provincial hotel, with a cosy atmosphere and well furnished, with a good restaurant. Right in the centre of town off Via Castello which runs into Via Emilia a short way west of Piazza del Monte. *Via Palazzolo 5, T: 0522 453500, albergonotarie.it.*

€€ **Hotel Mercure Astoria**. A large modern hotel overlooking the park of Piazza del Popolo, just north of Piazza Martiri 7 Luglio. Unimaginative décor but with restaurant and car parking. *Viale Nobili 2, T: 0522 435245, mercurehotelastoria.com.*

€ **Student Hostel Della Ghiara**. *Via Guasco, T: 0522 452323.*

RESTAURANTS

€€ **Caffè Arti e Mestieri**. Offers creative variations on traditional recipes. In a lovely walled garden courtyard. Closed Sun–Mon. *Via Emilia San Pietro 16, T: 0522 432202, giannidamato.it.*

€€ **Canossa**. An old-established family restaurant serving excellent pasta dishes, and roast meats. *Via Roma 37/B, T: 0522 454196, ristorantecanossa.com.*

€€ **Chiostro della Ghiara**. Atmospheric restaurant in an old cloister, known for its good fish. *Via Guasco 6 (part of the old church complex of the Madonna della Ghiara), T: 0522 452323.*

CAFÉS

Pasticceria Torinese, on Via Fornaciari (with a 'tearoom')

Caffè Royal, on the corner of Via Guido da Castello and Vicolo delle Rose (off Via Farini), with a pretty little old-fashioned interior.

FESTIVALS & MARKETS

Market on Tues and Fri in four *piazze*: Piazza Prampolini, Piazza San Prospero, Piazza Martiri 7 Luglio, and Piazza Fontanesi.

Festival of San Prospero (patron saint), 24 Nov. In the first week of September, Sagra della Giareda, on Corso Garibaldi, with artisans' stalls selling traditional ware. 7 January, Festa del Tricolore.

The Teatro Municipale has a renowned winter opera and ballet season, and music and prose at the Ariosto theatre (*for information on the theatre seasons, T: 0522 458811, iteatri. re.it*).

LOCAL SPECIALITIES

Many shops sell good salami, ham and parmesan, including the Antica Salumeria Giorgio Pancaldi (*Via Broletto 1/P near Piazza San Prospero*). Bread and snacks from 'Da Lucia' (*4 Via Samarotto 4*).

PARMIGIANO-REGGIANO CHEESE

Parmigiano-Reggiano comes from a strictly defined area: both the cheese and the milk from which it is made are produced only in the provinces of Parma, Reggio Emilia, Modena and Mantua, by a consortium of 600 small dairies. The cows graze in open pastures or are fed locally grown fodder, and all-natural fermenting agents are used to give the cheese its particular flavour and texture.

Today as eight centuries ago, the process is the same: milk, fire, rennet, and the skill and knowledge of cheese masters are the basic ingredients. The giant truckles are aged naturally for at least a year (usually two years or more), all the while being brushed and turned, and inspected daily to check that they match up to strict consortium standards.

Parmigiano-Reggiano is a DOP (*Designazione d'Origine Protetta*) product, which means it meets special EU quality standards. If buying a truckle (or, more likely, part of one), you should look for ID markings on the rind: the words PARMIGIANO-REGGIANO, the identification number of the dairy, the month and year of production, the acronym DOP in pin-dot stencil, and the fire-marked oval brand of the Consorzio Tutela. If you're buying a pre-packaged slice, the oval brand will appear on the wrapper.

Real Parmigiano-Reggiano is straw-coloured, and the colour is always uniform throughout the cheese. Inside, the cheese forms long, thin flakes radiating from, or converging towards, the centre. The internal mass tends to be soft, minutely granulated, and dotted with barely visible holes. Although these traits remain constant, it is still possible to detect differences between individual cheeses. As is the case with any hand-made product, each truckle has a touch of individuality.

Environs of Modena & Reggio Emilia

T he area described in this chapter was badly hit in the earthquake of 2012. Reconstruction has been underway since. Five years on, in April 2017, Pope Francis visited the region and praised the people for their courage and tenacity.

CARPI

The most interesting place in the province of Modena is the town of Carpi (*map B, B1*). It has an attractive centre and some fine palaces (though it was one of the towns worst hit by the earthquake), though surrounded by extensive industrial suburbs. From 1327 to 1525 it was a lordship of the Pio family, famous as patrons of the arts, who after 1450 were called Pio di Savoia. The huge **Piazza Martiri**, laid out in the 15th–16th centuries, with a lovely portico, is particularly handsome. Here the **Palazzo dei Pio** houses the town's museums (*open Thur, Sat–Sun and holidays 10-1 & 3-7; Tues, Wed, Fri 10-1; palazzodeipio.it*). The Museo della Cità contains some fine works in scagliola, a material made from selenite, which is used to imitate marble and *pietre dure* (the town was famous in the 17th–18th centuries for its production of scagliola works). The Museo del Castello houses works of art and the third museum commemorates the victims deported to Nazi concentration camps in the Second World War. The largest Nazi internment camp set up in Italy in 1944 was at **Fossoli**, 5km to the north Carpi on the way to Novi di Modena; it is described at the beginning of *Se Questo è un'Uomo* (*If This is a Man*) by Primo Levi, who was deported from here to Auschwitz in 1944. He survived to write about the ordeal.

Beneath the portico in the piazza is a 19th-century pharmacy. The **duomo** was begun in 1514. The Teatro Comunale (with a fine interior) dates from 1857–61. The Portico del Grano dates from the end of the 15th century.

Behind Palazzo del Pio is **Santa Maria in Castello** (known as La Sagra), with its tall campanile. The 12th-century church was greatly reduced in size in 1514. It contains the sarcophagus of Manfredo Pio (1351), a marble ambo attributed to Niccolò (12th century) and two frescoed chapels of the early 15th century.

On Corso Manfredo Fanti is the late 17th-century church of **Sant'Ignazio**, which contains a fine high altar in scagliola (1696) and a large 17th-century painting by Bonaventura Lamberti. It houses the Museo Diocesano (*still closed at the time of writing following earthquake damage*). To the south is the church of **San Nicolò**, built on a central plan in 1494. It also contains fine scagliola altars. Further south are the Rococo church of the **Crocifisso** (with a *Madonna* by Begarelli) and **San Francesco** (*closed since the earthquake*) with the tomb of Marco Pio attributed to the school of Jacopo della Quercia and a fresco of the *Enthroned Madonna* attributed to Giovanni da Modena.

Via Giulio Rovighi is on the site of the **ghetto**, where the Jewish community was forced to live between 1719 and 1796. The synagogue at no. 57 was in use until 1922.

NORTH & EAST OF MODENA

Nonantola (*map B, B2*) has two 14th-century towers and is famous for its abbey, founded in 752 and rebuilt in brick in the 13th century. The portal has reliefs (1121) by the school of Wiligelmus, who produced the famous decorations on the exterior of Modena's duomo. The church contains the tombs of popes St Sylvester and Adrian III. In the refectory are fresco fragments dating from the early 12th century. Adjacent is the Museo Diocesano.

Mirandola (*map B, B1*), at the epicentre of the earthquake, was a principality of the Pico family, the most famous member of which was Giovanni Pico (1463–94; known as Pico della Mirandola), the humanist and scholar noted for his learning, a famous figure of the Italian Renaissance. The church of San Francesco, with its tombs of the Pico family, was almost totally destroyed in the earthquake. There are scanty remains of the Pico ducal palace in the main piazza. The Collegiata (collegiate church) was also destroyed in the earthquake but a 15th-century wood Crucifix was extracted in many pieces from the rubble and has subsequently been restored.

San Felice sul Panaro (*map B, B1*) and the pretty little town of **Finale Emilia** (*map B, C1*) were also at the epicentre of the quake. Not only were there human casualties, but thousands of the inhabitants had to leave their homes and much of the damage was irreparable. The Este castle at San Felice was heavily damaged. Finale's castle was reduced to rubble.

SOUTH OF MODENA

On the Panaro river is **Vignola** (*map B, B2*), a fruit-growing centre famous for its cherries. It was the birthplace of the architect Jacopo Barozzi, called Il Vignola (1507–73). He became the most important successor to Michelangelo in Rome. The fine castle (*for opening times, see www.roccadivignola.it*) was built by Uguccione Contrari between 1401 and 1435. The chapel has very interesting late-Gothic frescoes by an unknown artist who was at work in the early 15th century and is known from these works as the 'Maestro di Vignola'.

At **Sassuolo** (*map B, A2*) is the Palazzo Ducale, rebuilt for the Este in 1634, with an interesting park. This gem of Baroque architecture is by Bartolomeo Avanzini, who also built the Palazzo Ducale in Modena. It contains decorations by Jean Boulanger, and by Angelo Michele Colonna and Agostino Mitelli in the *salone* (*for opening times, T: 0536 1844801, urp@comune.sassuolo.mo.it*). After the earthquake in 2012 the entire ground floor was been turned into a deposit for works of art from damaged buildings in Emilia and a restoration laboratory was set up here.

On the road to Abetone (the principal ski resort of Tuscany) across the Apennines is **Pavullo nel Frignano** (*map B, A3*), the 19th-century residence of the Dukes of Modena (now home to a small gallery of contemporary art, with works by local artists).

AROUND REGGIO EMILIA

Correggio (*map B, A1*) was the birthplace of the painter Antonio Allegri (1489–1534), nicknamed Correggio (*see p. 77*), whose house is in Borgovecchio. The Palazzo dei Principi, begun in 1507, contains the Museo Civico 'Il Correggio' (*for opening times, see museoilcorreggio.org or T: 0522 691806*), a small museum with 16th-century Flemish tapestries and a tempera *Head of Christ* by Mantegna. The 18th-century Teatro Asioli has been restored. The church of San Quirino (1516–87) has an interesting interior.

Novellara (*map B, A1*) has a castle (now the Town Hall) of the Gonzaga, dating in part from the 14th century. It contains a small museum (*usually only open on Sun*) with detached frescoes of the 13th–16th centuries and a remarkable series of ceramic jars made for a pharmacy in the 15th–16th centuries.

Gualtieri (*map B, A1*) has the vast Piazza Bentivoglio as its main square (with a garden in the centre). It was begun in 1580 by Giovanni Battista Aleotti. Palazzo Bentivoglio, also by Aleotti, has 17th-century frescoes in the Salone dei Giganti. Nearby **Guastalla** (*map B, A1*) was once the capital of a duchy of the Gonzagas. It was badly damaged in the 2012 earthquake. In the square is a statue of the mercenary captain Ferrante Gonzaga (d. 1457), by Leone Leoni. The Basilica della Pieve is an interesting Romanesque church.

Brescello (*map A, D2*) is a town of Roman origins. In the central piazza is a copy of a statue of Hercules by Jacopo Sansovino (the original is kept in the Museo Archeologico in Via Cavallotti; *only open at weekends, for information, T: 0522 482564 or look at visitbrescello.it*). Sir Anthony Panizzi (1797–1879), librarian of the British Museum, was born in the town. The church of Santa Maria Maggiore (1830–7) was used as the setting of the film of *Don Camillo* (based on the book written in 1950 by Giovanni Guareschi) and there is a little museum (Peppone e Don Camillo) with mementoes of the film (*T: 0522 482564 or ufficioturismo@comune.brescello.re.it*).

Parma

arma (*map A, D2*) is the second city of Emilia (the first is Bologna). All its most interesting buildings and museums are grouped close together in the centre, just ten minutes walk from the station, which makes it a very easy place to visit, and it is well organised to receive visitors. Correggio, who arrived in the city around 1520, frescoed three domes here (in the Camera di San Paolo, the cathedral and San Giovanni Evangelista) which are amongst the most memorable decorations in all Italy, and particularly delightful for the relationship the figures establish with the viewer far below. Parma's baptistery is a very unusual building, with fascinating 12th–13th-century sculptures by Antelami. Some of the best paintings by Correggio and Parmigianino can be seen in the Galleria Nazionale of Parma, as well as masterpieces by other Italian painters, including Leonardo da Vinci. The gallery is very well arranged in the huge Palazzo della Pilotta, which also contains a great wooden theatre constructed for the first Duke of Parma at the very beginning of the 17th century. Two centuries later Napoleon's second wife Marie Louise became duchess of Parma and she is fondly remembered in the town, where the Museo Glauco Lombardi is dedicated to her 'reign'.

Parma is well-known for its food industries and is a gastronomic centre, famous for Parmesan cheese and Parma ham, and a stroll down the Strada Farini which leads south from Piazza Garibaldi shows you what it has to offer in the way of excellent places to eat and shops with local products. Parma is also traditionally one of the best places in the country to visit if you wish to hear good music and opera.

HISTORY OF PARMA

There was a Roman station here, on the Via Emilia, and recent excavations right in the centre of town under Piazza del Duomo have unearthed a number of Roman artefacts. In the 12th–14th centuries the town had a republican constitution. It was the birthplace of Frate Salimbene in 1221, and his chronicle (the manuscript is preserved in the Vatican Library) is one of the most interesting historical sources for the 13th century. From around 1335 onwards Parma was ruled by a succession of ducal families: the Visconti, Terzi, Este and Sforza. In 1531 it became a papal dominion and in 1545 Paul III made it over, along with Piacenza, to his illegitimate son Pier Luigi Farnese, who was given the title of duke. From this time forward Parma was ruled by a succession of dukes, their names often complicated by the fact that they were also kings of European states. King Charles III of Spain, of the house of Bourbon, inherited the dukedom in 1731 from his Farnese mother and called himself Charles I of Parma, and the Spanish house of Bourbon-Parma held the duchy thereafter until 1801. For the history of the dukedom after the Congress of Vienna in 1815, see p. 82.

PIAZZA DEL DUOMO

This cobbled square (*map Parma East, 7*) is particularly peaceful since the centre of life of the town is to the southwest, in and around Piazza Garibaldi. The monuments in the piazza are: the pink-and-white **baptistery**, remarkable for its very original architecture as well as its sculptures and lovely interior; the **duomo**; Palazzo Vescovile, the bishop's palace with the **Museo Diocesano** (opposite the duomo), first built in the 11th century, with a portico beneath a row of three-light windows on its handsome façade, well restored in 1935 (its courtyard dates from the 16th century); and **San Giovanni Evangelista** (facing the duomo's lovely apse and transepts at the east end).

Access to the monuments
For opening times, see piazzaduomoparma.com. Combined tickets are available. Last entry 15mins before closing. No entry to the churches during services.

THE BAPTISTERY
This splendid octagonal building in red Verona marble has an extremely interesting design showing the influence of French Gothic architecture as well as ancient Roman buildings. Begun in 1196, it is the masterpiece of Benedetto Antelami, a Romanesque architect and sculptor whose works can best be appreciated here in Parma. His first work in the town was for the duomo, where a sculpted panel of the *Descent from the Cross* dated 1178 is preserved. He was particularly skilled in incorporating sculptural works into architectural settings, and is seen as one of the last great Romanesque sculptors preluding the Gothic era. Some works in France have been attributed to him, and it is thought he must have visited Provence. Other works by him for churches in Emilia Romagna can be seen at Ferrara and Fidenza.

However, recent research has shown that the baptistery is not all Antelami's work and that after 1216 he was no longer involved in the building, which was taken over by Campionese masters (Campionese being a term used to describe masons, sculptors and architects from the Campione d'Italia region, who were active in Italy and Switzerland up until the end of the 14th century, and are often documented at sites where work was already underway but required completion). The consecration of the completed baptistery is documented in 1270.

Exterior of the baptistery
The upper storeys have four tiers of delicate galleries, with small columns supporting architraves, which encircle the octagon (the little towers on the roof were added in the 14th century). At pavement level blind arches with Classical columns, and

a frieze of 79 small panels carved with stylised reliefs including fantastic animals alternate with the doorways.

The three grand **doorways** bear splendid carvings by Antelami. The lunette over the main north door on the piazza shows the *Madonna and Child Enthroned* between the *Three Kings* and the *Dream of Joseph*. In the architrave beneath are the *Baptism of Christ, Banquet of Herod* and *Beheading of the Baptist*. The date of the foundation, 1196 is also inscribed here. The genealogical trees of Jacob and the Virgin adorn the door jambs. The west door depicts the *Last Judgement*: Christ as Judge surrounded by angels in the lunette and the Saved and the Damned in the architrave below being called by angels with trumpets. The relief in the lunette of the south door illustrates the *Legend of Barlaam and Josaphat*. These are two characters of Buddhist origin who became popular at this time when they were worshipped as Christian saints.

The six statues in couples in three niches on the exterior which represent Solomon and the Queen of Sheba, David and Isaiah, as well as two angels, are copies of the originals now displayed in the Museo Diocesano in the piazza (*see below*).

Interior of the baptistery

The interior provides a surprise since its design is decastyle rather than octagonal, and it has a beautiful dome. It is entirely decorated with paintings and sculpture (and very well illuminated). A continuous series of niches (painted over time with votive frescoes) encircles the lower walls between columns with lovely capitals, and in the lunettes of the niches are statues or (above the three doors and the altar) biblical scenes. Tall slim columns link these niches to the upper storey, which has two tiers of plain brick matronei (or galleries) behind small columns. At the spring of the umbrella vault, each of the 16 cells of which corresponds to a niche below, begins the painted decoration of the dome, of extreme interest for its iconography.

Antelami was responsible not only for the architectural design of the building but also for much of the carving, which (both inside and out) follows a scheme carefully worked out by him to illustrate the parallels between Old and New Testament stories. He also carved some of the loveliest capitals, including one near the altar illustrating *Daniel in the lion's den* (Daniel, shown wearing a beret, embraces a lion whose paw rests on his knee while two others sniff at his feet). Simpler capitals by the same sculptor have characteristic 'waves' recalling water, a clear allusion to the liturgical function of the building.

There are reliefs (later coloured) over the doors by Antelami (sometimes with the help of his workshop): *Flight into Egypt* (with an angel showing Joseph the way); *David playing the harpsichord*; and the *Presentation in the Temple*. Between them are angels and the *Annunciation* figures, in the apses of the niches, and 14 figures of the *Months*, winter and spring (some with reliefs of the signs of the zodiac below) have been set in the lower gallery—all of these must once have belonged to other architectural settings (and were possibly part of another portal outside on the south side). The lunette of *Christ* flanked by the symbols of the Evangelists is by a later sculptor.

The very unusual red-porphyry square altar is carved with the figures of John the Baptist, between a priest and a Levite, by Antelami, and against the wall is his original font supported by a lion.

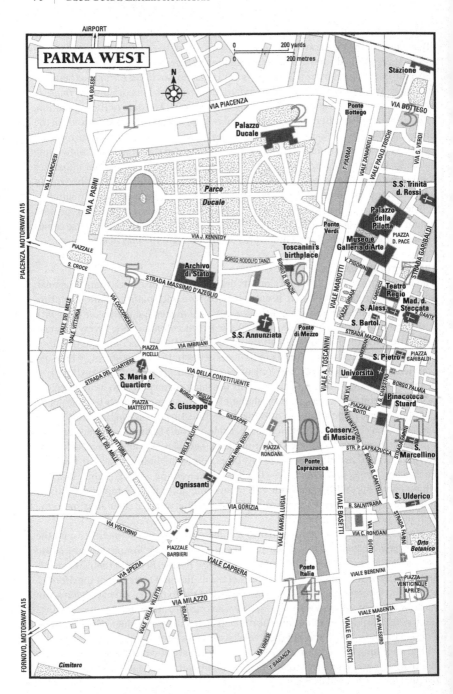

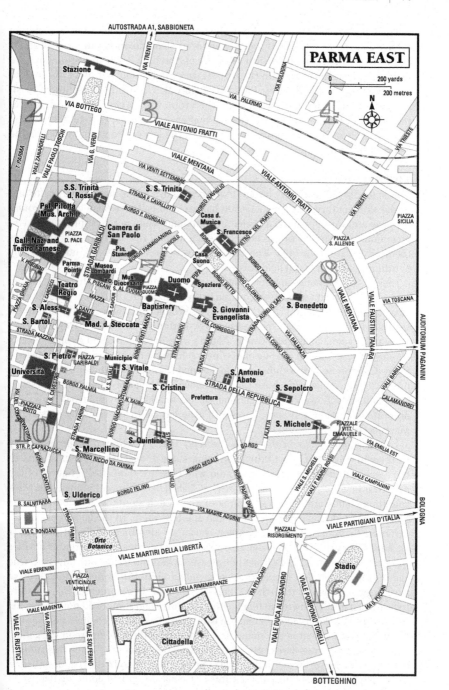

The cupola is totally covered with lovely tempera paintings almost certainly carried out in 1268–9, in a Byzantine style, in a composition unique in Italy. It begins with lunettes painted with the story of Abraham. In the register above are 16 scenes of the life of St John the Baptist (from the Annunciation of his birth to Zacharias and Elizabeth to the Banquet of Herod). The band above shows Christ, the Baptist, St John the Evangelist and the Virgin with twelve standing figures of the Prophets. Higher still are the twelve smaller seated Apostles together with the four symbols of the Evangelists. The stars in the key of the vault symbolise the celestial Heaven.

THE DUOMO

This splendid 11th-century church (*map Parma East, 7*) was modified by Antelami in the 12th century. The lovely façade has arcaded galleries (also carried around the apse and transepts) and a projecting pink-and-white porch, supported by two huge lions, with reliefs of the months added around the arch in 1281. The doors themselves date from 1494. The campanile was built in 1284–94, but, struck by lightning in 2009, it is still being restored.

Inside, the Romanesque structure is still clearly visible, with finely carved capitals, although it was entirely covered in the 16th century by frescoes in the vault, nave, aisles and west end (*light in the nave*). Around the stained-glass window on the west wall is a fresco of the *Ascension* by Lattanzio Gambara (1573). Gambara was a tailor's son taken under Giulio Campi's wing in Cremona and given an artist's training. These frescoes are one of his finest achievements, painted with the help of fellow Cremonese Bernardino Gatti. More good frescoes by Gambara, showing the life of Christ, can be seen above the matroneum in the nave. The vault is frescoed by a pupil and follower of Parmigianino, Girolamo Mazzola Bedoli (1557), who also decorated the choir and apse. The south aisle has ceiling frescoes by Alessandro Mazzola (son of Girolamo).

In the cupola (*light in the south transept*) is the celebrated **Assumption by Correggio** (1526–30), one of the most remarkable dome frescoes in existence. In the octagonal drum, between the round windows, are the colossal figures of the Apostles, in a crowd behind a *trompe-l'oeil* balustrade. Above, entangled in thick spiralling clouds are countless figures of angels and saints which dominate the scene—the Madonna can hardly be found amongst them. In the golden heaven an acrobatic figure descends to fetch her—variously identified as Christ himself or perhaps simply the Angel Gabriel. Understandably, perhaps, the Church authorities were taken aback and not altogether pleased when the dome was unveiled. One canon commented that the decoration seemed to him little more than a 'soup of frogs' legs', but it is said that when Titian saw the dome he commented that if it were to be turned upside down and filled with gold, Correggio would still not receive the recompense he deserved for such a masterpiece. The entire composition, almost too high up to be seen in any detail, is dominated by the lone figure in the golden dome, which provides an extraordinarily innovative iconography for this subject, which was for centuries one of the most popular with artists. In the spandrels below, Correggio painted the four patron saints of Parma: Joseph, St John the Baptist, St

Bernard (Bishop of Parma in 1106), and a St Hilary, all of them also atop cotton-wool clouds in which elegant youths are at play (and the artist didn't even bother to give these 'angels' wings).

In the south aisle, the fourth chapel has a lovely screen (c. 1507) in pink marble and remains of frescoes on the two side walls dating from the early 15th century, with amusing scenes from the busy lives of the two Roman martyrs, Sebastian (left wall) and Pope Fabian (right wall). The next (5th) chapel has monochrome frescoes on the lower side walls and an altarpiece of the *Madonna and Saints* with a donor the first work signed and dated 1496 by Alessandro Araldi, who lived and worked exclusively in Parma (*see the Camera di San Paolo, p. 79*). He was clearly influenced by Lorenzo Costa and Francesco Francia. At the end of this aisle, in the chapel by the side door, is a *Crucifixion with Saints* by Bernardino Gatti.

Steps lead up to the south transept, where on the wall is displayed a very moving relief (from the pulpit) of the **Descent from the Cross** by **Benedetto Antelami**, his earliest known work, signed and dated 1178. It includes a scene of the soldiers drawing lots for the tunic and the Angel Gabriel directing Christ's hand to comfort the Madonna, as well as two slightly smaller female figures representing the Church and the Synagogue. In the two rosettes are heads of the Sun and the Moon. Incised inscriptions help to interpret the scene.

In the sanctuary Antelami also carved the bishop's throne with telamones holding up the arms on which rest two lions, and the sides decorated with two reliefs of Saul falling from his horse and St George and the dragon. Here the beautiful stalls are signed by Cristoforo da Lendinara. The crypt has good capitals. The last chapel in the north aisle was entirely frescoed in the 15th century.

CORREGGIO (c. 1489–1534)

Antonio Allegri, born in Correggio, a small town near Modena, was always known by the name of his birthplace. He seems to have studied with Mantegna as a young man, and he was greatly influenced by the works of Raphael and Michelangelo, which he saw on a visit to Rome. One of the most important Italian artists of the early 16th century, his life is poorly documented, but he worked almost exclusively in Parma, where he frescoed the two magnificent domes of the duomo and San Giovanni Evangelista, where his use of the *sotto in sù* (literally 'upwards from under') technique, creates an extraordinary illusion of movement and suspension in space by a daring use of foreshortening. His influence on all later Baroque ceiling decorations is clear. The cupola he painted for the 'camera' of the abbess of the convent of San Paolo is on a more intimate scale but just as beautiful.

The town also possesses two of his most important oil paintings, in the Galleria Nazionale. He died aged only 45, and became extremely famous in the 17th and 18th centuries.

MUSEO DIOCESANO
Map Parma East, 7. Entrance in Vicolo del Vescovado, at the corner of Piazza del Duomo.

Inaugurated in 2003, the museum has finds from excavations here and sculptures from the exterior of the baptistery. In the first room is the original copper weathervane from the campanile in the form of the Archangel Raphael, dating from the last years of the 13th century (it has been replaced *in situ* by a copy). Stairs lead down to a room with Roman finds from excavations beneath the duomo and piazza, including a hoard of coins. In the large room in Palazzo Vescovile are sculptures by Antelami and his workshop, including six from the exterior of the baptistery (Solomon and the Queen of Sheba, two angels, and two prophets). There are also interesting sculpted panels from the duomo, including one in red Verona marble of Samson and the lion. Excavations dating from the Roman and medieval periods can be seen beneath the floor with a polychrome Paleochristian mosaic. An adjoining room exhibits the reliquary of the Florentine St Bernard ('degli Uberti'), who lived in Parma after he was appointed bishop here until his death in 1133. There is also a fascinating multimedia display showing the details of the decorations of the baptistery.

SAN GIOVANNI EVANGELISTA

Facing the prettily decorated Romanesque apse of the duomo, this church (*map Parma East, 7*), attached to its Benedictine monastery founded before 1000, was rebuilt in the early 16th century by an unknown architect but finished by Bernardino Zaccagni and his son Benedetto (whose works can only be seen in their native Parma). It was given its present façade a century later. It is famous for its dome frescoed by Correggio.

In the last north chapel a light illuminates (in sequence) the frescoes by Correggio (*see p. 77*) at the east end: over the sacristy door the lunette of the *Young St John Writing* (accompanied by his rather disgruntled eagle); the wonderful dome with the *Vision of St John at Patmos*; and in the main apse the *Coronation of the Virgin* (a copy made in 1587 by Cesare Aretusi of a larger composition later destroyed, but the original of which is kept in the Galleria Nazionale in Parma). Correggio frescoed the dome in 1521, just before the one in the duomo, which it resembles in the central figure suspended in space against a golden sky. This is Christ appearing to the Evangelist at his death: the Apostles, including the elderly St John, are all shown present in a circle of clouds accompanied by little putti. In the spandrels Correggio painted the Church Fathers. On the high altar is a *Transfiguration* by Girolamo Mazzola Bedoli. The stalls date from 1513–38.

The ribs of the nave vault are beautifully decorated by Michelangelo Anselmi and the nave walls have an exquisite frieze by Francesco Maria Rondani (on cartoons by Correggio) of prophets and sibyls. The entrance arches of the first, second and fourth north chapels have lovely frescoes by Parmigianino (*see p. 86*): the first chapel has a font made out of a large rectangular ancient Roman urn, and delightful frescoed putti with festoons of fruit and flowers. The fourth chapel has an altarpiece by Girolamo Mazzola Bedoli.

The frieze in the transepts dates from the late 15th or early 16th century. Two large statues by Antonio Begarelli adorn the south transept, and in the second south chapel there is an *Adoration of the Child* by Francesco Francia. In the sixth chapel in the north aisle is *Christ Carrying the Cross* by Michelangelo Anselmi.

The monastery

The Benedictine monastery, still operating as such, is approached through a portal in the piazza (*open daily 6.30–12 & 3.30–6.30*) with three lovely cloisters, a chapter house and a library with late 16th-century frescoes. The monks' ancient pharmacy, the **Spezeria di San Giovanni**, is entered from an old doorway in the lane behind (*Borgo Pipa 1, map Parma East, 7; open Tues–Sun 8.30–2, last entry 30mins before closing*). Founded in the 13th century it was in use up to 1881, and the three rooms preserve their 16th-century wooden furnishings, with 17th-century vases, mortars, and pharmaceutical publications. The old laboratory with its marble basin and well, where the apothecaries used to work, can also be seen.

THE CAMERA DI SAN PAOLO & PINOCATECA STUARD

CAMERA DI SAN PAOLO

Map Parma East, 7. Entrance at Via Melloni 3. Open Tues–Sun 8.30–2, Sat 8.30–5.30; www.parmabeniartistici.beniculturali.it.

In a peaceful corner of the centre of town, and since the mid-19th century approached by an avenue of japonica trees, this famous little room with its dome painted by Correggio (*see p. 77*) was once part of the Benedictine convent of San Paolo. It was in the private apartment occupied in the early 16th century by the Abbess Giovanna da Piacenza. The visit begins in a room with a copy of Leonardo's *Last Supper* by Alessandro Araldi (1516), 16th-century majolica, and engravings and watercolours by Paolo Toschi (1788–1854) of works by Correggio. A large room which used to be the convent refectory (and was later turned into a chapel) contains fine 17th-century carved wood stalls and 15th–16th-century detached frescoes from the convent (with appropriate scenes of nuns). Beyond is a little room with a very pretty vault adorned with grotesques against a deep blue ground by Alessandro Araldi. Here is displayed a late 15th-century *Nativity* with scenes from the life of the Virgin in polychrome terracotta. About six years after Araldi had painted this vault the abbess called in Correggio (in 1518 or 1519) to decorate the adjoining room, known as the Camera di San Paolo. His first commission in Parma, this is one of his most beautiful and charming works.

The Gothic umbrella vault is painted with a dome of thick foliage supported by wickerwork (canes cover the ribs of the vault). The abbess' coat of arms appears in the centre, surrounded by drapes off which hang festoons of fruit. Through 16 oculi in the arbour you can see groups of putti at play against the open sky. The dominant colour is a rich green. The monochrome lunettes below have painted *trompe-l'oeil* statues and reliefs of mythological subjects, and below is a frieze of rams' heads with veils stretched between them, in which are hung plates and pewterware (which may signify that the room was used as a refectory). The central theme seems to be Diana, goddess of Chastity; she was also painted (returning from the hunt) over the fireplace by Correggio.

The significance of these remarkable Humanist frescoes, in which the artist uses a careful play of light, is uncertain: the abbess was a particularly cultivated lady who lived in the convent for 17 years and was unsuccessful in her attempt to prevent it from becoming a closed community in 1524. The frescoes remained unknown to the outside world until the 18th century, which probably accounts for their excellent state of preservation.

There is a little public garden here, opened in 1994, and a remarkable puppet museum, not to be missed, however unexpected. Another part of the convent is now occupied by the Pinacoteca Stuard (*see below*).

IL CASTELLO DEI BURATTINI (MUSEO GIORDANO FERRARI)

Via Melloni 3/A. Open Mon and Wed–Fri 10–5, Sat–Sun 10.30–6.30. For details of events and shows, see castellodeiburattini.it.

From the little courtyard by the entrance to the Camera di San Paolo there is access to this delightful **puppet museum**. The collection was begun by Italo Ferrari, a shoemaker who then became a puppeteer, and his skills were passed on to his son Giordano (1905–87) who augmented the collection. The civic museum named after him was opened in 2002. Including both glove puppets and string puppets (marionettes) from all over Italy and beyond, this is the most important collection of its kind in the country. Beautifully displayed, there are also fascinating videos of historic performances.

PINACOTECA STUARD

Map Parma East, 7. On the corner of Via Cavour and Borgo Parmigianino. Open weekdays except Tues 10–5, weekends and holidays 10.30–6.30.

This collection of paintings was put together by Giuseppe Stuard, a wealthy landowner born in Parma in 1790, and it was left to the city on his death in 1834. Since 2002 it has been housed here, in part of the convent of San Paolo (*see above*), which was restored for the purpose. By the ticket office is a 10th–11th-century tower with a brick dome, and finds from excavations on the site are displayed here. Another room has a vault decorated in the 15th century by Alessandro Araldi. The earliest works in display cases are by Tuscan artists and include a *Madonna and Child* with a bullfinch on a gold ground by the Maestro della Misericordia, a *Lamentation* by Niccolò di Tommaso, four *Saints* by Bicci di Lorenzo, and a small *Christ carrying the Cross* attributed to Paolo Uccello. The early 15th-century Sienese school is well represented in Room 5 by Pietro di Giovanni d'Ambrogio's charming *Entrance of Christ into Jerusalem*. In Room 6 is a terracotta head of the Madonna attributed to an artist close to Antonio Begarelli, and in Room 7 the display of drawings includes a seated greyhound by Parmigianino (*see p. 86*). A particularly gory *Judith and Holofernes* in Room 8 is by Lavinia Fontana and here there are other works by the Bolognese school. Room 9 has a display relating to the history of the Congregazione della Carità, founded in 1500, to which Stuard left his collection. The last rooms (upstairs) are filled with later works, notably (Room 15) battle scenes by Francesco Monti, known as 'Brescianino delle Battaglie' because he was born (in 1646) in Brescia and his output was almost exclusively representations of imaginary battles, and (Room 16) three small works by Sebastiano Ricci, born just a few years later. The last rooms illustrate the work of local 19th-century artists.

THE MADONNA DELLA STECCATA

Map Parma East, 7. Entrance in Strada Garibaldi. Open 9–12 & 3.30–6.

This handsome Renaissance church was built in 1521–39 on a domed Greek-cross plan by the local architect Giovanni Francesco Zaccagni and his father Bernardino, whose work can only be seen in Parma. The elegant dome has a very fine exterior, and in the 18th century it was surrounded (at the level of the roof) by a balustrade with statues, an unusual feature. More statues and urns were installed a little lower down to decorate the top of the walls of the apse and transepts.

Inside, from 1530 to 1570, every inch of the surface of the walls and vault were covered with excellent frescoes by painters of the Parma school including Girolamo Mazzola Bedoli. Bernardino Gatti (inspired by Correggio) frescoed the *Assunta* in the dome. The *Crowning of the Virgin* in the apse is by Michelangelo Anselmi (based on a drawing by Giulio Romano, and also showing the influence of Correggio). But the most remarkable frescoes are those on the barrel vault between the dome and apse: six tempera figures of the three wise and three foolish Virgins, which are the superb last works by Parmigianino (*see p. 86*), completed in 1539. The six figures hold lamps and carry amphorae on their heads, and there are four monochrome figures in golden niches of Adam and Eve and Moses and Aaron. Parmigianino had also been asked to paint the apse but he took so long over this vault that the church authorities imprisoned him for breach of contract and he died the following year.

Parmigianino had already worked in the church as a young man when he was asked to decorate the organ doors: the outer ones, now on the wall of the transept, show the *Flight into Egypt* and St Joseph drawing water from a spring (with a lovely landscape and a white bird looking on), and the inner ones, with St Cecilia and David (later enlarged with barley-sugar columns by a Flemish painter), are now on the wall close to the entrance. The organ itself was built in 1574 by Benedetto Antegnati, and restored by Negri Poncini in 1780.

The late 14th-century fresco of the *Madonna* over the high altar, held to be miraculous, drew such crowds when it was in an oratory on this site that it had to be protected by railings (or a '*steccato*', hence the church's unusual name).

The tomb on the left as you enter the church of Field-Marshal Count Neipperg (1775–1829), second husband of Parma's well-loved duchess Marie Louise (*see below*), is by the important Tuscan sculptor Lorenzo Bartolini (1840). It includes a relief of Neipperg's horse in mourning.

MUSEO COSTANTINIANO DELLA STECCATA
Open 9–12 & 3.30–6, weekends only 3.30–6 (closed at weekends in July and August). T: 0521 282854.

The **crypt**, with its Neoclassical decorations, was commissioned in 1823 by Marie Louise (*see below*) as a fitting burial place for the Farnese and Bourbon rulers of Parma, and here is the simple tomb of Alessandro Farnese, who distinguished himself in 1571 at the Battle of Lepanto and as governor of the Spanish Netherlands captured Antwerp in 1585 (he died in 1592). The general's bronze helmet rests on the sarcophagus.

The great violin virtuoso Niccolò Paganini was a member of the Constantinian Order and his coat of arms is shown in a corridor here. He found early encouragement for his talent in Parma and returned to the town to perform many times throughout his brilliant career, which took him all over Europe. He died in Nice in 1840 but in 1876 his embalmed body was brought back to Parma and rests beneath a classical canopy in the Villetta cemetery, to the south of the town.

The **Sagrestia Nobile** (1670) has Baroque wood cupboards by Giovanni Battista Mascheroni from Lombardy, which contain numerous ex votos, Church silver and vestments (the drawers are opened by the guide). On the ground floor of the headquarters of the Constantinian Order a room has been arranged as a museum illustrating the Bourbon Duchy of Parma (*see below*).

THE '*BUONA DUCHESSA*' MARIE LOUISE

The Empress Marie Louise, born in 1791, eldest child of the Habsburg Emperor Franz I of Austria and Maria Teresa Bourbon of Naples, was forced to marry Napoleon (as his second wife) in 1810 in order to broker a peace. Their son, Napoléon François Charles Joseph, was born 'King of Rome' in 1811 (later known more simply as the Duke of Reichstadt), but he was obliged to live apart from his mother and predeceased her in 1832. At the Treaty of Vienna in 1815 Marie Louise was assigned the Duchy of Parma and Piacenza. She is remembered fondly in Parma for her wise government of the town from 1816 to her death 1847 and she also commissioned some public buildings, including the Teatro Regio. At Napoleon's death in 1822 she married her lover and minister Adam Albrecht Adalbert, Count of Neipperg, and then when he died she promptly married another of her councillors.

At her death the history of the Duchy remained complicated. It returned to Charles Louis of Bourbon, who became Parma's Charles II. He ruled just one year and abdicated in 1849 in favour of his son, who took the title Charles III—but in 1854 he was assassinated by his saddle-maker. His widow, named Louise, daughter of Ferdinand, Duke of Berry, acted as regent for her son Roberto until in 1859 Parma joined the united Italy and its long connection with the imperial families of Europe came to an end.

MUSEO GLAUCO LOMBARDI

Map Parma East, 7. Entrance at Strada Garibaldi 15. Open Tues–Sat 9.30–4, Sun and holidays 9.30–7; July–Aug 9.30–2. museolombardi.it.

Professor Glauco Lombardi, born in 1881, spent much of his life collecting objects to document the period when the Duchy of Parma was ruled by Marie Louise. It is fittingly arranged on the first floor of this 18th-century palace, known as Palazzo di

Riserva, which was redesigned in 1764 with a Neoclassical façade and provided with a ballroom and gaming rooms for Marie Louise's court. It contains mementoes of her time charmingly arranged in old-fashioned showcases. In the main *Salone* is a portrait of the duchess in 1812 by Robert J. Lefèvre and one of her magnificent ball-dresses. The gilded *corbeille de mariage* displayed here was presented by Napoleon to his bride for her trousseau.

TEATRO REGIO

Strada Garibaldi. Map Parma East, 7. Can be visited on a guided tour; for details, see teatroregioparma.it.

This theatre, with its Neoclassical façade, was begun for the duchess Marie Louise by Nicola Bettoli in 1821. For its inauguration in 1829 Vincenzo Bellini was commissioned to write the opening opera, but his *Zaira*, performed in the presence of the duchess, was a resounding flop. However, Teatro Regio very soon became one of the great opera houses of Italy and is still famous as such. The conductor Arturo Toscanini (1867–1957), who was born in Parma, played in the orchestra.

PIAZZA GARIBALDI

Strada Garibaldi and the parallel Strada Cavour, the main shopping street, end in the large Piazza Garibaldi (*map Parma East, 11*), site of the Roman forum and always the centre of the city. In the 17th century the Municipio with its portico, and Palazzo del Governatore with its clock tower, were built here. The monument to Garibaldi by Davide Calandra was set up in 1893. Divided in two by the busy Strada Mazzini and its continuation Strada della Repubblica, this huge square is not particularly attractive or peaceful. But it is worth exploring the Strada Farini, which runs south from the piazza and which has numerous crowded cafés, restaurants and food shops.

PALAZZO DELLA PILOTTA

Map Parma West, 6. Entrance from the stairs under the portico, off Piazzale della Pace. The huge palace houses two museums as well as the Teatro Farnese. The Teatro Farnese is open Tues–Sun 8.30–2. Galleria Nazionale and Museo Archeologico open Tues–Sat 8.30–7, Sun and holidays 8.30–2; last entry 30mins before closing. Combined tickets (tickets to Teatro Farnese only available for groups). For more information, see parmabeniartistici.beniculturali.it.

The enormous rambling Palazzo della Pilotta was built for the Farnese family c. 1583–1622, but left unfinished; it was badly bombed, and half of it was demolished in the Second World War. Numbering below refers to the plan overleaf.

TEATRO FARNESE

This huge theatre is an extraordinary sight. It was built in 1617–18 in wood and stucco by Giovanni Battista Aleotti for Rannuccio I, Duke of Parma. It has a

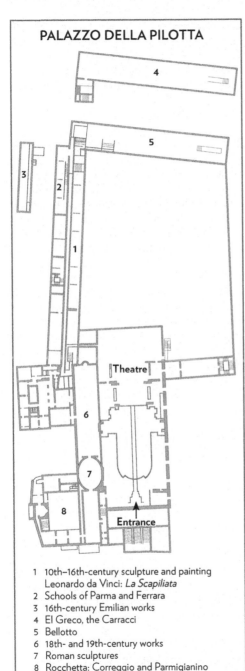

PALAZZO DELLA PILOTTA

Theatre

Entrance

1 10th–16th-century sculpture and painting
   Leonardo da Vinci: *La Scapiliata*
2 Schools of Parma and Ferrara
3 16th-century Emilian works
4 El Greco, the Carracci
5 Bellotto
6 18th- and 19th-century works
7 Roman sculptures
8 Rocchetta: Correggio and Parmigianino

U-shaped cavea that could seat 3,000 spectators. Above are two tiers of loggias, with arches modelled on Palladio's theatre at Vicenza, although the stage in this theatre had movable scenery. Used only nine times after its inauguration in 1628 (when it was flooded for a mock sea-battle), it fell into ruin in the 18th century and was almost entirely destroyed by a bomb in the Second World War, but was subsequently very beautifully reconstructed. Most of the painted decoration (including the ceiling fresco) has been lost, although two painted triumphal arches survive at the sides, with stucco equestrian statues of Alessandro and Ottavio Farnese.

GALLERIA NAZIONALE

From the stage of the theatre you enter the Galleria Nazionale, founded by Philip of Bourbon-Parma in 1752. A walkway leads into a **long gallery (1)**, with a chronological display of sculpture and paintings. The Romanesque section has the 10th-century wooden doors from San Bertoldo, decorated with birds and beasts, and three capitals and reliefs from the pulpit of the duomo, all carved by Benedetto Antelami. Beyond is a fine collection of early Tuscan gold-ground paintings in very good condition, many of them acquired in 1786 by Ferdinand of Bourbon-Parma (Agnolo Gaddi, Bernardo Daddi, Nicolò di Pietro Gerini, Bicci di Lorenzo). There is also an exquisite little portable altar by Paolo Veneziano, the *Crowning of the Madonna* by Starnina, and a very lovely *Madonna of Humility* by Fra' Angelico. Beyond the marquetry stalls by Lendinara are four detached frescoes of acts of Charity by a local painter working in the mid-15th century, and a polyptych with 18 episodes from the life of St Peter Martyr, a delightful work by the little-known Agnolo and Bartolomeo degli Erri. The last section has paintings by the famous Venetian painter Cima da Conegliano (two tiny tondi, including *Endymion Asleep* and a superb *Madonna and Child with two Saints*, including a wonderful landscape), and a *Deposition* by Francesco Francia. Beyond a passageway with tiles made in Faenza in 1482 from the monastery of San Paolo, the last room has an exquisite *Head of a Girl* (*La Scapiliata*) by Leonardo da Vinci (c. 1508), owned by the Gonzaga in 1531. The two marble bas-reliefs displayed here are by Giovanni Antonio Amadeo.

Another huge hall **(2)** displays paintings by the **schools of Parma and Ferrara** (15th–16th centuries). These include portraits by the little-known Francesco Zaganelli and four small works by the Emilian painter Garofalo (note particularly the *Annunciation*), and a small *Rest on the Flight into Egypt* by Dosso Dossi (with a lovely landscape—the secular appearance of the Madonna has led to this work being re-named 'the Gypsy'). Stairs lead up to another room **(3)** with **16th-century Emilian works** (Michelangelo Anselmi), and works by Giulio Romano, Holbein (*Portrait of Erasmus*), Sebastiano del Piombo and Bronzino. On the balcony above **(4)** are interesting works by Girolamo Mazzola Bedoli and El Greco, and large works by the Carracci.

Another huge hall, **(5)**, hung with permanent scaffolding, houses a vast collection of later works. Particularly notable here are 18th-century views of the Venetian lagoon and the Brenta canal by Canaletto's nephew Bernardo Bellotto, animals by Rosa da Tivoli, genre paintings, and (at the far end) portraits by Frans Pourbus the Younger. The two marble busts of the vastly over-weight Rannuccio II are by the workshop of Gian Lorenzo Bernini.

A walkway, with early maps and prints of Parma and 19th-century views of the city (many by Claudio Alessandri), leads down to a large Neoclassical hall **(6)** with **18th- and 19th-century works**, including portraits by Zoffany and Jean-Marc Nattier, and a seated statue of Parma's duchess, Marie Louise, by Canova. In the adjoining oval room **(7)** are two colossal statues of Dionysus and Hercules in very dark basalt, dating from the 2nd century AD found in the Farnese Gardens on the Palatine in Rome (they were dug up shortly after Parma's Duke Francis I had inherited the gardens in 1724). They are thought to be by Rabirius, one of just two named masters who were at work in Imperial Rome. They are an extraordinary sight—their vast dimensions and the very unusual stone making them almost ugly.

The last section of the gallery is in the small rooms of the Rocchetta **(8)**, and here are displayed the works for which the gallery is best known: the **masterpieces of Correggio and Parmigianino**. The detached frescoes by Correggio (*see p. 77*) include the lunette of the *Coronation of the Virgin* from the apse of San Giovanni Evangelista. His finest oil painting, dating from c. 1525–30, the *Madonna della Scodella* (named after the shiny pewter bowl) is here, as well as his *Madonna and Child, with St Jerome, an Angel, and Mary Magdalene* dating from the same period.

In the next room is his *Martyrdom of Four Saints*, and *Lamentation*. Parmigianino (*see below*) is represented by a famous female portrait of a woman in a turban (only partly hiding her coquettish curls) holding a fan. Known as the *Turkish Slave*, this is unquestionably one of the greatest portraits produced in Italy in the 16th century. Heavily made up, the sitter represents a type of female beauty which interestingly enough you can still sometimes see in the women of Parma. A tiny portrait of a man in a red hat is thought to be Parmigianino's self-portrait (you can turn it to see the drawing on the back), and there are also other drawings by him displayed here. The important **Palatine Library**, also housed in the palace, has editions and matrices of Giovanni Battista Bodoni, the famous printer who set up his office in the palace in 1768–1813. There is a small museum dedicated to him (*only open by appointment; T: 0521 220449*) and a section with musical MSS.

PARMIGIANINO (1503–40)

Francesco Mazzola, born in Parma into a family of artists, has always been known as Parmigianino, a diminutive of his birthplace. Vasari tells us that as a young man he appeared more angelic than human, but later in life the art historian accuses him of allowing himself to go to seed and neglecting to trim his beard. He was a contemporary of Correggio and was clearly influenced by him. He also looked closely at the works of the Tuscan *maniera*, and after a trip to Rome in 1524 at the decorations carried out there by Raphael and Michelangelo. A refined and sophisticated artist, Parmigianino perfected the stretched and elongated lineaments of the human form which were to become such a hallmark of Mannerism. But at the same time he paid enormous attention to detail, as can be seen in his portrait known as the *Turkish Slave*, but this cost him dearly when he failed to complete the decorations at the Madonna della Steccata, concentrating all his attention on the one little vault with the Wise and Foolish Virgins (for which numerous studies survive). He also decorated the entrance arches on two of the chapels in San Giovanni Evangelista—exquisite works but easy to miss. Perhaps the work for which he is best remembered, the supremely elegant *Madonna 'of the Long Neck'*, is in the Uffizi in Florence. Although he died aged only 37, he was to influence later generations of artists, as well as the French school. There are other works by him in some of the most important museums of the world—in Dresden, Vienna, Berlin and the National Gallery of London—but nearer at hand his paintings can also be appreciated in Bologna, where he lived for several years.

MUSEO ARCHEOLOGICO NAZIONALE

On the first floor of Palazzo della Pilotta; entrance from the staircase up to the Teatro Farnese (for times, see above).

This archaeological museum was founded in 1760 and the most important Roman pieces come from excavations at Veleia (*see p. 109*). Particularly interesting is the *tabula alimentaria*, which is the largest Roman bronze inscription known. The portrait busts include the bronze head of a boy (1st century BC), and there is a very fine collection of small bronzes including a winged Victory. One room contains an

Egyptian collection. On the lower floor is an excellent display of palaeolithic finds from the region around Parma and material from the pile-dwellings of Parma and the lake-villages of its territory. Also here are Roman inscriptions and mosaic pavements as well as local finds from the early Medieval period, including Lombard jewellery and coins.

ACROSS THE RIVER

On the other side of the Parma river, reached by Ponte Verdi, is the entrance to the huge **Parco Ducale** (*map Parma West, 5–6; open 7am–8pm; or until midnight from April–Oct*), pleasant public gardens created in 1560 when they were the private park of Palazzo Ducale. They have fine chestnut, beech and plane trees. **Palazzo Ducale** (*map Parma West, 2; open Mon–Sat 9–12; ring for admission*) was built as a summer residence for Ottavio Farnese in 1564; it has a wing furnished in the French Neoclassical style.

A pretty road leads south from Ponte Verdi towards Borgo Rodolfo Tanzi. The house at no. 13 in this street is the simple birthplace of Arturo Toscanini (born in 1867; *map Parma West, 6*). Renovated in 2007, it has a small **museum dedicated to Toscanini** with mementoes of the great conductor (*museotoscanini.it*). The nearby church of the **Annunziata** is an impressive Baroque building (1566); the graceful building which once housed the Ospedale della Misericordia, begun c. 1214 and enlarged in the 16th century, now houses the state archives, **Archivio di Stato**, important for their documentation of the duchy.

MUSIC MUSEUMS

The Museo dell'Opera on Piazza San Francesco and the Casa del Suono on Piazzale Salvo d'Acquisto are open Wed–Sun 10–6. operamuseo.parma.it, casadelsuono.it.

The **Museo dell'Opera** illustrates the history of opera in Parma, and in the Palazzo Cusani here is the **Casa della Musica** (*map Parma East, 7*), an institution dedicated to research and music history and which also organises concerts (*lacasadellamusica. it*).

Very close by, housed in the former 17th-century church of Santa Elisabetta, is the **Casa del Suono** (*map Parma East, 7*), which documents the history of sound technology from the phonograph and gramophone to CDs and iPods.

THE AUDITORIUM PAGANINI
Approached from Piazzale Vittorio Emanuele II by Viale Barilla and Largo Calamandrei (beyond map Parma East, 12), in the Parco 1° Maggio. Admission by appointment when not in use for rehearsals, T: 0521 039002.

Designed by Renzo Piano and inaugurated in 2001, this is a very remarkable building, renowned for its excellent acoustics. Surrounded by a park, it is on the site of a sugar beet factory erected in 1899 and in use up until 1978. Two of the factory walls built from the typical local yellow stone known as '*giallo Parma*' were retained by Piano in this excellent example of industrial conversion, and the entrance is through a glass screen 27m high. There is seating for 780. Exceptionally this concert hall was completed on time and within its original estimated budget. Next to it the former Barilla pasta factory, in use from 1902 to 2000, has been converted into a hotel and residential conference centre.

THE 'CERTOSA DI PARMA'

At Paradigna, north of Parma, this was first built in 1282 by the Cistercians but it has been enlarged and remodelled several times over the centuries (and is now occupied by a department of Parma University). But it is remembered since it gave its name to Stendhal's famous novel, published in 1839, *La Chartreuse de Parme*. Stendhal (the pseudonym of Henri Beyle, 1783–1842) spent much of his life in Italy: after the 1830 revolution he was appointed consul in Civitavecchia (the port of Rome) where he wrote his autobiography: *The Life of Henri Brulard*.

PARMA PRACTICAL TIPS

INFORMATION OFFICES

IAT. *Piazza Garibaldi 1, T: 0521 218889, turismo.comune.parma.it. Map Parma East, 11.*
Parma Point. Open every day 9.30–7.30 (run by the Province). Provides tourist information and also has a bookshop and sells local products. *Strada Garibaldi 18, T: 0521 931800. Map Parma East, 7.*

GETTING AROUND

• **By air:** Parma's small Giuseppe Verdi Airport, opened in 1991 less than 2km northwest of the town, has low cost flights from London Stansted, as well as internal flights. Bus 6 to the railway station.
• **By car:** Underground car parks: 'Toschi' on the river just behind Palazzo della Pilotta (*map Parma West, 6*) and (to the south, a little less central) 'Goito' in Via Goito (*map Parma West, 14*).
• **By rail:** Italy's main north–south line closely follows the Via Emilia from Milan to Bologna. Some *Frecce* and most Intercity trains stop at Parma (50mins from Milan, 1hr 20mins from Bologna) and there are some through trains from Rome and Florence. Parma station (*map Parma East, 3*) has been under renovation for many years.
• **By bus:** Buses from next to the

railway station to the main places in the province, operated by TEP (*T: 840 22 22 22, tep.pr.it*).

• **By bicycle:** Bicycles can be hired from Parma Punto Bici, from the square in front of the railway station. *T: 0521 281979. Map Parma East, 3.*

WHERE TO STAY

€€€ **Grand Hotel De la Ville**. Beside Renzo Piano's magnificent new auditorium, just east of the centre of the city. Convenient if you have a car as you can park outside (but you are charged extra if you use the garage). Part of a residential conference centre on a former industrial estate now surrounded by a park and so very peaceful. *Viale Barilla and Largo Calamandrei 11, T: 0521 0304, grandhoteldelaville.it. Map Parma East, 12.*

€€€ **Park Hotel Stendhal**. Modern and comfortable, with a restaurant. *Piazzetta Bodoni 3 (Piazzale della Pace). T: 0521 208057, hotelstendhal.it. Map Parma East, 7.*

€€ **Palazzo della Rosa Prati**. On the top floor of an historic palace, right beside the baptistery, this has seven self-catering suites, available also for short-term stays. *Strada al Duomo 7, T: 0521 386429, palazzodallarosaprati.it. Map Parma East, 7.*

€€ **Toscanini**. Overlooking the river Parma, with a restaurant. *Viale Toscanini 4, T: 0521 289141, hoteltoscanini.it. Map Parma West, 10.*

€ **Button**. In an excellent position, in a quiet street just off Piazza Garibaldi, this hotel has no pretensions but is efficiently run and very pleasant. Nice places to sit in the foyer, even if the rooms are a little dated. An excellent no frills choice. Frequented by dedicated opera goers. *Borgo della Salina 7, just out of Piazza Garibaldi. T: 0521 208039, hotelbutton.it. Map Parma East, 11.*

€ **Torino**. Friendly and centrally located. *Borgo Mazza 7, off the Strada Cavour. T: 0521 281046, hotel-torino.it. Map Parma East, 7.*

RESTAURANTS

€€ **Angiol d'Or**. A pleasant restaurant just off Piazza Duomo, with tables in a covered veranda on the street. Standard local food. Closed Mon. *Vicolo Scutellari 1, T: 0521 282632. angioldor.it. Map Parma East, 7.*

€€ **Il Cortile**. A typical *trattoria* in a quiet narrow lane on the other side of the river, specialising in traditional regional cooking. Good wine selection. Caters also for those on special diets. Closed Sun and Mon at lunch. *Borgo Paglia 3, T: 0521 285779, trattoriailcortile.com. Map Parma West, 9.*

€€ **Parizzi**. An elegant place renowned for its *cucina parmense*, run, together with a cooking school, by chef Marco Parizzi. The dishes are perhaps a touch too decorative, and the minimalist décor rather stark, but it has gained a place in all the famous food guides. Closed Mon. *Strada della Repubblica 71, T: 0521 285952. ristoranteparizzi.it. Map Parma East, 12.*

At Botteghino, 6km outside town (*beyond map Parma East, 16*) €€ **Da Romeo** is a *trattoria* with genuine Parmesan food and a good wine list. Closed Thur. *Via Traversetolo 185, T: 0521 641167.*

CAFÉS

Sorelle Picchi. Strada Farini 27 (with tables outside; *map Parma East, 11*). Its sandwich bar specialises in good ham and salami. **Le Delizie di Ori**. Strada Farini 19 (*map Parma East, 11; www.ledeliziediori.it*). Renowned for its cakes. A less grand but good quality *pasticceria* is **Pagani** (Borgo Venti Marzo 4; *map Parma East, 7*), popular with locals (closed Mon).

WINE BARS

€ **Enoteca Fontana**. Excellent *salumi* and traditional Parmesan sandwiches to accompany your drinks. Closed Sun–Mon. *Strada Farini 24a, T: 0521 286037. Map Parma East, 11.*
€ **Bottiglia Azzurra**. A charming place which also serves good food. Closed Sun and midday. *Borgo Felino 63, T: 0521 285842. Map Parma East, 11.*
€ **Ombre Rosse**. Wide selection of vintage wines and good food. Closed Sat midday–Sun midday. *Vicolo Giandemaria 4, T: 0521 289575, ombrerosseparma.it. Map Parma East, 11.* There is also a restaurant under the same management, at Borgo Tommasini 18.
€ **Tiffany**. Typical of today's popular places to have a drink in Parma. *Borgo Venti Marzo 8. Map Parma East, 7.*

REGIONAL SPECIALITIES

Parma is particularly well-known for its gastronomic specialities—notably Parmigiano-Reggiano cheese (*see p. 67*); Parma ham (*prosciutto di Parma*) and various salami (*salame di Felino, culatello di Zibello, spalla cotta di San Secondo*). An excellent place to buy these is La Prosciutteria (*Strada Farini 9/c; map Parma East, 11*).

FESTIVALS & EVENTS

Parma is a renowned centre for good music: opera at the Teatro Regio (*teatroregioparma.it, T: 0521 203999*) and concerts at the purpose-built Auditorium Paganini, opened in 2001. Verdi festival in Oct.

Street markets selling food, fresh produce and bric à brac are frequently held in Piazza Ghiaia (*map Parma West, 6*).

Piacenza

Piacenza (*map A, B1*) is a peaceful place, on a much smaller scale and less busy than nearby Parma, with which it is all too often associated. It has pleasant little houses and narrow well-paved streets, and is very well kept. It is visited for its beautiful cathedral and interesting churches, and it has some excellent museums where the exceptionally helpful custodians assist the visitor. It is easy to visit also by train since the station (beside a pleasant little public garden) is just a few minutes from the centre. Oddly enough it is unfortunately not very well equipped with places to stay.

HISTORY OF PIACENZA

Situated at the strategic point where the Via Emilia touches the Po, the town has been an important centre of trade since Roman times, and its name (the French for which is *Plaisance*) is derived from the Latin *Placentia*. The town has an uncanny way of popping up almost at random in European history. The peace negotiations ratified at Constance (1183) between Frederick Barbarossa and the Lombard League were conducted in the church of Sant'Antonino here. In 1545 Pope Paul III created the dukedom of Parma and Piacenza for his illegitimate son Pier Luigi Farnese; the pope's grandson, Alessandro Farnese (1545–92), was governor of the Low Countries from 1578 until his death. Piacenza was the first city to join Piedmont by plebiscite in 1848.

THE TOWN CENTRE

Piazza Cavalli (*map Piacenza, 3*) is named after its magnificent, dynamic pair of bronze equestrian statues of Duke Alessandro Farnese (1625) and his son and successor, Ranuccio Farnese (1620). They were commissioned from Francesco Mochi, who also designed the pediments which have two low reliefs in bronze showing a battle scene with Alessandro, when governor of the Spanish Netherlands, capturing Antwerp in 1585 and his meeting with English ambassadors; and (on that of Ranuccio) allegories of Peace and Wise Government. Mochi is an interesting sculptor showing a transition from the Mannerist style to the new Baroque era (he worked mostly in Rome) and these are considered his masterpieces.

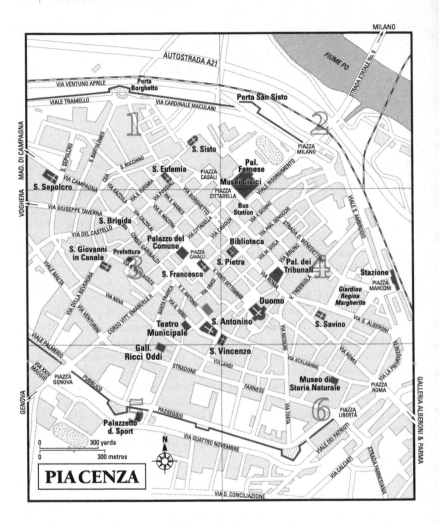

The piazza has a miscellany of buildings, the best of which is the **Palazzo del Comune** (often simply called **Palazzo Gotico**) begun in 1280, with five Gothic arches faced with marble leading into the ground-floor portico and six round Romanesque arches above the windows decorated with brick and terracotta, and battlements crowning the building. This is one of the most handsome town halls in northern Italy. The Madonna di Piazza in a niche, is a copy of the original by the school of Benedetto Antelami now in Palazzo Farnese. Opposite is the late 18th-century Palazzo del Governatore with a clock and statues on the roof. There are also two monumental buildings, one with a tower, from the pre-War Fascist era. The huge church of San Francesco, begun in 1278, has a transitional façade and an impressive vaulted Gothic interior with an ambulatory in the apse.

PIAZZA DEL DUOMO AND THE CATHEDRAL

Via XX Settembre, the town's main shopping street, which links Piazza Cavalli and **Piazza del Duomo** (*map Piacenza, 4*), frames a view of the cathedral and its bell-tower. The pleasant piazza with benches, is lined on two sides with uniform houses above porticoes, all of them painted in different colours, and next to the cathedral is the very grand Palazzo Vescovile in Neoclassical style, decorated with herms and statues on the roof.

The beautiful Lombard Romanesque **duomo** (1122–1240) has a lovely polychrome façade in sandstone and red Verona marble. The three **doorways** are well worth examining in detail. The left one is attributed to the school of Wiligelmus: telamones support the two columns of the porch and the architrave has reliefs with scenes from the life of Christ; above, more arches have very delicate carving and in the spandrels are two reliefs of the *Annunciation*. The central door is guarded by two dignified lions (replaced in the 16th century) which support two columns with lovely capitals. The architrave, supported in turn on the shoulders of two little human figures, bears more reliefs. The outer arch has more carvings with animals and the signs of the zodiac. The right door, by a local master known simply as Niccolò, has two telamones beneath the columns and in the architrave six scenes from the life of Christ, three of them particularly unusual for their iconography as they show Christ tempted by the Devil in the desert (the tormentor is present in all three panels).

On the right of the façade, beyond the lane called Chiostri del Duomo, you can see the exterior of the early 12th-century apse, a carved window with four figures, and pretty loggias above, as well as the drum and the 14th-century campanile, crowned by a gilded angel, a weather vane placed here in the early 14th century by Pietro Vago. There is another pretty side portal in Via Vescovado.

Interior of the duomo

Behind heavy velvet curtains at the door, the magnificent Romanesque interior has massive cylindrical pillars dividing the nave and aisled transepts, and a raised sanctuary at the east end. High up on the **west wall** are two capitals attributed to Niccolò, one with the story of Saul and David, and one showing the *Stoning of St Stephen*. The paintings here carried out in 1609 include a large *Transition of the Virgin* by Camillo Procaccini, and, below, *Isiah* and *David* both by Lodovico Carracci. There is a carved lunette dating from the 15th century above the main door.

Set into the pillars are little square reliefs by local sculptors (c. 1170), of interest because they show the work of the guilds that paid for the erection of each column. Above the arches, but too high up to see clearly, are 12th-century figures of saints, the Madonna (left) and prophets (right).

On the first right pillar, lit by votive candles, are three charming frescoes of the *Madonna della Misericordia*, dating from the 14th–15th century, and still greatly venerated today.

The frescoes in the vault of the central octagon (*light at the west end, essential to illuminate the crossing*) were begun by the artist known as Morazzone, who otherwise worked almost exclusively in Lombardy. He completed just two sections before his death in 1626. The frescoes in the rest of the vault (and the lunettes below) were completed by the much better-known Guercino. The frescoes in the four vaults of the sanctuary and in the apse, of the *Coronation* and *Assumption of the Virgin*, are by Camillo Procaccini (1629), with angels by Lodovico Carracci. The magnificent sculpted gilded wood reredos in the sanctuary dates from 1447 (by a certain Burlengo). The stalls were carved some 30 years later.

A lunette over the little door into the sacristy has a very sweet Giottesque *Madonna and Child with two angels*.

The crypt has 62 columns and, tied up in little bundles beneath the altar here, are the relics (supposed to have arrived in the town in 1001) of the virgin St Justina of Padua, martyred around AD 300.

SAN SAVINO AND SANT'ANTONINO

These two churches in the neighbourhood of the Duomo were the first to be built in the town in the palaeochristian era.

Although founded in the 12th century, **San Savino** (*map Piacenza, 4*) now has a portico and late Baroque façade facing a pleasant little triangular garden, with some fine trees. Inside the imitation Romanesque mosaic pavement and screen in front of the sanctuary were well made in 1902. But fragments of the original paving can be seen at the end of the north aisle (where the pair of dogs seem to be eating their tails), as well as in the sanctuary and in the crypt (here decorated with signs of the zodiac and the Months). The 10th–11th-century capitals of the columns are very fine. The most precious work of art in the church is the wood Crucifix in the sanctuary, dating from the 12th century.

Rebuilt in the 11th century, **Sant'Antonino** (*map Piacenza, 3–4*) has a particularly attractive brick exterior with an octagonal lantern tower, which dates in part from the 10th century, set in a pretty and secluded piazza (where a digital touchscreen has been set up for visitors). The Via Francigena pilgrim route to Rome (*see p. 105*) passed through here. Two ancient granite sarcophagi complete with their lids survive against the church wall. An exceptionally tall vaulted porch was added at the north end in 1350: the portal itself with its carved jambs (the two figures represent Adam and Eve) and red marble pilasters (but no architrave or lunette) dates from the previous century. Inside the church can be seen detached fragments of a very early fresco cycle (late 11th or early 12th century) discovered beneath the roof. In a chapel off the north side is a polychrome terracotta *Crucifixion* dating from the 15th century, and the church also owns a dossal with scenes from the life of St Anthony, made in the same century. Sixteenth-century works include a *Last Supper* by Bernardo Castello and a wood statue of St Lucy.

In the adjoining piazza is the **Teatro Municipale** (*map Piacenza, 3*), a handsome building dating from 1803–10, renowned for its music season.

From Piazza Sant'Antonino Via Scalabrini leads east, and some way along it, at no. 107, is a huge industrial building erected from 1892 to 1912 to produce ice for use in the adjoining slaughter-house. This is now home to the **Museo Civico di Storia**

Naturale (*map Piacenza, 6; open Tues, Wed and Fri 9.30–12.30, Thur, Sat and Sun 9.30–12.30 & 3–6, www.msn.piacenza.it*). The natural history collections from the province of Piacenza and the Po river basin, are extremely well arranged, with zoological, botanical, and geological sections.

GALLERIA RICCI ODDI

Via San Siro 13. Map Piacenza, 5. Open Tues–Sun 9.30–12.30 & 3–6. riccioddi.it. Very well labelled, also in English. Various interesting activities take place here throughout the year.

This gallery of modern art contains the collection begun in 1902 by Giuseppe Ricci Oddi (1868–1937), which was donated by him to the city in 1924. It provides an excellent over-view of Italian art between 1830 and 1930, including all the regional schools and the most important artistic movements. The charming building, with excellent overhead natural lighting, was built expressly in 1924 for Ricci Oddi's collection by his friend Giulio Ulisse Arata from Piacenza, and it survives as one of the best small museum buildings in Italy. It is on the site of a former convent which explains the presence of various cloisters.

The Salone d'Onore is used for temporary exhibitions. The collections are displayed as follows:

Room I: A selection of works by Emilian artists.

Room II: The Tuscan Macchiaioli school is well represented by all its most important protagonists: Giovanni Fattori, Vito d'Ancona, Giovanni Boldini, Vincenzo Cabianca, Cristiano Banti, Raffaello Sernese, Giuseppe Abbati, Telemaco Signorini and Silvestro Lega.

Room III: Works by artists of the lesser-known Ligurian and Piedmontese schools (although Giuseppe Pellizza da Volpedo's *Tramonto* (sunset) was sent to the Quadriennale of Turin in 1902 together with his much more famous *Il Quarto Stato*).

Room V is dedicated to landscapes by Antonio Fontanesi, born in Reggio Emilia in 1818, and **Room VI** has works by his followers.

Room VII: Here in the Rotunda are sculptures, including small bronzes by Vincenzo Gemito and Libero Andreotti.

Room VIII: Nineteenth-century Lombard artists: portrait of a man by Francesco Hayez; a Risorgimento scene by Gerolamo Induno; works by Mosè Bianchi and Giovanni Segantini.

Room XI: Sculptures by Medardo Rosso and Domenico Trentacoste.

Room XII: Forty small paintings on permanent loan to the gallery from an anonymous collector: works by Telemaco Signorini (*Marina di Viareggio*), Giovanni Fattori (*Casolari toscani*), Silvestro Lega, Vincenzo Cabianca, Giovanni Boldini, Giuseppe de Nittis, Corcos, Plinio Nomellini and Oscar Ghiglia.

Room XIII: Dedicated to the local painter Stefano Bruzzi.

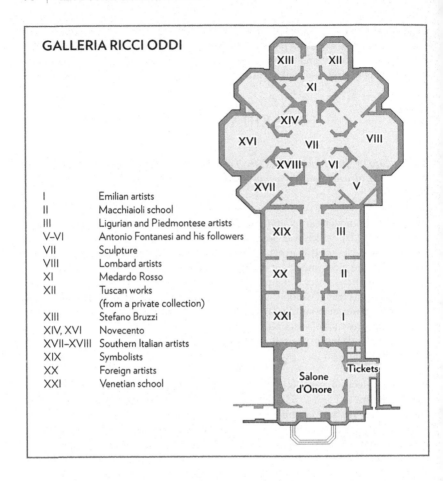

GALLERIA RICCI ODDI

I	Emilian artists
II	Macchiaioli school
III	Ligurian and Piedmontese artists
V–VI	Antonio Fontanesi and his followers
VII	Sculpture
VIII	Lombard artists
XI	Medardo Rosso
XII	Tuscan works (from a private collection)
XIII	Stefano Bruzzi
XIV, XVI	Novecento
XVII–XVIII	Southern Italian artists
XIX	Symbolists
XX	Foreign artists
XXI	Venetian school

Rooms XIV and XVI: The works here illustrate the important Novecento movement with (in Room XIV) Filippo de Pisis, Massimo Campigli, Bruno Saetti and Achille Funi and (in Room XVI) Felice Carena, Felice Casorati, Boccioni, Carlo Carrà, and four portrait heads in terracotta sculpted by Francesco Messina.

Rooms XVII–XVIII: Excellent painters from southern Italy are represented here: Domenico Morelli (*Portrait of Concettina*), Francesco Paolo Michetti, Filippo Palizzi, and in

Room XVIII is a delightful still life of fish by Vincenzo Irolli from Naples.

Room XIX: The Symbolist movement is recorded here, with works by Adolfo de Carolis, Cesare Maccari, Giulio Aristide Sartorio and Armando Spadini.

Room XX: The works by foreign artists seem to be here to emphasise the much higher quality of the Italian painters in the rest of this collection. Among them have been hung works by Federico Zandomeneghi and Giuseppe de Nittis (since they both worked in Paris) and they stand out as the most interesting.

A portrait by Gustav Klimt was stolen from this room in 1997 and has never been found.

Room XXI: The Venetian school: Ettore Tito, Luigi Nono, Guglielmo Ciardi, and Guido Cadorin.

PALAZZO FARNESE: MUSEI CIVICI

Piazza Cittadella 29. Map Piacenza, 2. Open Tues–Sat 9–1 & 3–6, Sun 9.30–1 & 3–6, palazzofarnese.piacenza.it. Combined ticket for all the museums otherwise separate ones for the Pinacoteca; the Carriage Museum and Risorgimento Museum; and the Archaeological Museum. Guided visits (included in the price of the ticket) are given at certain times (see the website for details).

This huge palace was begun in 1558 for Duchess Margaret of Austria, daughter of the emperor Charles V of Spain and wife of Ottavio Farnese, the second Duke of Parma and Piacenza. The architect was the little-known Francesco Paciotto from Urbino, but after 1559 the much more famous artist Jacopo Barozzi, always known as Vignola, was called in since he had worked for the Farnese on their villa of Caprarola in northern Lazio. However, he left it only half-finished since he was busy in Rome designing the church of the Gesù—his finest work, which was to have an enormous influence on later generations of church builders.

This palazzo has a grand if stark exterior, divided into three floors by protruding cornices and numerous well-proportioned windows. Inside Vignola provided a spiral staircase from the basement all the way up to the top of the palace. Building was continued throughout the 16th century by the Farnese, followed by various vicissitudes including, in the 19th century, its use as a barracks, and then as a refuge for families who had been rendered homeless during the Second World War. The Musei Civici were installed here during the 1980s and 1990s and major restoration work has been completed.

From the **entrance through the courtyard** you can see the monumental double loggia with niches of the palace (where Vignola had envisaged a theatre) as well as the smaller adjacent Cittadella Viscontea, which has a round tower (and a 15th-century loggia). This had been built by the Visconti rulers in the 14th century.

Various parts of the huge rambling palace house the civic museums, the most important of which is the Pinacoteca. Others are devoted to carriages, archaeology, armour and the Risorgimento. Some of the decoration of the rooms survives from the time of the Farnese, interesting for their paintings which celebrate the 'glories' of the dynasty. The signposting is generally good and the custodians particularly helpful. The display is excellent. Numbering corresponds to the plan overleaf and to the numbering *in situ* in the museum.

GROUND FLOOR
A large room off the ticket office displays the important Armoury, a huge collection

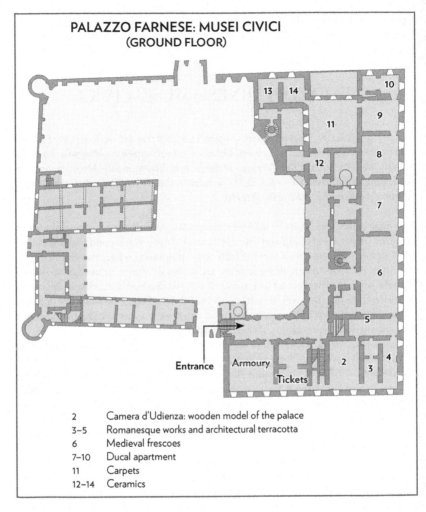

PALAZZO FARNESE: MUSEI CIVICI
(GROUND FLOOR)

2	Camera d'Udienza: wooden model of the palace
3–5	Romanesque works and architectural terracotta
6	Medieval frescoes
7–10	Ducal apartment
11	Carpets
12–14	Ceramics

of arms and armour mostly dating from the 16th and 17th centuries (and including some pieces made by Pompeo della Cesa). A flying bridge leads over a narrow staircase into the **Sala della Camera Udienza (2)**. Here is a wood model of the palace made in the 17th century by Giovanni Battista Bergonzoni and documents relating to the Farnese dynasty. **Rooms 3–5** contain Romanesque sculpture and epigraphs, as well as terracotta ornamentation dating from the 14th to the 17th centuries, salvaged from buildings in Piacenza. Displayed on its own is the 13th-century statue of the *Madonna di Piazza* by a follower of Benedetto Antelami, removed from the Palazzo Gotico. The large **Room 6** is filled with late medieval frescoes detached from churches of Piacenza, and lovely 14th-century frescoes of scenes from the life of St Catherine of Alexandria.

Rooms 7–10 were once part of the apartment of the Farnese Duke Ranuccio II, who commissioned the elaborate decoration of stuccowork and paintings on the upper part of the walls in the 1680s to celebrate the Farnese dynasty, and especially Pope Paul III and Duke Alessandro. Many of these illustrate the military exploits in the Netherlands of Duke Alessandro (where he awaited the Armada) and are by Giovanni Evangelista Draghi from Genoa (who died in Piacenza). Also here are some delightful painted wood fireguards dating from the same period. The last little room, the **alcova (10)**, used as a bedroom and private chapel, has the finest of all the decorations in the entire palace with exquisite stuccowork and a series of paintings by Sebastiano Ricci illustrating the life of the Farnese Pope Paul III: approving the Jesuit order, convening the Council of Trent, nominating his son Pier Luigi Duke of Parma and Piacenza, and culminating in his apotheosis.

Room 11 has a magnificent display of carpets from the Armani and Binecchio collections: there are five Turkish Ushak carpets made in the 19th century, and others dating from the 20th century from Morocco and Tibet. **Rooms 12–14** have the Agnelli and Anguissola donations of 17th- and 18th-century ceramics, including pieces from the Ginori manufactory of Florence and from the Marche.

UPPER FLOOR (PINACOTECA)

Rooms 16–17 contain 16th–17th-century works by Giovanni Battista Trotti (Il Malosso) from Cremona, Carlo Francesco Nuvolone, Justus Suttermans, and Giovanni Battista Merano (who died in Piacenza in 1698). Displayed on its own in **Room 18** (*automatic light*) is a superb tondo of the *Madonna in Adoration of the Child with the young St John*, shown in a rose garden, by Botticelli, in excellent condition and still in its beautiful original frame. It is documented in the Farnese collections from the early 18th century. Well displayed in **Room 19** are a group of three exquisite little portable altars of uncertain attribution, and two scenes which used to decorate marriage chests. The lovely *Madonna of Humility* here is by Sano di Pietro. **Room 20**, with a good ceiling, has 17th-century paintings by Antonio Tempesta and 'Brescianino delle Battaglie' (typical huge battle scenes). The following rooms (**21–23**) have paintings carried out at the time of Elisabetta Farnese, who became Queen of Spain in 1714, again celebrating the Farnese family's exploits, both at war and at peace (many of them by the local painter Pier Ilario Spolverini). The last rooms (**24–26**) have 18th- and 19th-century paintings, including some by Gaspare Landi. The deconsecrated **chapel** has a beautiful octagonal interior built in 1598, but it is now only open for concerts.

BASEMENT

Here, in remarkable vaulted rooms once used as kitchens and storerooms, is a splendid collection (one of the most important in Europe) of some 50 **carriages** dating from the 18th and 19th centuries. There are also prams, sedan chairs and even an old vehicle used by the fire brigade, with its incredibly long ladder.

A ramp leads up to the **Cittadella Viscontea**, where exhibitions are held. Dramatically displayed on its own in a circular room beneath its round tower is the celebrated **Fegato di Piacenza**, an Etruscan divination bronze representing a sheep's liver, marked with the names of Etruscan deities. It was found near Piacenza in 1877 and is a unique testimony to the mysterious religious practices which took place during the late Etruscan period (end of the 2nd or beginning of the 1st century BC).

In an adjoining building is the **Archaeological Museum**, founded in 1885 with finds from the territory dating from the Paleolithic era onwards (the neolithic finds from the Val Trebbia are particularly interesting). Also here is a museum dedicated to the Italian **Risorgimento**, with special reference to the dramatic events of 1848–9, when Piacenza joined Piedmont by plebiscite. The period of unification 1859–61, and the roles played by Mazzini and Garibaldi, is also very well documented.

TO THE MADONNA DI CAMPAGNA

Corso Garibald (*map Piacenza, 3*) leads past the 12th-century front of **Sant'Ilario**, with a relief of Christ and the Apostles on the architrave, and (at the end of the street) **Santa Brigida**, also 12th century. In a side street to the left is **San Giovanni in Canale** (*map Piacenza, 3*), a 13th-century church altered in the 16th century. Via Campagna leads northwest from beyond Santa Brigida to (a 15-min walk) one of the most important churches in Piacenza, the church of the **Madonna di Campagna** (*open 7–12 & 3–7; beyond map Piacenza, 1*), a graceful Renaissance building on a Greek-cross plan, with four little domed corner chapels. It is the best work of the local architect Alessio Tramello (1528), who was clearly inspired by both Alberti and Bramante. The interior has superb frescoes by Pordenone, who carried out numerous beautiful frescoes and altarpieces all over northern Italy. Towards the end of his life, in 1528–31, he worked here on the central dome, beautifully lit by small windows in a loggia, although the decoration of the drum and the pendentives was completed by Bernardino Gatti in 1543. Pordenone also worked in other parts of the church, including a corner chapel with beautiful scenes from the life of St Catherine, and another with scenes of the *Nativity*. The church also contains paintings by Camillo Boccaccino, and later works by Giulio Cesare and Camillo Procaccini and Guercino. On the high altar is a polychrome wood statue dating from the late 14th century of the Madonna, to whom the church is dedicated. The statue is held to be miraculous. There is also a statue of Ranuccio I Farnese, the first work of Francesco Mochi (1616).

SAN SISTO

Via Sant'Eufemia leads northeast past the church of Sant'Eufemia, with an early 12th-century front (restored) to **San Sisto** (*map Piacenza, 1*), another pretty church by Tramello (1511), inspired in part by Alberti's Sant'Andrea in Mantua. It was for this church that Raphael painted his famous *Sistine Madonna*, sold by the convent to the Elector of Saxony in 1754, and now at Dresden. On the north choir pier is the monument to Margaret, Duchess of Parma (1522–86), governor of the Netherlands from 1559 to 1567; the fine stalls date from 1514.

GALLERIA ALBERONI

The Galleria Alberoni (beyond map Piacenza, 6), in the southern suburbs of the city at no. 67 Via Emilia Parmense in the locality of San Lazzaro Alberoni, can best be reached by bus no. 2 or 3 in 10mins from the railway station. On foot it is an unattractive walk of about half an hour from Piazzale Roma (with its eccentric monument to ancient Rome) along Via Cristoforo Colombo and its continuation Via Emilia Parmense). It is only open from Oct–June on Sun at 3.30–6; guided tours at 4; galleriaalberoni.it.

The gallery forms part of the Collegio Alberoni, which has a library and scientific institutions. The college was founded by Giulio Alberoni (1664–1752), a gardener's son who rose to be a cardinal and the able minister of Philip V of Spain (whose marriage to Elisabetta Farnese he engineered), and he also put together this remarkable art collection.

Eighteen Flemish tapestries are displayed in a room specially designed for them in the 1960s. The two earliest with scenes of Troy were made in wool and silk in Brussels around 1520 possibly by Pieter Van Aelst. The eight which illustrate the story of Alexander the Great date from the late 17th century and are probably on cartoons by Jacob Jordaens. The other series with eight scenes from the myth of Dido and Aeneas were made in Antwerp around 1670 on cartoons by Giovan Francesco Romanelli.

The paintings purchased by the Cardinal in Spain include works by Sebastiano Martinez, who succeeded Velázquez at the court of Philip IV. Alberoni also commissioned works from contemporary artists in Piacenza such as Gian Paolo Panini, and he purchased a work by another contemporary, Sebastiano Conca. The vestments and Crucifixes used by the Cardinal are also preserved. In three rooms of the Cardinal's apartment the most precious and earliest works are exhibited. The *Ecce Homo* is a famous masterpiece, signed and dated 1473 by Antonello da Messina, extremely well preserved. It was presumably purchased by the Cardinal when he was in Sicily in 1718, where he was sent to attempt to reconquer the island for Spain. Antonello painted several other versions of this subject (today in collections in Genoa, Vienna and the Metropolitan Museum in New York), but this is perhaps the finest. Also here are a diptych by Jan Provost and an exquisite still life of flowers in a niche. There are later works here, too, by Guido Reni and Luca Giordano.

PIACENZA PRACTICAL TIPS

INFORMATION OFFICE

Quinfo (IAT). *Piazza Cavalli 7 (in the courtyard of Palazzo del Comune), T: 0523 492224. Open Mon–Sat 8.30–6pm.*

GETTING AROUND

• **By air:** The nearest airport is at Parma, 60km away, the same distance as Milan's Linate airport.
• **By rail:** Piacenza is on the main line between Milan (40mins) and Bologna (1hr 10mins).
• **By bus:** Services by SETA from Piazza Cittadella to places in the province and cities in Emilia (*T: 840000216, setaweb.it*).
• **By car:** Free car parking in Viale Sant'Ambrogio, close to the railway station.

WHERE TO STAY

€€ **Grande Albergo Roma**. The only hotel in the historic centre. Provincial elegance and a pleasant restaurant with views. *Via Cittadella 14, T: 0523 323201, grandealbergoroma.it. Map Piacenza, 3.*
€ **B&B del Borgo**. As its name suggests, a simple and economical bed and breakfast. *Via Poggiali 24, T: 0523 385436, www.bedandbreakfast.it. Map Piacenza, 3–1.*
€ **Affittacamere Morselli**. Officially in the category of places to rent, but in fact another place offering simple accommodation. *Via Frasi 20, T: 0523*

712420, 0523 712080. Map Piacenza, 3.

RESTAURANTS

€€ **La Pireina**. A typical *trattoria* which has been a sound place to eat for many years. Closed Sun evening and Mon. *Via Borghetto 137, T: 0523 338578. Map Piacenza, 3.*
€€ **Peppino**. This has also been for long a favourite place to eat and is still good. Closed Mon. *Via Scalabrini 49a, T: 0523 329279. Map Piacenza, 6.*
€ **Trattoria La Carrozza**. A simple place but a good choice. No closing day. *Via X Giugno 122, T: 0523 326297. Map Piacenza, 4.*
€ **Osteria del Trentino**. Run by Marco who prepares good local dishes. Closed Sun. *Via Castello 71, T: 0523 324260. Map Piacenza, 3.*
€ **Osteria d'una volta**. Popular with the locals for its simple no frills cuisine. Closed Sun. *Via San Giovanni Bosco 36, T: 0523 304034. Map Piacenza, 3.*
€ **Pizzeria Orologio da Pasquale**. In this peaceful piazza, with tables outside (for pizza). Closed Thurs. *Piazza Duomo 39, T: 0523 324669. Map Piacenza, 4.*

CAFÉS

Pasticceria Galetti. With excellent cakes, this is the place where the locals come to buy their pastries and it is especially crowded before lunchtime on Sun. It has a few tables outside. *Corso Vittorio Emanuele 62. Map Piacenza, 3.*

Il Barino. An old-established place, and the most central café, but rather stark for all that. *Piazza Cavalli/Corso Vittorio Emanuele. Map Piacenza, 3.*

FESTIVALS & EVENTS

General market in Piazza Cavalli and around the Duomo in the mornings on Wed and Sat.

The Teatro Municipale has an excellent programme of music, opera and dance, and the pretty little Teatro Comunale dei Filodrammatici, a 16th-century church converted into a theatre in 1908, has been restored (Via Santa Franca; *map Piacenza, 3*). For all listings see *teatripiacenza.it*.

Fiera di Sant'Antonio 4 July, with markets of local food and crafts.

Jazz festival April–May.

In Sept there is the important *Festival del diritto*, dedicated to human rights issues, with conferences open to all, *www.festivaldeldiritto.it*.

Around Parma & Piacenza

FIDENZA

Fidenza (*map A, C2*) is the most important town in the province of Parma. Known as Borgo San Donnino from the 9th century to 1927, it occupies the site of the Roman Fidentia Julia, where St Domninus was martyred by the Emperor Maximian in 291. It was on the Via Francigena (*see below*), and there are several carvings of pilgrims on the façade of its cathedral.

THE DUOMO

The duomo, built during the 13th century, has a **façade** with particularly interesting Romanesque sculptures by Antelami and his school. On the left tower are two reliefs, one showing *Herod enthroned*, and the other the *Three Kings* on horseback. In the tympanum of the left door are *Pope Adrian II* and *St Domninus*, with *Charlemagne* on the left and a *Miracle of St Domninus* on the right. The arch is carved with figures of animals. The column on the right has a capital ingeniously carved with a scene of *Daniel in the Lions' Den*. On either side of the central door are fine statues of *David* and *Ezekiel*, both by Antelami. The doorway has beautifully carved capitals and a relief of the *Martyrdom of St Domninus* in the architrave, with prophets, apostles and Christ in the lunette. On the right of the door is a relief showing an angel leading a group of poor pilgrims towards Rome. The right door is crowned by the figure of a pilgrim, and beneath, in the tympanum, is *St Domninus*. The lunette is carved with figures of animals. On the right tower is another frieze showing a group of pilgrims.

In the beautiful **interior**, on the first right pillar (above the capital) is the figure of Christ with a relief of a battle of angels below, both by Antelami. The fourth south chapel (1513) has good terracotta decorations and frescoes. The stoup by the school of Antelami includes the figure of Pope Alexander II. In the last chapel on this side is a wooden statue of the *Madonna and Child* of 1626, and remains of very early frescoes. In the raised choir, high up between the apse vaults, are good sculptures, including a figure of *Christ as Judge* by Antelami and a fresco of the *Last Judgement* dating from the 13th century. The crypt has interesting capitals, including one of *Daniel in the Lions' Den*. Here is displayed a seated statue of the *Madonna and Child* by Antelami (damaged in 1914) and the Arca of St Domninus, with carved scenes of his life (1488). Nearer the altar is a 3rd-century Roman sarcophagus.

Just off the piazza is the medieval **Porta San Donnino**. The restored Town Hall and the theatre, dating from 1812, face the main Piazza Garibaldi. At the end of Via Berenini, Palazzo delle Orsoline hosts the **Museo del Risorgimento**, entered from the street on the left, at no. 2 (*entrance at 2 Via Costa; for opening times see comune. fidenza.pr.it/museomusini*), with an interesting collection relating to the period from 1802–1946. The huge Jesuit college and church date from the end of the 17th century.

THE VIA FRANCIGENA: A MEDIEVAL PILGRIMS' WAY

The Via Francigena was the pilgrims' way from France and northern Europe to Rome. In the 8th century the road was used by the Lombards as a safe route from their capital Pavia to the south, avoiding Byzantine territory, and in the following century it became known as the Francigena because it originated in Frankish territory (it was called the Strata Romea in 990 and this name was usually used by medieval chroniclers up until the 12th century). The route across France started at Wissant in France (near Calais) and traversed Picardy, Champagne and the Ardennes, then from Switzerland, the Alps were crossed at the Great St Bernard Pass. From Aosta it passed through northern Italy (Ivrea, Vercelli, Pavia, Piacenza, Fidenza and Parma) and from the Passo della Cisa on the Emilian border it entered Tuscany. It continued south to Lucca, crossed the Arno at Fucecchio, and then passed through the towns of San Gimignano, Siena, San Quirico d' Orcia, and left Tuscany at Radicofani to cross Lazio (Bolsena, Montefiascone and Viterbo) before reaching Rome.

Sigeric (also called Siric) travelled along it on his way to Rome from Canterbury to receive the pallium, symbol of his investiture as Archbishop of Canterbury, from the hands of Pope John XV. He described his return journey in 990, with its 79 stopping places, and the manuscript of his chronicle is still preserved in the British Library in London. Born around 940, Sigeric had been a monk at Glastonbury with Dunstan.

The Francigena was one of three pilgrimage routes in medieval Europe; the other two led to Santiago de Compostela and Jerusalem. The journey from England to Rome took about two and a half months, and most pilgrims probably made the entire trip on foot (carrying a characteristic staff), although prelates such as Sigeric would have travelled on horseback. The road was rough and only paved in places, therefore unsuitable for wheeled vehicles. Numerous *ospedali* or stopping places grew up along the way which offered help and accommodation to travellers, some of them run by the Church. Castles and villages were also built near the route, and towns such as Fidenza prospered as a result of their proximity to it. Apart from pilgrims, the road was used by merchants and traders, and goods as well as works of art were transported along it. The importance of the Via Francigena diminished after the 13th century, when other routes were opened over the Alps.

The Via Francigena today

With the growth of interest in the history of medieval pilgrimage and the celebration of the Jubilee Year of 2000, Sigeric's route has been described in many publications and there are now specific guidebooks to it also in English (the first serious study of the Francigena was by Renato Stopani in 1988, and this has often been reprinted). In 1994 the Francigena was designated a 'European Cultural Route' by the Council of Europe and in 2009 the official itinerary was approved and signposting begun, and it is now widely promoted by local tourist offices. However, there are many variants to the route and only sections of it are at present waymarked as part of the long-distance footpath which it is hoped may one day exist all the way from the Alps to Rome. Alternative routes will have to be created where new roads have intruded (for instance from Piacenza to Fiorenzuola d'Arda the historic route follows the Roman Via Emilia, now a busy main road). There is still a very real problem of defining a pleasant route for walkers, so it is sadly still a long way from being a great pilgrimage itinerary like the route to Santiago.

From Fidenza the Francigena followed the broad valley of the Taro south through the village of **Fornovo di Taro** (*map A, C3*), which still has a Romanesque church with fine 13th-century sculptures on its façade. Further south it passed through **Berceto** (*map A, C3*), where there is a church also built at the same time. The Francigena then crossed the Apennines over the Passo della Cisa (1039m) before descending into the Magra valley in Tuscany.

SALSOMAGGIORE TERME

Salt was extracted from the waters of Salsomaggiore Terme (*map A, C2*) from the Roman era until the mid-19th century. After 1839 Salsomaggiore became one of the most famous spas in Italy; its saline waters are still used today to treat rheumatic, arthritic and post-inflammatory disorders. The Grand Hotel des Thermes (now a congress centre) was opened in 1901 and bought in 1910 by César Ritz. It contains Art Nouveau works by Galileo Chini, who also decorated the spa building, which opened in 1923. There are still several Art Nouveau and Art Deco buildings in the town.

VERDI'S HOME GROUND: RONCOLE & BUSSETO

In 1813 at Roncole (north of Fidenza; *map A, C1*), Giuseppe Verdi was born into a simple family: his father was a grocer there. It was after Verdi became world famous that the little town changed its name to **Roncole Verdi**. Verdi had his first great success only in 1843 with Nabucco but he went on to become Italy's most famous operatic composer, producing in the 1850s *Rigoletto* and *La Traviata*. *Aida* was first performed in 1871, and *Otello* (1887) and *Falstaff* (1893) both had their premières at La Scala in Milan. But Verdi also continued to enjoy a simple country life here, right up until his death in 1901. His house at Roncole can be visited (*open April–Sept Tues–Sun 9.30–12.30 & 3–7; Oct–March Tues–Sun 9.30–12.30 & 2.30–5.30*).

BUSSETO

Just 5 kilometres away is Busseto (*map A, C1*), a small town which was the fief of the Pallavicini in the 10th–16th centuries. The Villa Pallavicino houses the (very disappointing) **Museo Nazionale Giuseppe Verdi** (*open Tues–Sun 10–5.30, 7.30 in summer*). On two floors the rooms are decorated—in questionable taste—to illustrate Verdi's operas but there are no original artworks. The church of **Santa Maria degli Angeli** was built by the Pallavicini in the 15th century in front of their villa. It contains a *Deposition* group by Guido Mazzoni (1470s). The little **Teatro Verdi** was inaugurated in 1868 with a performance of *Rigoletto* (but in the absence of the composer). The Neoclassical **Palazzo Orlandi**, where Verdi lived for a time, was purchased in 2013 by the SIAE (the Italian Society of Authors and Publishers) and may be restored.

A few kilometres north, at **Sant'Agata di Villanova sull'Arda**, is the Villa Verdi, built by Verdi in 1848 as a summer residence for himself and the soprano Giuseppina Strepponi, who became his second wife in 1859. The rooms are more or less as he left them (*it is open for most of the year, Tues–Sun 9.30–11.45 & 2.30 or 3–6.15; villaverdi. org*).

CASTLES OF THE DUKEDOM OF PARMA & PIACENZA

The provinces of Parma and Piacenza are particularly rich in feudal strongholds. Those that are open to the public are shown on guided visits only (*for the latest information on visiting hours see also castellidelducato.it. The 'Castelli del Ducato' card provides discounts*).

IN THE ENVIRONS OF PARMA

The Reggia di Colorno at **Colorno** (*map A, D1*) is the grand ducal palace of the Farnese (*opening hours vary each month: see comune.colorno.pr.it or T: 0521 312545*). It is surrounded by a park with an orangery. The church of San Liborio was begun in 1777 and there are some 18th-century oratories in the grounds.

Fontanellato (*map A, C2*) has a moated 13th-century castle of the Sanvitale family (*open April–Oct daily 9.30–11.30 & 3–6, Nov–March Tues–Sat 9.30–11.30 & 3–5, Sun 9.30–12 & 2.30–5; fontanellato.org*). It contains a little room with delightful frescoes (1524) by Parmigianino (*see p. 86*) as well as 16th–18th-century furnishings, and a collection of ceramics.

Further northwest, the Rocca Meli Lupi at **Soragna** (*map A, C1*) has 16th-century works of art (*open daily 9–11 & 2.30 or 3–5.30 or 6*). The synagogue has a Jewish museum (*open on Sun and holidays 10–12.30 & 3–6, Tues–Fri 10–12 & 3–5*). Nearer the Po are the fortresses of the Rossi family at **Roccabianca** (*map A, D1; open at weekends, T: 0521 374065*) and **San Secondo Parmense** (*map A, D1; closed for structural repairs at the time of writing; T: 0521 873214, cortedeirossi.it*), with interesting frescoes.

Southeast of Parma is **Montechiarugolo** (*map A, D3*), with a good castle of 1406 (*open on some weekends; T: 0521 686643, castellodimontechiarugolo.it*), and **Montecchio Emilia** (*map A, D2*), which preserves parts of the old ramparts. **Torrechiara** (*map A, D3*) has the finest castle in the province of Parma (*open Tues– Fri 9–4.30, Sat–Sun 10–5; T: 0521 355255*), built for Pier Maria Rossi (1448–60), with its 'golden room' frescoed by Benedetto Bembo (c. 1463). Other rooms are decorated by Cesare Baglione and his followers.

Mamiano (*map A, D3*) lies near the Parma River south of Parma. The village itself is not very interesting, nor does it have a castle, but the nearby **Villa Mamiano**, surrounded by a beautiful park, is well worth the visit. It was the residence of the connoisseur, musicologist and art historian Luigi Magnani (d. 1984). His collections are now held by the Fondazione Magnani Rocca and there is a remarkable private museum here (exhibitions are held periodically; *open mid-March–Nov Tues–Sun 10–5; magnanirocca.it*). The paintings include works by Dürer (*Madonna and Child*); Carpaccio (*Pietà*); Filippo Lippi (*Madonna and Child*); Gentile da Fabriano (*St Francis Receiving the Stigmata*); Van Dyck (*Equestrian Portrait of Giovanni Paolo Balbi*); Titian (*Madonna and Child with St Catherine, St Dominic and a Donor*, c. 1512/14); and Goya (allegorical family portrait of the *Infante Luis de Bourbon*, a conversation piece of 1789). There is also a splendid modern collection, with works by Monet, Renoir, Cézanne and Giorgio Morandi.

The ruined castle of **Canossa**, still further south (*map A, D3; open summer Tues– Sun 9–12.30 & 3–7; winter 9–1 & 1.30–4.30*) was the home of Countess Matilda of Tuscia, who was responsible for the submission of Emperor Henry IV to Pope Gregory VII in 1077. Only the foundations of the castle of that time remain; the ruins above ground date from the 13th century and later.

IN THE ENVIRONS OF PIACENZA

Near **Gazzola** (*map A, B1*), west of the Trebbia river, is the medieval **Castello di Rivalta** (*open Feb–Nov usually only at weekends; T: 0523 978104, castellodirivalta. blogspot.it*), enlarged in the 15th and 18th centuries, which retains its original furnishings and paintings by Pordenone. **Grazzano Visconti** (*map A, B1*) is a medieval village built at the beginning of the 20th century by Giuseppe Visconti.

On the northern border of Piacenza Province, on the Po, is **Monticelli d'Ongina** (*map A, C1*), with a 15th-century castle (*open Sun and holidays 3–6.30, winter 2.30– 5 but closed Dec, Jan, July and Aug; T: 0523 827048*). with a chapel frescoed by Bonifacio Bembo in the 15th century and 18th-century frescoes and stuccoes in the main rooms. An ethnographic museum illustrates life on the river.

Cortemaggiore (*map A, C1*), a 15th-century 'new town' built by the Pallavicini family, has two fine churches; the former Franciscan church has frescoes by Pordenone.

CASTELL'ARQUATO, CHIARAVALLE & BOBBIO

CASTELL'ARQUATO

In the pretty Arda valley this picturesque hill-town (*map A, C2*) has double gates. In the attractive piazza stand the Palazzo Pretorio of 1293 and the Romanesque Collegiata, with a 14th-century cloister off which is a museum with Church silver, sculpture and paintings. The 14th-century **Rocca Viscontea** (*open Tues–Sun 10–1 & 2–6.30; in winter only at weekends; T: 0532 803215, castellarquatoruismo.it*) overlooks the river valley. The 16th-century **Torrione Farnese** is in the lower town, near a 13th-century fountain. A **geological museum** with marine fossils from the area is housed in the former hospital (16th century). Another museum is dedicated to Luigi Illica, in the librettist' s house.

THE ABBEYS OF CHIARAVALLE AND BOBBIO

At **Alseno** (*map A, C2*) the Cistercian abbey of Chiaravalle della Colomba (*open Mon–Sat 8.30–11.30 & 2.30–5.30, Sun and holidays 8.30–12 & 2–6; T: 0523 940132*) has a Romanesque church and a particularly fine 13th-century Gothic cloister with coupled columns.

At **Bobbio** (*map A, A2*) is the abbey of San Colombano, founded in 612 by the Irish St Columbanus, who died here in 615. The monastery was famous for its learning. The current basilica (*usually open 8am–7pm*), a 15th–17th-century building, has a crypt with some traces of the primitive church and the tomb of St Columbanus (1480). The museum (*usually open at weekends*) contains a remarkable Roman ivory bucket with a representation of Orpheus (or David) in high relief (4th century). The heavily-restored cathedral is 12th-century, and beyond, a humpback bridge, possibly Roman, probably 7th-century in part, crosses the River Trebbia.

VELEIA

Near Lugagnano Val d'Arda, in pretty countryside, is Veleia (*map A, B2; open daily 9–dusk*), the picturesque ruins (including the forum and basilica) of a small Roman town which flourished in the 1st century BC, first excavated in the 18th century. There is a small antiquarium here but the most important finds are preserved in the Museo Archeologico Nazionale in Parma.

AROUND PARMA & PIACENZA PRACTICAL TIPS

GETTING AROUND

• **By rail:** Fidenza is connected by frequent trains to Parma (in 10mins) and to Piacenza (in about 25mins).

• **By bus:** Buses from Parma leave from next to the railway station (*map Parma East, 3*), serving most places in the province (Colorno, Fornovo di Taro, Fidenza, Fontanellato,

Montechiarugolo, Roccabianca, Salsomaggiore Terme, San Secondo Parmense and Soragna). They are operated by TEP (*T: 840 222222, tep. pr.it*). From Piacenza, buses leave from Piazza Cittadella (*map Piacenza, 3–4*) to Bobbio, Busseto, Cortemaggiore and Salsomaggiore Terme. They are run by SETA (*T: 840 000216, setaweb.it*).

RESTAURANTS

BOBBIO (*map A, A2*)
€€ **San Nicola**. Restaurant offering excellent regional food and wines, in a former convent. Closed Mon evening and Tues. *Contrada dell' Ospedale, T: 0523 932355, www.ristorantesannicola. it.*

FIDENZA (*map A, C2*)
€€ **I Gemelli**. An interesting seafood restaurant. Closed Mon. *Via Gialdi 14, T: 0524 528506.*
€ **Astoria**. Good Emilian home cooking, in a restaurant and pizzeria attached to the hotel of the same name. Closed Mon. *Via Gandolfi 5, T: 0524 527663, hotelastoriafidenza.it.*

ROCCABIANCA (*map A, D1*)
€€ **Hostaria da Ivan**. Simple *osteria* popular with locals. Closed Mon–Tues. *Via Villa 73, Località Fontanelle, T: 0521 870113, hostariadaivan.it.*

SORAGNA (*map A, C1*)
€€ **Antica Osteria Ardenga**. Good local *osteria*. Closed Tues evening and all day Wed. *Via Maestra 6, Località Diolo (north of Soragna), T: 0524 599337, osteriardenga.it.*

FESTIVALS & EVENTS

Castell'Arquato Medieval market and banquet, May.
Fidenza Classical music and opera season, spring. *La Gostra di Maggio*, theatre festival, May.
Fontanellato Classical music and opera season, winter–spring.
Grazzano Visconti *Il Corteo*, historic pageant, May. *Alla Corte del Re*, music and dance in historic costume, first Sun of every month, April–Sept. *Notte di Faba*, medieval market and banquet, July.

Ferrara

Ferrara (*map C, A1*) is one of the most pleasing towns in northern Italy, well administered and with a peaceful atmosphere. Cycling is the main means of getting about. The city is divided into two distinct parts: the southern district retains many attractive cobbled streets and medieval houses, whereas the area to the north has a spacious plan laid out in the 15th century by Ercole I d'Este, when the Este court was one of the most illustrious of the Italian Renaissance; the very long, dead straight Corso named after the great ruler is still one of the most beautiful residential streets to be found anywhere in Europe. Jacob Burckhardt defined Ferrara as the first modern city in Europe. The huge Este castle survives right in the centre at the dividing line between the two areas of the town, and the walls, also built by the Este, which surround the entire town today provide a wonderful recreation area for walkers and cyclists. There are numerous parks as well as excellent museums, and important exhibitions and concerts are often held in the town.

HISTORY OF FERRARA

A settlement on the northern banks of the Po first became important under the Exarchate of Ravenna towards the end of the 7th century. The name Ferrara appears in history from around 760. The Guelph family of Este, after a decisive defeat of the Ghibellines by Azzo Novello at Cassano in 1259, established the earliest and one of the greatest northern Italian principalities here. The Este dukes remained in power until the end of the 16th century, and their court attracted a great many poets, scholars and artists, while trade and commerce flourished. Nicolò II (1361–88) gave hospitality to Petrarch; Alberto (1388–93) founded the university; Nicolò III (1393–1441) was the patron of Pisanello, and during his rule, in 1438, the Eastern emperor John VI Palaeologus met Pope Eugenius IV here at the Ecumenical Council later transferred to Florence. Lionello (1441–50) inaugurated the age of artistic pre-eminence that Borso (1450–71) continued. Ercole I (1471–1505) laid out the northern district of the town; and Alfonso I (1505–34), husband of Lucrezia Borgia, was the patron of Ariosto and Titian. Ercole II (1534–59) married Renée, the daughter of Louis XII of France; and Alfonso II (1559–97) was the patron of Tasso and began the reclamation of the marshes.

In 1598, on the pretext that Cesare d'Este, heir apparent to the duchy in a collateral line, was illegitimate, the town was annexed to the States of the Church. Without the Este Ferrara soon lost its importance. The town lies in

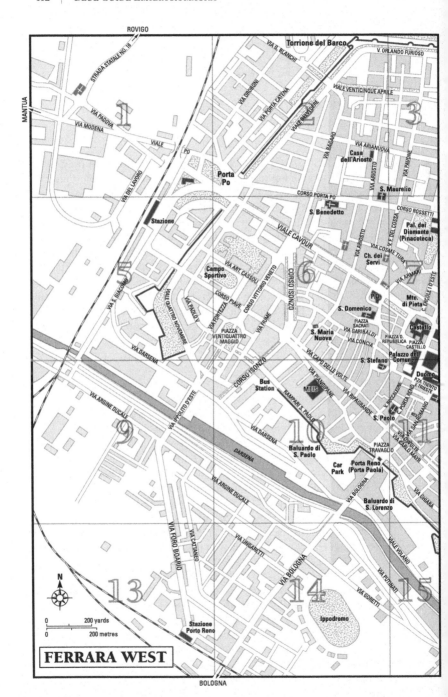

FERRARA WEST

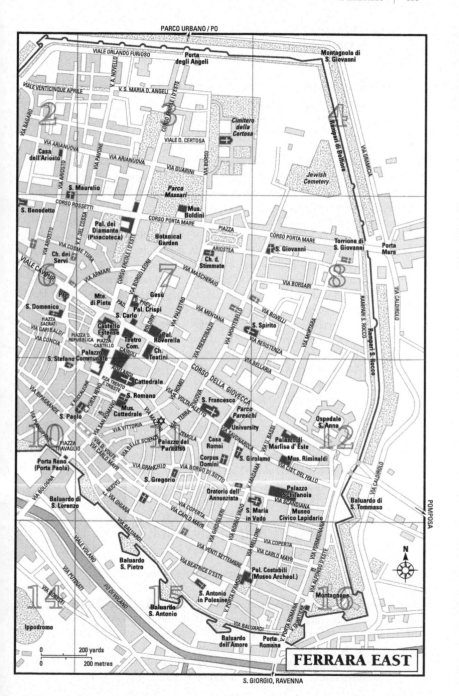

PARCO URBANO / PO

VIALE ORLANDO FURIOSO

Porta
degli Angeli

Montagnola di
S. Giovanni

VIALE VENTICINQUE APRILE

V.S. MARIA D. ANGELI

VIA BAGARO

2

VIA ARIANUOVA

Casa
dell'Ariosto

VIA ARIOSTO

VIA PAVIONE

VIA ARIANUOVA

VIA GUARINI

3

CORSO ERCOLE D'ESTE

VIALE D. CERTOSA

Cimitero
della
Certosa

4

Rampari di Belfiore

VIA GRAMICIA

S. Maurelio

CORSO ROSSETTI

Parco
Massari

Jewish
Cemetery

S. Benedetto

VIA V. E. DEL COSSA

Pal. dei
Diamante
(Pinacoteca)

Mus.
Boldini

CORSO PORTA MARE

PIAZZA
ARIOSTEA

CORSO PORTA MARE

Torrione di
S. Giovanni

Porta
Mare

VIA ARIOSTO

VIA COSME TURA

Ch. dei
Servi

VIALE CAVOUR

6

Botanical
Garden

Ch. d.
Stimmate

S. Giovanni

8

VIA BORSARI

VIA ARMARI

CORSO ERCOLE D'ESTE

VIA BORGO LEONI

7

VIA MASCHERAIO

P.D.

S. Domenico

Mte.
di Pieta

PAD.

Gesù

BOLDINI

PREL.

Pal. Crispi

S. Carlo

VIA PALESTRO

VIA MENTANA

VIA MONTEBELLO

VIA BOVELLI

S. Spirito

VIA MORTARA

RAMPARI S. ROCCO

Rampari S. Rocco

VIA CALDIROLO

PIAZZA
SACRATI

VIA GARIBALDI

VIA CONCIA

PIAZZA D.
REPUBBLICA

Castello
Estense

Teatro
Com.

PIAZZA
CASTELLO

Pal.
Roverella

VIA FRESCOBALDI

VIA RESISTENZA

VIA MUNARI

PIAZZA
CAIROLI

Ch.
Teatini

S. Stefano Communale

Palazzo

ADELARDI

VIA ROMEI

VIA VOLTAPALETTO

CORSO DELLA GIOVECCA

VIA BELLARIA

VIA RIPAGRANDE

VIA BROCASALE

C. PORTA RENO

PZA TRENTO
TRIESTE

Cattedrale

S. Romano

Mus.
Cattedrale

VIA TERRA NUOVA

VIA MAZZINI

S. Francesco

Parco
Pareschi

Ospedale
S. Anna

12

S. Paolo

VIA SAN ROMANO

VIA VITTORIA

VIA VOLTE

VIA BELLE SCIENZE

University

VIA SAVONAROLA

VIA U. BASSI

Palazzoldi
Marfisa d'Este

10

VIA PANISPERNA

PIAZZA
TRAVAGLIO

VIA CARLO MAYR

Palazzo del
Paradiso

Casa
Romei

VIA MADAMA

S. Girolamo

Mus. Riminaldi

Porta Reno
(Porta Paola)

VIA BOLOGNA

VIA NUOVA

VIA GHIARA

Corpus
Domini

VIA BRANCHIO

VIA BORGO DI SOTTO

VIA CIST. DEL FOLLO

S. Gregorio

Oratorio dell'
Annunziata

VIA GHISIGLIERI

VIA BORGO VADO

S. Maria
in Vado

Palazzo
Schifanoia

VIA SCANDIANA

Museo
Civico Lapidario

Baluardo di
S. Tommaso

POMPOSA

Baluardo di
S. Lorenzo

VIALE VOLANO

VIA BALUARDI

VIA COPERTA

VIA CARLO MAYR

VIA VENTI SETTEMBRE

VIA MELLONE

VIA COPERTA

VIA CARLO MAYR

VIA PRIMARIA

VIA ALFONSO D'ESTE

N

Baluardo
S. Pietro

VIA PUTINATI

PO DI VOLANO

VIA BEATRICE D'ESTE

Pal. Costabili
(Museo Archeol.)

14

VIA PORETTI

Ippodromo

15

Baluardo
S. Antonio

S. Antonio
in Polesine

VIA PORTA D'AMORE

VIA PORTA ROMANA

V. P. PORTA ROMANA

V. BATTIFERRO

Montagnone

16

Baluardo
dell'Amore

Porta
Romana

VIA BALUARDI

0   200 yards
0   200 metres

FERRARA EAST

S. GIORGIO, RAVENNA

a fertile plain near the right bank of the Po and extensive land-reclamation operations in the delta area in the early 20th century brought back some of its old prosperity, and it is now an important market for fruit.

ART, ARCHITECTURE, LITERATURE AND MUSIC

Ferrara had a productive school of painting, much of it overlapping with Bologna, where the court of the Bentivoglio attracted artists of talent and repute. One of the finest Ferrarese masters was Cosmè Tura—a great painter, of whose work all too little survives. With his hard outlines and vigorous modelling, there is a lack of Italian sweetness and sensuality to his work, but its glyptic astringency is difficult to forget. Unjustly treated both by posterity and by his patron (who replaced him with Ercole de' Roberti), Tura died penniless in 1495. Ercole worked both in Ferrara and in Bologna. He partnered another great Ferrarese artist, Francesco del Cossa, on the zodiac frescoes in the Palazzo Schifanoia (*see p. 122*), then followed Cossa to Bologna, until he was appointed court painter at Ferrara. The deceptively crude, spiky naïvety of his art masks great sophistication and emotion. Other important names associated with Ferrara include Dosso Dossi and his brother Battista, and Il Garofalo, a follower of Raphael, and high priest of the High Renaissance.

Ferrara was also the birthplace of an important sculptor, Alfonso Lombardi (1497–1537), and of a great architect, Biagio Rossetti (c. 1447–1516). Rossetti's most famous achievement is the 'Addizione', the northern extension of the city, one of the greatest feats of town planning of all time. The extraordinary Palazzo dei Diamanti, with its exterior covered with sharply-pointed rustication imitating diamonds (*see p. 126*), is also his.

The court of the Este was also noted for its music. The composer Girolamo Frescobaldi (1583–1643) was born in Ferrara. At the end of the 16th century the '*Concerto delle donne*' at the Este court had an important influence on the development of the madrigal. Robert Browning wrote several poems about Ferrara, and *My Last Duchess* (written in 1842) probably refers to Alfonso II and his wife. The writer Giorgio Bassani was born in Ferrara in 1916, and his novel *The Garden of the Finzi-Continis* is set here.

THE CASTELLO ESTENSE

Map Ferrara East, 7. Open daily 9.30–5.30. www.castelloestense.it.

In the centre of the town rises the castle, once the palace of the Este dukes. It is a massive quadrilateral surrounded by a moat (still filled with water) and approached by drawbridges. It was begun in 1385 for Duke Nicolò II by a certain Bartolino da Novara, who incorporated the 13th-century Torre dei Leoni into the northern corner of the fortress and added three more identical towers. It was altered for Duke Ercole II and his successor Duke Alfonso II in the 16th century by the better-known architect Girolamo da Carpi (also a painter) and today it is particularly interesting for its painted ceilings commissioned by these two Este dukes with the help of Pirro Ligorio, the Neapolitan antiquary and architect. They are the work of the local painter Camillo Filippi and his son Sebastiano (better-known as Il Bastianino), as well as Girolamo da Carpi. The castle was readapted in the 20th century to house the administrative offices of the province.

Interior of the Castello

Off the lovely courtyard, the ground-floor rooms (where a large model of the castle is displayed) are interesting for their architecture with brick vaulting and herring-bone pavements. They include the kitchen and the grim dungeons beneath the Torre dei Leoni, where Parisina, wife of Nicolò III, and her lover Ugo, his illegitimate son, were imprisoned and murdered; the cells were last used for political prisoners in 1943.

An artillery ramp, by which cannons were taken up to the bastions, leads round the Torre dei Leoni past another prison, and a modern iron staircase continues up to the **first floor**. Here a loggia opens onto the **Giardino degli Aranci**, a charming little walled hanging garden designed by Girolamo da Carpi, still with pots of citrus trees, where the Este duchesses could watch, unobserved, life in the town below. In the vault of the tiny **Camerino dei Baccanali** are three scenes painted on one of the walls of the *Triumph of Ariadne* and the *Triumph of Bacchus* on either side of a grape harvest. These were painted in oil at the end of the 16th century which accounts for their poor condition. The austere **Chapel of Renée of France** is named after Renée, the daughter of Louis XII of France and the protectress of John Calvin (who lived for a while in Ferrara under the assumed name of Charles Heppeville). Her husband, Ercole II, soon sent Renée into exile. The chapel has polychrome marble on the walls. The 16th-century ceiling frescoes of the four Evangelists were repainted in the 19th century. The adjoining three rooms all have delightful ceiling frescoes, seen with the help of large mirrors, painted in the 16th century by Camillo Filippi and his sons Cesare and Sebastiano (Il Bastianino), with deocative elements by Leonardo da Brescia. From the Saletta dei Giochi there is access to an iron staircase (with 122 steps) which leads up to the Torre dei Leoni. A little enclosed loggia called the Saletta dei Veleni has a vault painted by Carlo Parmeggiani in 1927 of allegorical figures and personifications (including a portrait of Italo Balbo on the wall opposite the entrance).

In the **Appartamento della Pazienza** the most interesting rooms are the two where Ercole II held court: the Sala del Governo and the adjoining antechamber, with a lovely ceiling with *grottesche* by Girolamo Bonaccioli (1556). Four rooms here were at the time of writing used to exhibit the Malabotta collection of paintings by Filippo de Pisis (1896–1956), from the Museo d' Arte Moderna in Palazzo Massari, which has been closed for a number of years. De Pisis was born in Ferrara and was one of the most important Italian artists of the 20th century: his works dating from the 1920s and 1940s are perhaps the most interesting.

The exit is through the 19th-century Salone degli Stemmi down a handsome 15th-century spiral staircase. The very beautiful little *Stanzina delle Duchesse* can only be visited from the Palazzo Comunale (*see below*).

PALAZZO COMUNALE

Beyond the monument to the preacher and theocrat Savonarola, born in Ferrara in 1452 and burned at the stake in Florence in 1498, is the huge Palazzo Comunale (*map Ferrara East, 7–11*). It was first built here for Azzo Novello (1243) but was considerably altered in the late 15th century by Pietro Benvenuti and Biagio Rossetti. The bronze statues of Nicolò III and Borso d'Este, on the Classical arch (to a design attributed to Leon Battista Alberti) and column in front, are 20th-century reproductions of the 15th-century originals destroyed in 1796. The arcaded courtyard has a fine staircase by Pietro Benvenuti (1481). From here you can visit (*usually on request in the morning at the municipal offices*) the tiny **Stanzina delle Duchesse** in the Castello, entirely decorated with exquisite grotesques by the Filippi (1555–65).

THE CATTEDRALE

The cathedral (*map Ferrara East 11, closed 12–3.30*), begun in 1135 by the architect and sculptor Master Niccolò, was almost complete by the end of the 13th century. The exterior and enclosed narthex are its most interesting features. The precincts are guarded by four fantastic animals carved in red marble. The church was dedicated to the Virgin Mary and to St George, both of whom feature prominently on the façade, which is divided vertically into three parts of equal height. Protecting the central portal is a magnificent tall projecting tabernacle with sculptures representing the *Last Judgement*. It is crowned by a tympanum with the *Redeemer*, between angels holding the symbols of the Passion, and the two kneeling figures of the *Virgin* and *St John the Evangelist*. Amongst the standing figures in the architrave below are angels blowing trumpets and weighing souls while the blessed proceed to the left on their way to Heaven (depicted in the lunette a little lower down on the façade itself) and the damned are banished towards Hell on the right (depicted in the lunette on the right). In the four spandrels below are the extraordinary figures of four of the dead actually emerging from their tombs. These are all the work of an unknown 13th-century master.

Within the tribune below is a statue of the *Madonna and Child* by Michele da Firenze (1427). The tabernacle is supported by four carved and knotted columns held up by crouching figures and two huge pink marble lions. The **central portal** itself has more beautiful carving dating from the previous century by Master Niccolò, with *St George and the Dragon* in the lunette and a frieze in the architrave with scenes from the life of Christ.

In a niche, the grim hooded figure of Alberto, the Este duke best remembered as the founder of Ferrara's university, dates from 1393. The south side is partly obscured by a charming little portico of shops added in 1473. The massive, unfinished **campanile**, southeast of the church, was built from 1412 to 1596 to a plan attributed to Leon Battista Alberti. The enclosed **narthex** has two ancient sarcophagi, and two more splendid lions carrying the tall columns which once decorated the main portal.

The gloomy **interior** was remodelled in 1712–18. The two stoups have life-size angels by Andrea and Ferdinando Vaccà from Ferrara (1745), and on either side of the main door are two detached frescoes by Garofalo, representing St Peter and St Paul. The last altarpiece in the north aisle by Francesco Francia depicts the Coronation of the Virgin and saints below but includes the Christ Child lying on the ground with no-one taking any notice of Him. In the transepts are very interesting painted terracotta busts in tondos of the Apostles by Alfonso Lombardi. The south transept has a *Martyrdom of St Lawrence* by Guercino (1629) and the Altar of the Calvary, composed in 1673 from large 15th-century bronze of Christ on the Cross flanked by the Virgin and St John by Niccolò and Giovanni Baroncelli, with St George and the Dragon and St Maurilius by Domenico di Paris. Below is the effigy tomb of Bishop Bovelli (d. 1954). A fresco of the *Last Judgement* by Bastianino (1580–3) adorns the apse.

MUSEO DELLA CATTEDRALE

This museum (*open Tues–Sun 9.30–1 & 3–6; artecultura.fe.it*) is housed in the former church and convent of San Romano, off a little modern piazza opposite the south side of the cathedral. The very interesting collection is beautifully displayed. Upstairs there is a wonderful collection of 22 illuminated choirbooks (1477–1535). The sculpture in this room includes a splendid large 8th-century ambo with reliefs of birds and grapevines, and a relief in profile of Cardinal Bessarion, who was in Ferrara in 1438 for the Ecumenical Council. Below, off the pretty little cloister, with attractive paving and twisted columns, is the entrance to the former sacristy where the ribs of the vault are painted with flowers. Here are displayed some interesting reliquaries, including silver busts from the 17th and 18th centuries, the arms of St Maurilius (in silver; 1455), and of St George (1388); and a lovely reliquary Cross in rock crystal, quartz, silver and gilded copper, made in 1437. Also here are some (framed) fragments of embroidery from 16th-century vestments. The tiny mosaic fragment of the head of the Virgin is a Veneto-Byzantine work of the 12th century from the ancient cathedral.

In the former church of San Romano, in the sanctuary, is a **superb work by Jacopo della Quercia**: the seated Madonna holding a pomegranate, with the Christ Child standing on her knee holding the scroll of the Law. Both of them appear to be gazing far into the future. This was the great Sienese artist's first work, commissioned in 1403 and the beautiful marble is still in pristine condition. In the centre of the church there is a wonderful display of **eight Flemish tapestries** made by Johannes Karcher, who was called to work (with his brother) at the Este court in 1552. On a design by Garofalo and Camillo Filippi, they illustrate the lives of St George and St Maurilius and used to decorate the cathedral. The huge organ doors are the earliest work (1469) of Cosmè Tura (who may also have designed the statuette of St Maurilius beside them). The doors have the *Annunciation* on the wings (with a particularly beautiful angel, and a squirrel above the Virgin), and *St George and the Dragon* inside.

The reliefs displayed around the walls are of the greatest interest: the delightful high reliefs of the Months come from the Porta dei Pellegrini on the south side of the cathedral, which was demolished in 1736. They are almost free-standing sculptures and are by an unknown early 13th-century master named from these the 'Maestro dei Mesi'. He worked in Forlì and Venice besides Ferrara and was clearly influenced by Benedetto Antelami. A capital from the baptistery in Verona stone, with carvings of the *Banquet of Herod* and *Beheading of the Baptist*, is the work of another unknown master (c. 1200), named from this piece. On the opposite wall are more very interesting sculptures, including a 13th-century relief of the *Presentation in the Temple*, *Christ in Maestà*, and three damaged statuettes by Bernardo Rossellino.

AROUND THE OLD GHETTO

The pretty, arcaded Via San Romano (*map Ferrara East, 11*) leads south from the Museo della Cattedrale through an interesting medieval part of the town. The street ends at Porta Reno (or Porta Paolo), built in 1612 to a design by the native architect Giovanni Battista Aleotti. Nearby is the imposing church of **San Paolo** (*map Ferrara East, 11*), begun in 1575 by the local architect Alberto Schiatti. It contains 16th–17th-century paintings and frescoes, some by Girolamo da Carpi (*St Jerome*) and Bastianino. In the presbytery are the *Adoration of the Magi, Conversion* and *Martyrdom of St Paul* by a certain Domenico Mona and, in the apse, a fresco of the *Abduction of Elijah* by Scarsellino. Along the aisles are some beautiful 18th-century terracotta sculptures by the otherwise unknown artists Filippo Bezzi and Francesco Casella.

The street ends at Porta Reno (or Porta Paola), built in 1612 to a design by the native architect Giovanni Battista Aleotti. At Via Piangipane 81 (*map Ferrara West, 10*) is the **Museo Nazionale dell'Ebraismo Italiano e della Shoah (MEIS)**. (*Open Tues–Sun 10–1 & 4–6; meisweb.it.*) Inaugurated in 2011, the museum, which illustrates the history of the Jewish people in Italy and the Shoah, is still under construction on the site of the former prison of Ferrara (in use until the 1990s). At the time of writing three rooms were open, but numerous interesting events are held here while work is in progress to restore another prison building and create more exhibition space (a firm of architects from Bologna won the international competition for the design). There will be a garden within the walls (and another entrance on Via Rampari). Work is expected to be completed by 2020. (*For the Ghetto of Ferrara and history of the Jewish community, see below.*)

Before the gate the pretty **Via delle Volte**, a peaceful cobbled lane which runs beneath numerous arches, leads left. It crosses Via Scienze, in which (at no. 17) is **Palazzo Paradiso**. The building dates from 1391 but it was given a façade in 1610 by Giovanni Battista Aleotti. In the library (Biblioteca Ariostea; *open Mon–Fri 9–7, Sat 9–1*) are manuscript pages of Ludovico Ariosto's epic poem *Orlando Furioso*, and autographs by him as well as his funerary monument. At Via Gioco del Pallone 31 is the house that belonged to Ariosto's family (the poet built himself another house in Ferrara, the Casa dell'Ariosto; *see p. 129*).

You can see well preserved old houses of the 15th-century city and little churches in the narrow lanes lying between Via Scienze and Via Borgo Vado.

At Via Mazzini 95 is the **Synagogue** (*map Ferrara East, 11*), in the area which was the **ghetto** of Ferrara from 1627 to 1848. The Museo Ebraico here has been closed since 2012 (*for the new museum dedicated to Italian Judaism and the Shoah, see above*). A few typical tall houses with iron balconies in Via Vignataglíata recall the architecture of the Ghetto.

THE HISTORY OF THE JEWS IN FERRARA

Jews are first documented in the town in 1227, and the Este court welcomed them and encouraged their influence in the field of economics (by 1393 it seems that all the banks in the town were in their hands). Many of them also practised as doctors and were later occupied in the printing trade. After their expulsion from Spain in 1492, many more were given a safe haven here. But when in 1597 Este rule came to an end and Ferrara was absorbed into the Papal States, their presence was no longer encouraged and in 1627 a ghetto was built for them where the five gates were locked at night. They remained segregated here right up until the Unification of Italy in 1859. In the 20th century the Jews of Ferrara suffered the same terrible fate as those in Germany: under laws introduced by Mussolini in 1938, Jewish teachers and pupils were no longer able to attend school or university and in the end their citizenship was denied them and their deportation began. It is believed that some 430 inhabitants of Ferrara were interned in Nazi concentration camps.

This tragic history has been recorded on a national basis in the new museum of Ferrara which is still being completed on the site of the former prison. It was in this prison that Giorgio Bassani (1916–2000) was interned in 1943 as an anti-Fascist. When, as a Jew, he lost his teaching post at a public high school in Ferrara in 1938, he taught at a private Jewish school set up in Via Vignatagliata until 1943, when he was temporarily imprisoned. His most famous novel, *The Garden of the Finzi-Continis*, is set in Ferrara and decribes the plight of the Jewish community (as do his other works). However, the film with the same title, released in 1970 by Vittorio De Sica, met with Bassani's strong disapproval. In 1955 he was one of the founders of Italia Nostra and to the end of his life remained deeply concerned about the conservation of the beauty of Italy. He is buried in the Jewish cemetery (*see p. 129*), where there is a bronze memorial to him by Arnaldo Pomodoro.

FROM THE CATHEDRAL TO CASA ROMEI & PALAZZINA DI MARFISA D'ESTE

Via degli Adelardi (*map Ferrara East, 11*) follows the north side of the Cattedrale. Opposite the Palazzo Vescovile is a wine bar (Al Brindisi), with tables outside on the site of the ancient Hosteria del Chiucchiolino, which is known to have been in operation here by 1435. The lane leads into the attractive Via Voltapaletto, with Palazzo Bevilacqua Costabili (no. 11), which also existed in the 15th-century town although it was given its façade, decorated with busts and trophies, in the 17th century. Beyond is the spacious church of **San Francesco** (at the time of writing, only the east end was accessible). It was partly rebuilt in 1494 by Biagio Rossetti, following the plan devised by Brunelleschi for his church of San Lorenzo in Florence. The frescoed frieze of Franciscan saints above the arches and on the vault are good Ferrarese works of the 16th century. In the north aisle is a polychrome wood *Pietà* attributed to Alfonso Lombardo, and a *Rest on the Flight into Egypt* by Scarsellino. The first chapel in the south aisle has a high relief of 1521 of the *Prayer in the Garden*, with two kneeling donors and a fine fresco of the *Seizure of Christ in the Garden* (1524) by Garofalo. Also in this aisle is a high relief in terracotta of *Christ at the Column*, with frescoes of the flagellants also attributed to Garofalo.

CASA ROMEI

Casa Romei (*Via Savonarola 30; map Ferrara East, 11; open Tues–Fri 8.30–7.30, Sat 2–7.30, Mon and Sun 8.30–2*) is one of the best examples of an aristocratic home from 15th-century Ferrara. It was begun around 1440 for the wealthy Giovanni Romei, who served the Este court as a diplomat and whose successful career culminated in 1474 when he married Polissena d'Este (daughter of Meliaduse d'Este, the illegitimate daughter of Niccolò III). In keeping with Giovanni's will, the house was donated after his death to the Poor Clare nuns of the adjacent convent of Corpus Domini and was used to house pilgrims and other visitors to the city (and at one time one of the guests was Lucrezia Borgia; *see below*). It remained in the nuns' hands until the confiscation of monastic properties under Napoleon.

Off the central courtyard are two rooms with very interesting frescoes representing respectively the *Prophets*, with philosophical truths and biblical prophecies written on scrolls, and the *Sibyls* (probably executed after Romei's marriage to Polissena). The twelve sibyls are depicted standing in a garden enclosed by a hedge of roses: these monumental figures are also fascinating for their dress. They hold long scrolls on which their oracles are written in Gothic characters. The frieze continues across the chimneypiece. In a room (*usually shown only on Fridays*) thought to have been Romei's *studiolo*, more very rare painted decorations, probably by the same artist who painted the sibyls, have been discovered on both sides of a wooden partition wall. Here there are ladies in roundels (note Europa's splendid hairdo) representing the known continents, between friezes of pomegranates.

The ceilings of some of the other rooms have very delicate paintings on paper. The frescoes in the courtyard date from the 16th century, and here are two 14th-century lions in red Verona marble. Architectural fragments and sculptures from demolished buildings in Ferrara are exhibited in two rooms, and another room has ceramics found during excavations in the grounds of the Sant'Antonio in Polesine (*see p. 124*).

Off the upper loggia is a display of ruined detached frescoes mainly of the 14th century, from Ferrarese churches. The frescoes and grotesques in two handsome vaulted rooms here are by the Filippi, commissioned by Cardinal Ippolito d'Este in the mid-16th century when he was in residence.

CORPUS DOMINI

Across Via Savonarola is the seat of the University, founded in 1391. The church of **San Girolamo** (1712) faces the house (no. 19) where Savonarola spent the first 20 years of his life. The church of **Corpus Domini** has a 15th-century façade in Via Campofranco (*for admission, 3.30-5.30 except Sat and Sun, ring at the convent round the corner in Via Pergolato 4; the Franciscan nuns of the closed order of the Poor Clares open the door by remote control*). This convent was where the most illustrious

Ferrarese families would send their daughters to take the veil in the 15th and 16th centuries and it was the place where the Este family chose to be buried. Today, in the nuns' choir of the 18th-century interior, their simple pavement tombs can be seen. Here lies Lucrezia Borgia, famous as the daughter of Pope Alexander VI and sister of Cesare Borgia, who came to Ferrara to marry Alfonso I (after two previous marriages) and died here in childbirth at the age of 39. Lucrezia's two sons lie here beside her. Other famous dukes who rest here are Alfonso I, Ercole I and his wife Eleanor of Aragon, Ercole II and Alfonso II.

MUSEO RIMINALDI AND PALAZZINA DI MARFISA D'ESTE
At the end of Via Savonarola can be seen the brick Palazzo Diotisalvi Neroni (Bonacossi) with its tower. This houses the rather gloomy **Museo Riminaldi** (*map Ferrara East, 12; open Tues–Fri 9–6, Mon 9–1*) with a curious 18th-century collection including busts and mosaics in the style of ancient Rome (the one of Cicero by Bartolomeo Cavaceppi is particularly notable). Off the *salone* is a room with a collection of small bronzes by Girolamo Carpagna, Giambologna and Algardi (who also made the bronze head of an angel).

Via Ugo Bassi, to the left, leads to Corso della Giovecca. At no. 170 is the **Palazzina di Marfisa d'Este** (*map Ferrara East, 12; open Tues–Sun 9.30–1 & 3–6*). Built in 1559 on the commission of Francesco d'Este for his daughter Marfisa, it was well restored in 1938. The ceilings are decorated with grotesques and mythological scenes by Camillo Filippi and his sons Sebastiano and Cesare, extensively restored in the late 19th century. The charming little house also has a good collection of period furniture (including a pair of Venetian cupboards with carved figures probably designed by Jacopo Sansovino, and a pair of Tuscan benches with delicate Ionic columns). Works of art include ceramics, a supposed portrait of James I of England and a damaged bust in profile of Ercole I d'Este, by Sperandio. The Loggia degli Aranci in the little walled garden has a barrel vault painted with trellised vines and birds. Adjacent is an area where concerts were held and the musicians would practise in the Sala della Musica, with its coffered ceiling. A huge old magnolia tree survives here and behind the hedge is a tennis court. The original bronze putto made by Giuseppe Virgili in 1935 for the fountain is preserved in a room of the house.

PALAZZO SCHIFANOIA

Map Ferrara East, 12. Open Tues–Sun 9.30–6. Entrance at Via Scandiana 27.

The palace was one of a number of '*delizie*' used by the Este family as places where they could enjoy themselves and hold banquets and parties. A 14th-century building, it was enlarged in 1469 by Pietro Benvenuti and Biagio Rossetti, and the following year the **Salone dei Mesi** was decorated for Borso d'Este, one of the most important rulers of the town, to celebrate his conferment with the title of 'Duke', a recognition which crowned his political ambitions. The delightful frescoes are the work of Francesco Cossa and other masters of the Ferrarese school (maybe with the intervention of Ercole de' Roberti) and are the most extensive cycle of secular frescoes in Italy produced in the Renaissance.

Each wall is clearly divided into three registers depicting the months of the year. The most visible are those on the lower walls which illustrate life at the new duke's court as well as pastoral scenes of the inhabitants enjoying cultivating the land during what we know was a particularly peaceful time for Ferrara. There are numerous portraits of the genial Borso himself in the act of dispensing justice, of generously rewarding the court jester, conversing with visitors, receiving the sombre Venetian ambassadors, or, in his favourite pastime riding out to the hunt, or hawking. The courtiers mingle amongst numerous horses and dogs, beautifully painted.

The middle register, relatively well preserved, bears the signs of the Zodiac for each month against a dark ground of blue-green and maroon, accompanied by three enigmatic figures who were first interpreted at the beginning of the 20th century by Aby Warburg as following an Egyptian scheme which divided each month into three, each period associated with a different divinity in a complicated astrological scheme. Virgo is represented by a memorably elegant lady dressed in white stretched out in a languid pose.

The top register illustrates Triumphs: Mercury, Zeus, Ceres, Vulcan and others are all shown in chariots drawn by animals (including swans, monkeys, and unicorns). The month of September has a charming scene of a couple in bed under a white counterpane, with the lady's dress discarded on the floor beside the knight's empty armour. Unfortunately the scenes for January and February on the west wall are very ruined, and those for October, September and December on the south wall are almost totally obliterated.

The adjoining **Sala delle Virtù** (or Sala degli Stucchi), has a coffered ceiling beautifully decorated two or three years earlier (attributed to Domenico di Paris), and a frieze with reliefs of the Virtues on the upper walls.

The rest of the palace, which has the city's collection of arts and antiquities, has been closed since 2012.

LAPIDARIO CIVICO, SANTA MARIA IN VADO AND THE ORATORIO DELL'ANNUNZIATA

Across the street from Palazzo Schifanoia is the **Lapidario Civico** (*map Ferrara East 12; same opening hours as Palazzo Schifanoia*), arranged in the 15th-century former church of Santa Libera. The collection of Roman works was formed in 1735 by Marchese Bevilacqua. Among the funerary stelae and sarcophagi are those of Annia Faustina and of the Aurelii (both dating from the 3rd century AD).

On the left of Palazzo Schifanoia, Via Borgo Vado leads south past the church of **Santa Maria in Vado** by Biagio Rossetti (1495–1518), with a handsome interior covered with 17th- and 18th-century paintings, including works by Carlo Bononi, the most important local painter at work in the city in the 17th century, responsible for the decoration of the ceiling of the nave and transepts as well as the apse (1617), and whose Baroque style here was greatly admired by Guercino. Nearby, at Via Borgo di Sotto 47, is the **Oratorio dell'Annunziata** (*map Ferrara East 11; closed* *at the time of writing*). The elegant façade is by Gian Battista Aleotti (1612). The rectangular interior was decorated in 1548 with frescoes attributed to Camillo Filippi, Pellegrino Tibaldi and Nicolò Rosselli, and *trompe-l'oeil* perspectives by Francesco Scala. The paintings were commissioned by the Confraternità della Buona Morte (who assisted the condemned) and represent the *Legend of the True Cross* according to the apocryphal text of Jacopo da Varagine. On the altar wall is a 15th-century *Resurrection* with members of the confraternity, and on the opposite wall an *Assumption* signed by Lamberto Nortense.

PALAZZO COSTABILI
(MUSEO ARCHEOLOGICO NAZIONALE)

Map Ferrara East 15–16. Open Tues–Sun 9.30–5. Entrance at Via XX Settembre 124.

The palace itself is of extreme interest for its courtyard and painted ceilings and the archaeological collection, beautifully displayed, with its magnificent Attic vases, is one of the greatest museums of its kind anywhere.

The **building**, also called the Palazzo di Lodovico il Moro, was commissioned in 1495 from Biagio Rossetti by Antonio Costabili, who was the ambassador of the Este at the Sforza court of Lodovico il Moro in Milan (Lodovico married Beatrice d'Este in 1490). It is one of Rossetti's masterpieces, though left unfinished in 1504. The magnificent (unfinished) courtyard has porticoes with beautifully carved capitals on two floors on two of the sides with unusual carved pilasters in relief below the middle floor. At the back of the courtyard is an eccentric brick archway with lovely decorations in painted marbles. The Sala del Tesoro, probably a music room, has a stunning illusionistic ceiling by Garofalo (1503–6) depicting a polygonal dome and balcony hung with carpets with members of the Costabili family looking down at the viewer. The inspiration is clearly derived from Mantegna's *Camera degli Sposi* in the Palazzo Ducale at Mantua. The grisaille decoration in the lunettes illustrates the myth of Antiope and Eros, based on an interpretation by the Humanist Celio Calcagnini who was a friend of Costabili. In the centre is a gilded wood rosette.

On the opposite side of the portico (*the closed door is not locked*) are exhibited two huge canoes dug out of single oak trunks probably in the 3rd or 4th century AD and found in the Valle Isola (Comacchio). Beyond another room with a lovely 16th-century ceiling can be seen a little walled garden with beds of roses inside box hedges, and surrounded by another portico.

THE ARCHAEOLOGICAL COLLECTIONS

The Museo Archeologico Nazionale was established in 1935 for the finds from the necropolis of Spina near Comacchio (*see p. 135*), which was an extremely rich port that traded extensively with Greece and Etruria. The collection of Attic vases is one of the most important in the world.

Ground floor

Splendid displays using all the latest multimedia devices, illustrate daily life in Spina (including fishing and commerce, water transport, artisans workshops, hunting, etc.). The tomb artefacts date from between the 6th and the 3rd centuries BC and are mainly linked to the idea of banquets and symposia intended to accompany the dead to the afterlife. In a room with a ceiling with scenes from the life of Joseph by an assistant of Garofalo is a display illustrating the various cults and myths present in the civilisation of Spina, including terracotta votive statuettes and small bronzes.

Upper floor

From the main courtyard a beautiful staircase with charming incised decoration on the risers leads to the upper floor where the finds from the necropolis of Spina are displayed. Over 4,000 tombs dating from the 6th–3rd centuries BC have been discovered and the vases found in them, made in the 5th century BC in Athens, are extraordinarily fine. There are explanations of how the tombs were arranged and the different burial practices. The best vases, some of them exceptionally large **kraters attributed to the Berlin Painter**, and both red- and black-figure, are displayed in Rooms II–VI. In Room V are very unusually shaped amphora and two global vases complete with their stands, which were used for mixing wine and water. There are also two pairs of bronze candelabra and two bronze situlae. In Room XI there is a magnificent display of **jewellery** dating from the late 5th–mid-4th century BC: diadems, earrings, necklaces in amber and glass paste, perfume flasks in molten glass, rings, and even marble pots where the jewellery was kept. The last room, the dark Room XVII, contains the ten most beautiful and best-preserved **red-figure vases**, some of them attributed to the Niobid Painter and the Polygnotos Painter. The huge Sala Geografico was decorated with maps in 1935.

Beyond a room where you can rest and handle some original ceramics (in a display devised also for the blind) is the huge **Sala Geografico**, which was decorated with maps in 1935.

SANT'ANTONIO IN POLESINE & SAN GIORGIO

Near Palazzo Costabili, off Via Beatrice II d'Este, is the Benedictine convent of **Sant'Antonio in Polesine** (*map Ferrara East, 15; ring for admission, 9.30–11.30 & 3.30–4.30 or 5; closed Sun*). The monastery was originally established in the late Middle Ages by the Eremitani di Sant'Agostino on what was then an island in the River Po. It subsequently passed to a community of Benedictine nuns founded in 1254 by Beatrice II d'Este, who promoted the reconstruction of the buildings. Beatrice died in 1264 and was beatified in 1270; her relics and marble tombstone (from which miraculous water issues) are kept on the side of the cloister flanking the church. The extremely interesting frescoes are shown by one of the 15 nuns who still live here (and are well-known locally for their singing, to the accompaniment of a lyre).

The church is divided into two parts, of which the oldest, to the east, houses the **nuns' choir** (with beautiful wooden stalls decorated with intarsia work of the late 15th century) and three chapels with frescoes dating from the 14th–16th centuries. The frescoes in the **north chapel**, executed in the early 14th century, were clearly influenced by the works of Giotto and represent the lives of Christ and the Virgin. The iconography of some scenes is unusual: the *Visitation* includes Zacharias, who normally is not present; the *Nativity* follows a Byzantine prototype with a double representation of Christ, one spiritual and prefiguring his death (hence the tomb), the other temporal and in need of human care (he is being washed by the midwives). The charming *Flight into Egypt* is absolutely unique in its representation of Jesus on Joseph's shoulder, instead of the Virgin's lap. On the left wall, the *Dormition of the Virgin* again follows a Byzantine scheme with Christ in a mandorla holding the personification of the Virgin's soul.

The cycle continues in the **south chapel**, with the scenes of the *Garden of Gethsemane*, *Judas's Betrayal* and the *Mocking of Christ* on the left wall, all belonging to the same school of painters that decorated the north chapel. The representation of Christ ascending the ladder to the Cross, painted in the lunette on the right wall, is highly unusual. Somewhat later in date (mid-14th-century) and belonging to a different school of painters (and showing the influence of Bologna painters) are the scenes of the *Dance of Salome*, *Christ in Limbo*, *Crucifixion*, *Deposition* and *Entombment*, as well as the *St John the Baptist* and *St John the Evangelist* on either side of the window.

The frescoes in the **central chapel** date mainly from the 15th century, whereas the vault is decorated with grotesques of the late 16th century. The lunettes on the side walls depict the scallop shell of Santiago de Compostela: pilgrims travelling to the saint's shrine in Spain along the Via Romea departed from this church. On the walls are representations of the *Virgin Enthroned among Saints*, as well as martyrs and Doctors of the Church. Particularly interesting are a scene of the *Stoning of St Stephen* on the right wall, and the *Coronation of the Virgin*. The wooden Crucifix at the top has been ascribed to the school of Cosmè Tura.

Behind the central chapel is a room decorated with 17th-century paintings inserted in the ceiling, a 16th-century panel with the *Virgin* and the *Mysteries of the Rosary* over the altar, and a fresco of the *Flagellation* attributed to Ercole de' Roberti on the entrance wall.

At the other side of the choir is the newer part of the church, with an illusionistic ceiling painted in the 17th century by Francesco Ferrari.

SAN GIORGIO

At **Via XX Settembre 152** is the house which Biagio Rossetti designed as his own home. Just beyond, Via Porta Romana leads south to the site of the gate in the walls and across the Po di Volano canal to the church of **San Giorgio** (*beyond map Ferrara East, 16*), which was the cathedral of Ferrara in the 7th–12th centuries, then rebuilt in the 15th century and partly renovated in the 18th. The campanile is by Rossetti (1485). In the sanctuary is the magnificent tomb of Lorenzo Roverella, physician to Julius II and afterwards Bishop of Ferrara, by Ambrogio da Milano and Antonio

Rossellino (1475). Cosmè Tura is buried in a pavement tomb in the chapel at the entrance to the bell tower. His will is kept in the archives of the monastery: the monks commissioned a beautiful triptych of the *Pietà* from Tura for the high altar of their church (now in the Louvre).

THE 'ADDIZIONE'

The area of the city north of the broad, busy Corso della Giovecca (once a canal) was developed by Ercole I d'Este in the early 15th century with wide thoroughfares and fine palaces and gardens. It was planned and laid out by Biagio Rossetti, and its splendid main corso named after Ercole runs due north from the castle all the way to the walls. At the beginning of Corso Giovecca, on the south side is the **church of the Teatini** (1653; *map Ferrara East, 7*), which contains a *Presentation in the Temple* by Guercino. Almost opposite is **Piazzetta Sant'Anna**, where a well in a little garden which is all that remains of the 15th-century cloister of the former Basilian convent attached to the old Arcispedale Sant'Anna, where Tasso was confined as a lunatic in 1579–86. The fine church of **San Carlo** is by Giovanni Battista Aleotti (1623). Nearby, at Via De Pisis 24, is the **Museo Civico di Storia Naturale** (*open Tues–Sun 9–6*). The ground floor has an old-fashioned natural history display, and upstairs a more up-to-date arrangement.

The handsome, cobbled **Corso Ercole I d'Este** (*map Ferrara East, 7–3*) is dead straight and passes lovely palaces and their walled gardesn. Devoid of shops, it is extremely peaceful. In Piazza Tasso is the **Gesù**, which contains a dramatic *Pietà* in painted terracotta by Guido Mazzoni. The seven life-size figures were made in 1485 and include Nicodemus and Joseph of Arimathea. The altarpieces in the south aisle are by Giuseppe Mazzuoli (Bastarolo) and Giuseppe Maria Crespi (Lo Spagnuolo), and there are delightful little devotional stauettes in the niches of the aisles.

Further up the Corso is Palazzo di Giulio d'Este (no. 16), attributed to Biagio Rossetti. Opposite is the **Museo del Risorgimento e della Resistenza** (*open Tues–Sun 9.30–1 & 3–6*). The ground floor retains its old-fashioned arrangement of exhibits relating to the history of Italy from 1796 up until the end of the First World War, with particular reference to the Risorgimento period. The newspapers and posters are exhibited for easy consultation. Another set of rooms is dedicated to the post War period up to the end of the Second World War, with the tragic deportation of the Jews from Ferrara carefully documented.

PALAZZO DEI DIAMANTI AND THE PINACOTECA

This great palace was begun by Rossetti for Sigismondo d'Este c. 1492 and remodelled around 1565. It takes its name from the diamond emblem of the Este which covers the entire façade (the rustication is cut into 12,600 diamond-shaped points). The palace contains the **Pinacoteca Nazionale** (*open Tues–Sat 9–2, Thur*

9–7; *www.gallerie-estensi.beniculturali.it/pinacoteca-nazionale*), especially notable for its paintings of the Ferrarese school. The rooms are unnumbered, but the works are all labelled. Excellent exhibitions are held on the ground floor. Although in simple bare brick, the courtyard and portico are also beautiful.

PINACOTECA

In the Pinacoteca on the upper floor the works come from various sources, notably the Vendeghini-Baldi and Sacrati-Strozzi collections, as well as churches in Ferrara. Some of them are by obscure painters little known outside Ferrara but the quality is extremely high (and the iconography often particularly interesting). Since the rooms are un-numbered and the labelling kept to a minimum the following description attempts to point out some of the most interesting paintings.

First room (on the left): (Right wall) Garofalo, *Portrait of a Lady*; Michele Coltellini, *The Saviour*. (Window wall) Vicino da Ferrara, *St John the Baptist*; Ercole de' Roberti, *St Petronius* (a tiny work in a lovely frame).

Second room (with a fine wood ceiling): Large detached fresco from the church of San Domenico with stories from the life of St John the Evangelist by an unknown master, named from this work, who was active in Ferrara in the early 15th century. On the left wall are two works by another artist, of around the same date, who is also named from the *Pietà* here from the Massari collection (his is also the panel with four saints). On the entrance wall is a *Trinity* dating from the first years of the 15th century by an artist who signed his works with the initials 'GZ' and paintings, including the *Dream of the Virgin*, by Simone dei Crocifissi (Simone di Filippo), who was active in Bologna in the late 14th century.

Third room: (Entrance wall) Giovanni di Pietro Faloppi (also called Giovanni da Modena), *Madonna and Child*. On the opposite wall are hung two tondos in their orignal frames by Cosmè Tura

(scenes from the martyrdom of St Maurilius). The two lovely enthroned Muses are thought to be by Tura's workshop. On the wall opposite the windows are very interesting detached frescoes dating from the mid-15th century of St Sebastian and St Christopher.

Fourth room: Detached fresco fragment of three worshippers by Baldassare d'Este, and a dossal (with the *Crucifixion* and Passion scenes) as well as a large *St Jerome*, both by Vicino da Ferrara. The small severed head of St John the Baptist is by Giovan Francesco Maineri.

Fifth room: Two very interesting townscapes by Girolamo Marchesi (known as Girolamo da Cotignola), who died around 1531.

Sixth room: Here are 16th-century works and on the upper walls three scenes from the life of Christ by Gisueppe Mazzuoli (Bastarolo).

Rooms 7–9: Late 16th-century works by Scarsellino and Carlo Bononi, as well as four exquisite small panels by El Greco.

Salone d'Onore (beyond a room with works by Garofalo and Girolamo da Carpi): It has a fine wooden ceiling of 1567–91. Very large detached frescoes are displayed here: the *Apotheosis of St Augustine* is by Serafino de' Serafini (at work in Ferrara in the late 14th century) and another by an unknown master active in the 13th century, is divided into three distinct registers, with a remarkable depiction of the heavenly Jerusalem at the top, and stories from the life of St Bartholomew at the bottom. But the fresco dating from 1523 of the Old and New Testament here by Garofalo has the most unusual iconography of all: on either side of the Crucified Christ there are curious allegories of the Christian and Jewish faiths. On the window wall are two paintings of the *Adoration of the Magi* also by Garofalo, and a very dramatic *Deposition* by Bastarolo. Also here is the *Martyrdom of St Maurelius* by Guercino.

Last five rooms: These have recently been renovated to display (against apple-green walls) works (here well-labelled) by artists who were painting in Ferrara just at the time when Ariosto was writing his *Orlando Furioso* (c. 1505–32). This area of the palace was once the apartment of Virginia de' Medici, wife of Cesare d'Este, and it preserves its 16th-century ceilings. Artists represented include Battista Dossi (note the delightful tournament scene above the fireplace) and Garofalo (*Finding of the True Cross, Raising of Lazarus, Massacre of the Innocents, Noli me tangere*). The *Death of the Virgin* was painted by Carpaccio for the church of Santa Maria in Vado. The painting of the *Assumption of Mary Magdalene* by an unknown master named from this work includes a remarkable landscape with a rabbit and birds. There are also works by Ortolano and Bachiacca, and, displayed in a room on their own, small works by Garofalo and Dosso Dossi, one of which was only purchased by the Italian state in 2015.

The last room displays the large Costabili polyptych by Dosso Dossi and Garofalo, dated around 1520. It was commissioned by Antonio Costabili (*see p. 123*) for the church of Sant'Andrea.

THE NORTHERN STRETCH OF CORSO ERCOLE I

Across the busy Corso Rosselli from Palazzo dei Diamanti is **Palazzo Prosperi Sacrati**, with lovely carved pilasters at its four corners and putti sitting beneath the balcony above the portal. In Corso Porta Mare which leads east are the **Orto Botanico** (*open Mon–Fri 9–1; Sun 10–6*) and, on the opposite side of the street (no. 9), Palazzo Bevilacqua Massari, but this has been closed for a number of years. It houses the **Museo d'Arte Moderna e Contemporanea** as well as the **Museo Boldini** (*map Ferrara East, 7*). The palace was built in the 16th century, but in the late 18th it was given a first-floor enfilade of 14 rooms that follows the model of French royal palaces. These richly-decorated apartments have been used to display paintings by Giovanni Boldini (1842–1931), born in Ferrara. After his move to Paris in 1870, Boldini became established as a painter of Parisian high society. The museum also owns works by Giorgio de Chirico (who was confined to hospital as a conscript at Ferrara in 1915) and the Metaphysical School. Works also normally displayed here by Filippo de Pisis are at present exhibited in the Castello (*see p. 115*).

THE NORTHERN DISTRICTS AND THE WALLS

Corso Ercole I continues north, passing the gate (no. 40) into the delightful public garden of **Palazzo Massari** (taken by Vittorio De Sica in his film based on Bassani's *Garden of the Finzi-Continis* as the setting for the garden). A detour along Via Arianuova to the left brings you to the little **Casa di Ludovico Ariosto** (*map Ferrara West, 2; Via Ariosto 67, open Tues–Sun 10–12.30 & 4–6*), the house purchased by the poet Ariosto in 1526, ten years after finishing his famous epic poem *Orlando Furioso*. He and his son lived here until the poet's death in 1533. It has a little garden and museum dedicated to his memory.

ARIOSTO AND *ORLANDO FURIOSO*

Ariosto is the author of a long epic poem *Orlando Furioso*, which he published at his own expense in Ferrara in 1516. Describing the legendary exploits of Charlemagne and his paladin Roland in the 8th century, it became extremely famous. There were numerous successive editions of it, revised by the author himself, up until 1532. Ariosto frequented the Este court where Alfonso I was his patron.

The **last stretch of the Corso Ercole I** is particularly lovely and peaceful. Trees line the approach to the Certosa with the church of San Cristoforo (*closed at the time of writing*) and the cemetery. The Corso is now lined with poplars and paths on either side of the cobbled road which passes delightful two-storied houses before ending at the walls. Here the **Porta degli Angeli** (*map Ferrara East, 2; open Tues–Sun 10–12.30 & 3.30–5.30*), which was the gate by which the Este left Ferrara in 1598, never to return (it was closed the following year). You can climb the short iron staircase inside to the (roofed in) terrace at the top. The view north extends across the former Barco, the ducal hunting reserve, as far as the Po, an area of some 1,200 hectares, now an unenclosed public park (**Parco Urbano Giorgio Bassani**). It is entered by a path under the road midway between the Port degli Angeli and the Torrione del Barco at the northwest angle of the walls (*map Ferrara West, 2*).

The low **walls** were begun in 1451 at the southern limit of the city, and in 1492 Biagio Rossetti was commissioned to build the walls around Ercole I's northern extension. Alfonso I and Alfonso II strengthened the fortifications, and more work was carried out on them by the popes in the 17th and 18th centuries. Their total length is 9.2km and they are surmounted by paths and avenues for nearly their entire circumference, and provide a delightful public park.

One of the most interesting and best-preserved stretches of walls (followed by a picturesque path open to cyclists) is from Porta degli Angeli to Porta Mare (*map Ferrara East, 8*). From here another path, also open to cyclists, leads down into the rural area within the walls which includes the old, grass-grown **Jewish Cemetery** (the earliest tomb is dated 1549) and the beautiful countryside of Terra Viva near the Certosa (also approached by Via Erbe and Via delle Vigne from Corso Porta Mare).

FERRARA PRACTICAL TIPS

INFORMATION OFFICE

IAT, Castello Estense. *T: 0532 209370, ferrarainfo.com and ferraraterraeacqua. it. Map Ferrara East, 7.*
See also *ferraradeltapo-unesco.it.*
The MyFE, Ferrara Tourist Card, can be purchased at the Tourist Office (and some museums). Valid for 2, 3 or 6 days, it gives free entrance to all the museums.

GETTING AROUND

• **By air:** Ferrara lies 45km from Bologna Airport. Bus services 8 times a day from the airport via the railway station to Ferrara city centre in 1 hour (Bus&Fly, *T: 333 200 5157, ferrarabusandfly.it*).
• **By rail:** Ferrara is on the main rail line from Padua (50mins north) to Bologna (25mins south). From most other places to the south, east and west the quickest way to get there is via Bologna. Commuter trains connect to Rimini via Ravenna, and to Mantua via Suzzara. The railway station is in the west of town (*map Ferrara West, 5*), 20mins walk from the centre.
• **By bus:** From the station Buses 1 and 9 along Viale Cavour to the Castello; no. 11 also passes the Castello and then turns right past the Duomo (stop in Corso Porta Reno). Services also to the province run by Tper (*tper.it*) depart from the bus station on Corso Isonzo (*map Ferrara West, 6*).
• **By bicycle:** Ferrara is famous for the number of cyclists and numerous cycle lanes are provided. Cycles can be hired near many of the car parks, as well as

outside the duomo and at Porta Paola in the walls to the south (*map Ferrara West, 10*). You can cycle round the walls and beyond the Parco Urbano outside the northern stretch of walls there is access to the river Po, with a very fine long cycling route along its banks. See *ferrarabike.com.*
• **By car:** There are car parks outside the walls to the south by Porta Paola (*map Ferrara West, 10*): the most convenient is Kennedy, approached from Via Bologna.

WHERE TO STAY

€€€ **Duchessa Isabella**. In an historic old townhouse this has a rather kitsch atmosphere, with antique style furniture beneath coffered ceilings and frescoes in the Ferrarese manner. But for all that it has for long been considered Ferrara's best hotel and has a good restaurant. *Via Palestro 70, T: 0532 202121, duchessaisabella. it. Map Ferrara East, 7.* It has a *dépendence*, with five rooms, called La Duchessina, in Vicolo del Voltino 11 (*T: 0532 206981, laduchessina. it*). It has a *dépendence*, **Principessa Leonora**, in Via Mascheraio, *principessaleonoraferrara.it.*
€€ **Annunziata**. A friendly, family-run place, quiet and comfortable. *Piazza Repubblica 5, T: 0532 201111, www. annunziata.it. Map Ferrara East, 7.*
€€ **Astra**. Comfortable and well-managed, with antiques here and there. *Viale Cavour 55, T: 0532 206088, astrahotel.info. Map Ferrara West, 6.*
€€ **Ripagrande**. In a Renaissance townhouse, with garden

restaurant seating in summer. *Via Ripagrande 21, T: 0532 765250, ferrarahotelripagrande.it. Map Ferrara West, 10.*

€ De Prati. Small with friendly staff and very central. *5 Via Padiglioni, T: 0532 241905, hoteldeprati.com. Map Ferrara East, 7.*

€ Locanda Borgonuovo. With just 4 rooms. *Via Cairoli 29, T: 0532 211100, borgonuovo.com. Map Ferrara East, 7.*

€ Locanda della Biscia. One of the cheapest places to stay in Ferrara, in an excellent position. *Via Palestro 57, T: 0532 242817, locandadellabiscia.it. Map Ferrara East, 7.*

RESTAURANTS

€€ La Provvidenza. A very popular restaurant known for its hearty local fare. One of the best places to eat in Ferrara. Good mushrooms and truffles in season. Closed Sun evening and Mon. *Corso Ercole I d'Este 92, T: 0532 205187, ristorantelaprovvidenza.com. Map Ferrara East, 3.*

€€ Quel Fantastico Giovedì. Oddly named ('That fantastic Thursday') but considered, together with La Provvidenza, a very good place to eat. It serves Emilian dishes with an innovative twist, and has good fish. Closed Wed. *Via Castelnuovo 9, T: 0532 760570, quelfantasticogiovedi.it. Map Ferrara East, 11.*

€€ Ristorante Raccano. Close to the Music Conservatory this has simple but excellent quality fare, with home-made pasta and desserts. Frequented by those in the know at lunch, when there is a special-price menu. It takes on a more elegant air in the evenings. Closed Thur. *Piazzetta Sant'Anna 9, off Corso Giovecca near Via Boldini (map Ferrara East, 7), T: 0532 1825685, ristoranteraccano.it.*

€€ Trattoria il Mandolino. A typical Ferrarese *trattoria* with local dishes with a pleasant rather old-fashioned atmosphere. Closed Mon evening and all day Tues. *Via Carlo Mayr 83, T: 0532 760080, ristoranteilmandolino.it. Map Ferrara East, 11.*

€€–€ Il Don Giovanni. A restaurant and bistrot right in the centre of town, at the beginning of Corso Ercole d'Este, with good food (the seasonal produce comes from the proprietors' local vegetable garden), and organic wines. Special diets catered for. The restaurant with just six tables occupies the former strong room of the bank which was once on this site, and next to it in the very well restored ex Borsa (exchange building) is the large bistrot, much frequented by the young who come here not only for a good reasonably priced meal but also for concerts and events (it has seating for 400). Closed Mon. *Corso Ercole I d'Este 1, T: 0532 243363, ildongiovanni.com. Map Ferrara East, 7.*

€ Il Bagattino del Setaccio. A simple *trattoria*, but a sound choice. Closed Wed. *Via Correggiari 6 (off Via Boccaleone), T: 0532 206387. Map Ferrara East, 11.*

€ Balebuste. In the area of the Ghetto this also serves Jewish dishes, and is a place very popular with the young, and well worth trying if you don't mind a rather chaotic atmosphere. Closed Thurs. *Via Vittoria 44, T: 0532 763557, balebuste.it. Map Ferrara East, 11.*

€ Al Brindisi. A wine bar which serves good cold meals. It is in a building in an old lane by the cathedral on the site of an ancient hostelry. Always busy and open every day. *Via Adelardi 11, T: 0532*

*471225, albrindisi.net. Map Ferrara
East, 7.*

€ **Tre Pennelli**. A wine bar, renowned
for its wine which serves simple meals
accompanied by exceptionally good
Tuscan olive oil. Closed Sun. *Via
Gaetano Previati 9, T: 0532 206703.
Map Ferrara East, 7.*

CAFÉS

Among Ferrara's many good cafés are
Roverella (*8 Via Boldini, off Corso
Giovecca; map Ferrara East, 7*), with a
few tables outside in Piazza Sant'Anna)
and **Europa**, at Corso Giovecca 51 (*map
Ferrara East, 7*). The latter has tables
where you can sit for no extra charge,
as well as a smarter more comfortable
room at the back where you are given
table service. But for the best coffee
in town, don't miss the **Artlife Caffè
Penazzi**, close to the Castello at Piazza
della Repubblica 27. Closed Sun (*map
Ferrara East, 7; artlifecaffe.com*).

FESTIVALS, MARKETS
& EVENTS

Street markets in Ferrara Mon and
Fri; antiques and crafts markets, first
weekend of the month (except Aug),
in Piazza Municipale and Piazza
Savonarola, both just south of the
Castello.

The Palio of Ferrara (San Giorgio)
is held at the end of May with races
(horses, mules, etc.) in Piazza Ariostea
(*map Ferrara East, 7*); Buskers Festival,
street musicians' festival, last week in
Aug.

The Teatro Comunale (*map Ferrara
East, 7*) has an excellent concert and
opera season. There is a summer
festival of music, and concerts are
sometimes held in palace courtyards.

The Province of Ferrara

Ferrara has a small province, most of which is to the east of the town in the southern part of the Po Delta, where the Po di Volano reaches the sea in a nature reserve. See *ferraraterraeacqua.it*. The northern Po delta belongs to the Veneto region and is covered in *Blue Guide Venice and the Veneto*.

THE PO DELTA

The Po is the longest river in Italy (652km). Its source is at Piano del Re (2050m) in Piedmont, on the French border, and it is joined by numerous tributaries as it crosses northern Italy from west to east on its way to the Adriatic. The wide open plain—the largest in Italy—through which it runs and which separates the Alps from the Apennines, is known as the *pianura padana*. In the late Middle Ages the Po was navigable and was one of the principal waterways of Europe. In 1599 the Venetian Republic carried out major works to deviate the course of the river south to prevent it silting up the Venetian lagoon. It now reaches the sea by seven different channels: and the delta so formed is the largest area of marshland in Italy. Tthe flat open landscape, with wide views over the reedy marshes and wetlands (known as *valli*), is remarkably beautiful, whether in typical misty weather or on clear autumnal days. Rice and sugar beet were once intensely cultivated here, and some attractive old farmhouses survive, although most of them have been abandoned.

The once marshy country between Ferrara and the sea, where the Po enters the Adriatic, has been the subject of land-reclamation schemes ever since the time of Alfonso II d'Este (16th century). It is a place of wild natural beauty: the dunes in the Po di Goro delta, in particular (*map C, B1–C1*), are of great interest to naturalists. The **Gran Bosco di Mesola**, one of the last wooded areas in the Po Delta, is part of the Parco Regionale del Delta del Po, a nature reserve that you can explore by boat (*navideldelta.it*), or by bike (*ferrarabike.com*) along the marshland banks (*open March–Oct Tues, Fri, Sat, Sun 8–dusk; information: parcodeltapo.org*). Yellow iris, waterlily and ditch reed offer a natural setting for numerous bird species, and the meanders of the delta host a large colony of European pond turtles. There is also sport fishing for eels, carp and perch. The soil of the delta is especially good for growing asparagus. On the Po di Goro is the splendid **Castello di Mesola** (*open Tues–Sun 9.30–12.30 & 2.30 or 3–5.30 or 6; T: 339 193 5943, prolocomesola.it*), a hunting lodge of Alfonso II, built in 1583 by Antonio Pasi (to a design by Giovanni Battista Aleotti), and it contains a museum dedicated to the Este family, and material relating to the woods and fauna (including the deer which still survive here) of the Po delta.

THE ABBEY OF POMPOSA

Map C, B1. Branch railway line from Ferrara to Codigoro and from there by taxibus no. 8 (c. 6km).

This famous isolated Benedictine abbey was founded in the 7th–8th century on what was then an island, but was gradually deserted in the 17th century because of malaria. It is still one of the most evocative sites on the delta, marked by its fine campanile, 48m high. The church (*open daily 8.30–6.30; T: 0533 719110 or 0533 719119*) dates from the 8th–9th centuries, and was enlarged in the 11th century. It is preceded by an atrium with beautiful Byzantine sculptural decoration. The fine basilican interior, with good capitals and a mosaic floor from the 12th century, is covered with charming 14th-century frescoes representing *Scenes from the Old and New Testament* and the *Apocalypse*. Some of these, including the *Christ in Glory* in the apse, have been attributed to Vitale da Bologna.

The monastic buildings (*open as for the church, but closed on Mon*) include the chapter house and refectory, both with important frescoes of the Bolognese school. There is a small museum above the refectory. Guido d'Arezzo (c. 995–1050), inventor of the modern musical scale, was a monk here. The Palazzo della Ragione (abbot's justice court) is a beautiful 11th-century building, altered in 1396.

To the south are fields where rice is cultivated, and the marshes of the Valle Bertuzzi (visited by migratory birds).

COMACCHIO

Comacchio (*map C, B1*) is an interesting little town that grew to importance because of its salt-works. It is now important for fishing and curing eels—the huge shoals of eels that make for the sea in Oct–Dec are caught in special traps. The town was continuously attacked by the Venetians and destroyed by them in 1509. Comacchio's pretty canal-lined streets (plastic swans and ducks rather surreally float in the canal waters) are crossed by numerous bridges, notably the 17th-century **Trepponti**, which traverses no fewer than four canals.

Museo Delta Antico

This exceptionally fine museum (*Via Agatopisto 2; seasonal opening times, see museodeltaantico.com*) housed in the fine old 18th-century Ospedale degli Infermi (Antonio Foschini, 1784). The upper floor traces the history of Spina and has necropolis finds, including fine imported Greek pottery, and explores Comacchio's origins as a commercial centre (emporium), importing goods from around the Mediterranean and trading inland with the Lombards. On the ground floor is the fascinating **cargo of the Comacchio wreck**, a Roman ship that foundered c. 19–12 BC and which was found and recovered in 1980–1. The cargo includes Spanish lead ingots marked with the stamp of Agrippa and numerous amphorae. Also among the finds are pieces of the ship itself (ropes, block and tackle, its anchor), cooking and fishing utensils, weighing scales, items of basketwork and leather, and personal items belonging to the passengers, inlcuding portable temple shrines and well-preserved pieces of footwear.

On the opposite side of the canal, **Palazzo Bellini**, once a well-to-do residence attached to a fish-processing facility, holds temporary exhibitions.

Manufattura dei Marinati

From Piazza XX Settembre, with the cathedral and bell-tower, Corso Mazzini leads west to the votive church of **Santa Maria in Aula Regia**, dedicated to the Virgin as a prayer to preserve the city from the Po floodwaters (a high levée now separates Comacchio from the waters of the canals and valli). The church is approached by a long colonnade (mid-17th century), off which, at no. 200, opens the entrance to the **Manufattura dei Marinati**, an old factory for processing, curing and canning eels, now reopened. The visitor trail follows the process (*open March–Oct Tues–Sun 9.30–12.30 & 3–7; Nov–Feb Tues–Sun 9.30–1 & 2.30–6; T: 0533 81742, parcodeltapo. it*).

SPINA AND THE COAST

On the sandy coast are a line of popular resorts, known as the Lidi Ferraresi, with numerous hotels and camping sites, crowded in summer.

In the drained lagoon northwest of Comacchio the burial-ground of the Greco-Etruscan city of **Spina** (*map C, B2*) yielded a vast quantity of wonderful vases and other pottery (displayed in the archaeological museum in Ferrara). Founded c. 530 BC, it was a port carrying on a lively trade with Greece, but it barely outlasted the 4th century BC. Part of the city itself, laid out on a regular grid plan with numerous canals, was located by aerial survey in 1956

The dwindling **Valli di Comacchio** (*map C, B2*) are now more than two-thirds drained, to the detriment of the egrets, herons, stilts, terns and avocets that were once found here in profusion. The area is part of the Parco Regionale del Delta del Po. At **Porto Garibaldi** (formerly Magnavacca) the Austrian navy captured the last 200 'Garibaldini', leaving Garibaldi alone with Anita (his Brazilian wife and companion in arms) and his comrade Leggero. Anita died at Mandriole, on the southern shore of the lake, where there is a monument to her.

Argenta is on the western side of the Valli di Comacchio (*map C, A2*). The Museo delle Valli di Argenta in the Campotto Nature Reserve illustrates the morphology of the marshes and the Museo della Bonifica in the Saiarino pumping station documents the history of land reclamation between the Reno and Sillaro rivers (*for information about access to either, T: 0532 808058 or check www.vallidiargenta.org*).

CENTO

On the western border of the province is the little town of **Cento** (*map B, C2*), badly hit in the 2012 earthquake. It was the birthplace of Isaac Israeli, great-grandfather of Benjamin Disraeli, and of Guercino, whose painting is well represented in the Pinacoteca Civica, but all its contents had to be removed from the building following damage to its structure in 2012 and at the time of writing it was still closed (*see guercino.comune.cento.fe.it for updates*). The church of the Rosario contains a chapel built for Guercino and a fine *Crucifixion* by him. Above the town rises the 14th-century Rocca. At **Pieve di Cento** is a small Pinacoteca Civica in the main square, with paintings by the Bolognese and Ferrarese schools (15th–19th centuries), a wooden 14th-century *Madonna* and 18th-century reliquaries.

PROVINCE OF FERRARA PRACTICAL TIPS

INFORMATION OFFICE

The Tourist Office in **Comacchio** is in the same building as the Museo Delta Antico (*Via Agatopisto 2, T: 0533 314154, turismocomacchio.it*). They have maps and a useful information booklet, *Comacchio Po Delta Park Riviera,* with contact numbers for boat trips, fishing trips, birdwatching and deer-spotting safaris.

GETTING AROUND

By bus: Ferrara and Ravenna are linked by bus to Comacchio and Porto Garibaldi. Buses also link the smaller towns with each other and with the beach resorts. For routes and timetables, see *tper.it*.

RESTAURANTS & CAFÉS

Comacchio (*map C, B1*)
€ **Al Cantinon**. Welcoming place very close to the Trepponti and old fish market, with tables out on the canal in fine weather and a cosy interior.

Excellent fish (including eel), good fresh salads, light and crispy tempura vegetables, and a selection of typical desserts. Closed Thur. *Via Muratori. T: 0533 314252, alcantinon.com.*
€ **Bar Ragno**. Simple, authentic place under the arcades of the 17th-century Loggia del Grano, built as part of a papal initiative to renovate the town. Built of Istrian stone and brick, a handsome loggia supports an upper floor, once the town granary. The bar is a good place to sit out in fine weather with a coffee or an aperitif, and a view of the Torre Civica clock tower.

FESTIVALS & EVENTS

Comacchio (*map C, B1*)
Sagra dell'anguilla (Eel Festival) held over two weeks in late Sept–Oct. Tastings of eel and other fish, street markets and music. *sagradellanguilla. it.*

Faenza

F aenza (*map C, A3*) is a very pleasant old town which has long been famous for the manufacture of the glazed and coloured pottery known as majolica or 'faïence', and there are still numerous working potteries in the town. The street names are indicated by faïence plaques, and several houses from the Art Nouveau period are decorated with ceramic tiles. But Faenza is above all visited for its huge museum, founded in 1908 (and continuously expanding), dedicated to majolica and ceramics. This provides the best historical introduction to this art in all of Italy, and includes not only examples from every region of the country but from all over the world and from all periods right up to the present day. The town has attractive peaceful streets, off which there are numerous spacious courtyards, and two adjoining central *piazze* with arcades.

> **HISTORY OF FAENZA**
>
> The ancient Roman Via Emilia (now Corso Mazzini and Corso Saffi) cuts straight through the middle of the town, which preserves its Roman plan. The Manfredi family were the powerful rulers of Faenza from the early 13th century up until 1501, though they did not prevent the city from being severely damaged in 1241 by Holy Roman Emperor Frederick of Hohenstaufen, and it was again sacked in 1376 by the mercenary soldier Sir John Hawkwood, then in the papal service. In 1501 Cesare Borgia took the town and killed the last of the Manfredi, and from 1509 Faenza was included in the States of the Church.

THE CERAMICS MUSEUM

At no. 19 Viale Baccarini, a very pleasant broad avenue with paths for pedestrians and cyclists, which connects the station with the centre of the town. Open Tues–Fri 10–1.30, Sat, Sun and holidays 10–5.30). There is a room for childrens' activities and a large exhibition hall. micfaenza.org.

The **Museo Internazionale delle Ceramiche**, in the huge former monastery of San Maglorio and adjoining new buildings, contains the best and most extensive collection of Italian majolica in Italy, covering all periods but with particularly superb examples of 15th–16th-century Faentine ware. The 20th-century works, most of them donated by the artists themselves, include pieces by Picasso and Matisse from the 1950s. Since its foundation in 1908 by Gaetano Ballardini, the museum's policy has been to attempt to illustrate typical Italian and foreign ceramics, and this has been made possible over the decades by numerous donations. Today the huge collection, which includes a whole section devoted to modern and contemporary ceramics, is so big that it is difficult to take in on a single visit.

A CONNOISSEUR'S GUIDE TO FAÏENCE

The so-called archaic ware produced from the mid-13th century to the first half of the 15th has a white tin-glazed body decorated with two colours only (brown and green), which after 1350 were gradually replaced by blue. In the late 14th and early 15th century the so-called Zaffera ware made its appearance, decorated with cobalt blue and manganese brown thickly applied on a white ground to produce a relief effect. In the 15th century, the import of tin-glazed wares from the island of Majorca (hence the Italian name for faïence, majolica) introduced the lustre technique as well as Islamic decorative motifs. Their combination with the existing Italian tradition gave rise to an Italo-Moresque style which is particularly evident in the blue Zaffera ware that includes yellow and purple details to imitate the lustre effects of Hispanic wares.

Further influences in the 15th century came from Chinese porcelain imported from Venice. The immediate consequence was the development of more delicate shapes (imitating Ming porcelain) and an enriched decorative repertoire, which found expression in a blue monochromy on white ground. From the mid-15th to the early 16th century, the most splendid examples of Faentine majolica were produced when there were some 40 potteries in the town, including the brothers Pirotti (the Ca' Pirota). The earliest authenticated dated specimen of faïence, in the Cluny Museum in Paris, is a votive plaque of 1475, though the technique is documented as early as 1142.

The typically Faentine motif of the curled leaf (or 'Gothic foliage') was developed in the late 15th and early 16th centuries. The first historiated wares made their appearance around the same time, thanks to the crosslinks between potters and painters and to the circulation of illustrated books (after the invention of printing), which made famous paintings and woodcuts available to the *maiolicari* and introduced new themes such as stories from mythology. The discovery of the grotesques of the Domus Aurea in Rome, and the decoration of the Vatican loggias by Raphael, provided further inspiration for subsequent ceramic production.

Monochrome ware was also highly valued from the 16th century onwards. Examples include the beautiful Faenza white, with its characteristic shapes obtained from plaster moulds, and the blue-ground majolica called *smalto berrettino*, decorated with delicate grotesques.

First floor
At the top of the stairs the Paolo Mereghi (1871–1953) collection is exhibited with a few choice examples of ceramics from many different periods and different countries. Room 6 opens the display of Faentine ceramics displayed strictly chronologically from the 14th century onwards. The immense long former dormitory corridor has the most important pieces produced in the town up until the 17th century, including magnificent examples from the greatest period of production from 1450 to 1520. Displayed on its own is a very fine and perfectly preserved goblet (1529) in the *istoriato* style, which reproduces a painting of Marcus Curtius riding into the abyss against a rich blue ground. Many other examples of this style are present. In the cells off one side the pieces are arranged by type (pharmacy jars, tableware, ecclesiastical vessels etc). At the far end the *bianco di Faenza* ware is illustrated, which has a hard, thick white glaze and takes on forms which are at first Mannerist in style and later, in the 17th century, Baroque.

In the next two halls (Rooms 8 and 9) there is a modern display of ceramics from all over Italy: a huge collection displayed strictly chronologically and by region from the Renaissance period up to the 19th century (arrows on the floor indicate the route you should take). Superb examples from the most important potteries are naturally present, including those of Umbria (Deruta, Gubbio), the Marche (Urbino, Casteldurante) and Tuscany (Montelupo). In a separate building (Rooms 13 and 14) begins the 20th-century collection of Italian ware from the Art Nouveau period to the present day, which even includes (in the basement approached down a ramp) terracotta pots from Impruneta, crêche figures from southern Italy, and a bust of a saint by Andrea della Robbia next to an imitation Della Robbian *Madonna* produced by the Cantagalli workshop in Florence in the 20th century.

Ground floor
The halls here display works of the greatest interes from outside Italy: pre-Columbian, Minoan, Greek and Etruscan ceramics, and an Oriental and Middle Eastern collection, with a notable Islamic section.

THE TOWN CENTRE

Viale and Corso Baccarini continue from the Ceramics Museum to end at Corso Mazzini. Here is the Loggia della Beneficienza (c. 1425 with 19th-century additions), with an impresssive long portico decorated in brick. To the left, at no. 62, is Casa Matteucci with Art Nouveau ceramic tiles made by the Fratelli Minardi, and pretty cast-iron balconies on the upper floors made by the Matteucci workshop.

The Corso ends at the centre of the town, with its two adjoining *piazze*, **Piazza della Libertà** and **Piazza del Popolo**. The eccentric clock-tower (reconstructed in 1944) and rather fussy fountain were both designed in the early 17th century by Domenico Paganelli. The castellated **Palazzo del Podestà** built in 1157–1256, has a long loggia above its portico (the brick exterior with its outside staircase can be seen in the pretty piazza behind it, approached through an archway). Opposite is the **Municipio**, once the palace of the Manfredi, with a matching loggia and portico. Beneath it, the **Voltone della Molinella** is an arcade with a beautiful frescoed vault and *grottesche* by Marco Marchetti (1566). The Galleria Comunale d'Arte here holds exhibitions, often of ceramics. In a pleasant cobbled courtyard is the Neoclassical Teatro Comunale Masini. Designed by the local architect Giuseppe Pistocchi (1780–87), it has a charming interior with statues and reliefs by Antonio Trentanove. The end of Piazza del Popolo is closed by a building from the Fascist period with a characteristic long inscription on its tower.

THE CATHEDRAL
Raised above steps, the building was never given a façade so it still has a rough-hewn front. It was begun by Giuliano da Maiano in 1474, but little of its Renaissance spirit survives in the interior, even though the proportions are good.

On the south side, the fourth chapel has a painted altarpiece of the *Madonna and Saints* by Innocenzo da Imola (1526). Next to it is the chapel of San Terenzio, with a reliquary urn with beautiful carvings in very low relief depicting miracles of the titular saint by an unknown master, named after this work. In the last chapel off this aisle is a wood Crucifix and (on the left wall) a *Madonna and Child* by the workshop of Biagio d'Antonio (1480), and (on the right wall) a 17th-century painting of *St Sebastian*.

Very high up in the vault of the sanctuary are majolica tondi by Andrea della Robbia. In the chapel to the left of the sanctuary (*light, 50 euro, essential*) is the very unusual tomb of St Savinus (first bishop of Faenza, early 4th century), with exquisite reliefs attributed by Vasari to Benedetto da Maiano (1474–6) but now thought by some scholars to be the work of Antonio Rossellino. The chapel in the north transept is extremely elaborate and has two huge statues of St Peter and St Paul dating from the 17th century. In the last chapel on the north side, dedicated to St Emilianus, a 15th-century monument to the saint has very unusual carvings of the Madonna and Child with saints attributed to the 'Master of San Terenzio' (*see above*). In the two niches on either side are Neoclassical allegorical statues. In the fifth chapel on this side is a painting of the *Ecce Homo* with two angels by Biagio d'Antonio (c 1480). In the first chapel, the baptistery, the vault frescoes are attributed to Giovanni Tonducci (1562). In the 1530s the local sculptor Pietro Barilotti carved the stoup and the Bosi funerary monument in the first chapel on the south side.

Just out of Piazza della Libertà, in Palazzo Laderchi (Corso Garibaldi 2) is the **Museo del Risorgimento e dell'Età Contemporanea** (*open Sat and Sun 10–12 & 3–7*), a museum founded in 1904 illustrating the 19th-century history of the town and its surroundings. A grand gallery of the palace was decorated in 1794 with painted decoration by Felice Giani, and stuccowork by Antonio Trentanove.

THE PINACOTECA AND PALAZZO MILZETTI
From Piazza del Popolo Via Severoli leads west passing the neo-Gothic Casa Valenti (no. 8; now converted into apartments) with very unusual terracotta decoration

on its exterior dating from 1867. Via Severoli is continued by Via Santa Maria dell'Angelo where at no. 9 is the entrance to the **Pinacoteca Comunale** (*only open Sat and Sun 10–6*). Upstairs the Sala Manfredi records the rulers of Faenza through some works commissioned by them. The standard with a *Pietà* is by a painter close to Melozzo da Forlì. Two 15th-century marriage chests, carved and gilded, and three paintings by Biagio d'Antonio—and most importantly a very fine marble bust of the young St John formerly attributed to Donatello but now thought to be by Benedetto da Maiano—all illustrate the presence of Florentine artists at their court.

The Sala Donatello exhibits the most famous work in the collection, a polychrome wood statue of St Jerome, a late work by the great Florentine sculptor Donatello. It shows the elderly saint in a highly dramatic attitude (belabouring himself with a stone), his age clearly illustrated by his flabby skin. This was probably commissioned by the Manfredi in 1444. There is another painting by the Florentine Biagio d'Antonio here, and a delightful altarpiece of the *Madonna and Saints* by an unknown artist named after the 'Pala Bertoni' who was at work at the end of the 15th century, particularly memorable for its four playful putti making music. But the most important painting here is that of the *Madonna Enthroned with Saints* by Marco Palmezzano, one of this painter's best works. He was born nearby in Forlì around 1459 and was influenced by the Veneto school. The pedestal of the throne is particularly intriguing as well as the various scenes in the background.

The long 'vestibule', a corridor with windows on one side, has a striking sculptural group in dark glazed terracotta of the *Madonna and Child*, shown seated between St John the Baptist and St John the Evangelist (with his eagle), by Alfonso Lombardi. The small gold-ground panel by Giovanni da Rimini dating from the early 14th century is particularly lovely with the Child lying back to caress the Madonna's face, and below a row of five saints. Next to it is hung another precious little work with the *Crucifixion and Descent into Limbo* by an anonymous master from Faenza, probably painted even earlier. The painted 13th-century Crucifix has two very beautiful mourning figures of the Madonna and St John in the terminals.

The Sala del Magistrato is named after a striking portrait of a Judge, with his bright white collar, by an anonymous 17th-century master. The largest hall is hung with 16th–17th-century altarpieces.

Next to the Pinacoteca is the church of **Santa Maria dell'Angelo** built for the Jesuits by Girolamo Rainaldi in 1621. In the sanctuary the marble altar flanked by two obelisks was designed by the great Roman Baroque architect Francesco Borromini as a funerary monument to Paolo and Giacomo Filippo Spada, who are recorded in the two bronze busts by Borromini's famous contemporary Alessandro Algardi. Opposite the church, the brick Casa Ghidieri dates from the early 16th century.

MUSEO NAZIONALE DELL'ETÀ NEOCLASSICA IN ROMAGNA

Via Cavour leads due south to Via Tonducci where at no. 15 is **Palazzo Milzetti**, the Museo Nazionale dell'Età Neoclassica in Romagna (*open Mon–Sat 8.30–6.30, Sun 12.30–6.30; palazzomilzetti.jimdo.com*). This is the grandest Neoclassical palace in Faenza, reconstructed for the Milzetti family in 1794–1802 by Giuseppe

Pistocchi (who also added its façade). It was decorated inside with delightful painted and stucco decorations on the walls and vaults from 1801–5 by Felice Giani, Gaetano Bertolani and the sculptor Antonio Trentanove, as well as Gianbattista and Francesco Ballanti Graziani. Their work is today preserved intact and make this one of the most interesting 'house-museums' in Italy of its period. There is some Neoclassical furniture still in the rooms.

On the **ground floor** you can visit the kitchens and the dining room above, with its delicate painted decoration, overlooking the garden. The other rooms on this floor were used by Count Francesco Milzetti. The reception room has ceiling tondi with emperors and winged victories on a rust-red ground, and a *trompe l'oeil* frieze of marble trophies at the top of the walls. The oval vestibule to the bathroom is decorated with copies of the wall paintings of Herculaneum on a black ground all related to the theme of water. The Pompeian bathroom has a sunken tub. The library, lined with bookcases, was provided with a single reading desk for the count. The two twin bedrooms are adjoined by octagonal anterooms, one in dark blue and one with very delicately painted dragonflies and butterflies. The last room, with deep red decorations contains a neoclassical statuette of Psyche by Cincinnato Baruzzi.

A grand staircase with a stucco vault by Giovanni Antonio Antolini leads up to the huge octagonal **atrium**, called the Temple of Apollo, with pairs of Corinthian columns also by Antolini. The stuccoes here are by Antonio Trentanove. The decoration of the ceilings of the adjoining rooms is superb and the Galleria, or ballroom, with its painted barrel vault has stucco panels on the walls. The octagonal boudoir of Countess Giacinta is totally covered with Pompeian-style painted decoration. A bust of Proserpine by Hiram Powers decorates the Sala di Compagnia, with scenes from Roman history. The two statues of Venus are by Baruzzi or Tadolini.

ACROSS THE LAMONE RIVER

In Borgo Durbecco, beyond the bridge over the Lamone, is the small Romanesque **church of the Commenda**, with a remarkable fresco in the apse by Girolamo da Treviso (1533). The next street to the right, Via Carchidio, crosses Via Trento into Via Santa Lucia, where there is a **Commonwealth War Cemetery**, with 1,152 graves of those who fell in the fighting in this area during the German retreat in the Second World War.

FAENZA PRACTICAL TIPS

INFORMATION OFFICE

IAT. *Voltone della Molinella 2, prolocofaenza.it.*

GETTING AROUND

By train. Faenza is reached from Florence in 1 hr 45min on a branch line across the Apennines via the Mugello. This is one of the prettiest railways in Italy, stopping at all stations and terminating in Faenza (although one train a day goes on to Ravenna). Faenza also has frequent services from Bologna.
Car park off Via Cavour near the Pinacoteca.

WHERE TO STAY

€€ **Vittoria**. Comfortable rooms and a good restaurant, in a 16th-century palace. *Corso Garibaldi 23, T: 0546 21508, hotel-vittoria.com.*

RESTAURANTS

Osteria del Mercato. An old-established place, also a pizzeria. Open every day. *Piazza Martiri della Libertà 13 (just east of Piazza del Popolo), T: 0546 046656, osteriamercato.it.*
Enoteca Astorre. A wine bar and restaurant with tables outside in Faenza's main piazza in good weather. *Piazza della Libertà 16/a, T: 0546 681407, enotecaastorre.it.*

LOCAL SPECIALITIES, FESTIVALS & EVENTS

Numerous **ceramic workshops** still operate in and around the town. See *www.comune.faenza.ra.it.* The *Palio del Niballo*, a Renaissance tournament, takes place in June. At certain periods of the year (usually between June and Oct) a portable kiln (with a wood fire) is set up outside the cathedral, and pottery is fired on the spot to be sold for charity.

Ravenna

There is no other place in western Europe which has such a profusion of beautiful Byzantine churches, world famous for their magnificent mosaics. These were built when Ravenna (*map C, B2*) was first capital of the Western Empire in the 5th century and then capital of an Exarchate of the Eastern Empire in the following century. They have all been remarkably well preserved and can be visited with ease, given that they all have exceptionally long opening hours.

Although the appearance of the town was altered irreparably in the 20th century when some undistinguished new buildings were erected and there was untidy industrial expansion on the outskirts, today Ravenna has a peaceful atmosphere since most of the well-paved streets are pedestrian and the bicycle is the most popular form of transport. It has a number of parks and gardens, good restaurants and cafés, some interesting new museums, and an air of well-being which makes it a very pleasant place to visit (and it is justifiably a proud candidate for European capital of culture in 2019). The railway station is just 10mins away from the heart of the town and all the monuments are close together except for Sant'Apollinare in Classe (easily reached by public transport) and the Mausoleo di Teodorico.

HISTORY OF RAVENNA

Ravenna today stands several kilometres inland, but in ancient times it was situated on a marshy lagoon. Its importance began with the construction, by the emperor Augustus, of the port of Classe, south of the city, as one of the two bases for Rome's Adriatic fleet. Ravenna, linked to the port by a canal, thus gained the trappings of a prosperous Roman town. Its greatest period, however, began much later, in 401, when the emperor Honorius moved the imperial court and civil administration here from Milan, where his father Theodosius I had been conducting the military operations of the empire. The move was largely prompted by the need to be readily defensible: Ravenna, surrounded as it was by marsh and salt flat, was not otherwise an advantaeous spot and drinking water was scarce. Honorius in fact was much criticised for removing himself from the front line, but the move meant that Ravenna became in effect the capital of the Western empire, and over the next hundred years was adorned with palaces and churches.

This first period of glory for Ravenna lasted for less than a century, for in 476 the last of the Western emperors, Romulus Augustulus, was deposed by the German commander Odoacer, whose capital the city became. It was here, in 493, that he was murdered at a banquet by the Ostrogoth Theodoric, in a deed which ushered in Ravenna's second period of splendour. Theodoric proved to be a strong and effective ruler, respecting the traditions of Rome. In one important respect he was different, however: the Christianity he professed was Arianism, which goes against the Nicene Creed in asserting that Christ is not 'of one substance with the Father' but subordinate. The churches he built and adorned were consecrated in the Arian faith, although orthodox (with a small 'o'; meaning belonging to the established tradition) congregations were allowed to co-exist in Theodoric's Ravenna. He died in 526, and the next year, in a desperate attempt to regain the Western empire, the Eastern emperor Justinian ordered an invasion of Italy. Ravenna fell to his general Belisarius in 540. Thus began the third period of Ravenna's glory. In 568 authority in the West was delegated to an exarch, a local ruler who combined civil and military powers but who remained subordinate to Constantinople. Ravenna's churches, with their brilliant array of mosaics from the Roman, Arian and orthodox periods, remain the glory of the town, their importance enhanced because so many of the contemporary rivals in Constantinople were destroyed by iconoclasts in the 8th century

The Eastern empire's hold on Ravenna was precarious however, with the main threat coming from the Lombards, to whom the town finally fell in 751. Anxious about this intrusion, Pope Stephen II called on the Franks, under Pepin the Short, father of Charlemagne, to retake the city. This they did in 756 and in 757, by the so-called Donation of Pepin, transferred it and all other territories wrested from the Lombards to the papacy, forming the nucleus of the later Papal States. Pepin's successor, Charlemagne, received permission from the pope to remove works of art from Ravenna to adorn his own capital at Aachen.

From then on Ravenna's history revolves around battles for control between popes, Frankish emperors and Ravenna's own archbishops. During the Ottonian period of Frankish rule (9th–10th centuries), the characteristic cylindrical bell-towers were built beside many of the basilicas.

Even though the port of Classe began to silt up, Ravenna emerged as one of the numerous city communes of northern Italy in the 12th century, and like many of them it passed into a seigniory, with local families emerging as overlords. The Traversari were in command in the 12th–13th centuries. Traversara Traversari was by tradition the mother of St Romuald, founder of the Camaldolese order of monks. In the 13th–14th centuries the city was governed by the Da Polenta family, distinguished for their hospitality to Dante. Ravenna was subsumed into the Venetian Republic in the 15th century, but Venice lost control after its defeat at the battle of Agnadello in 1509. A massacre of Ravenna's citizens followed at the hands of the invading French armies in 1512, and the city then passed by treaty to the papacy. Now outside the mainstream of Adriatic commerce, it entered a long decline and was transferred, like the rest of papal territory outside Rome, to the new kingdom of Italy in 1861. After the Second World War an industrial district was built beyond the railway and its port flourished.

THE MOSAICS OF RAVENNA

With so many of the early mosaics of Constantinople destroyed in the iconoclasm of the 8th century, those of Ravenna have special importance. There are earlier wall mosaics in Italy, for instance in Santa Costanza in Rome, where the iconography of the mid-4th century is as much pagan as Christian. However, by the 5th century, Christian imagery became more developed. The mosaics of Ravenna include scenes from the Old Testament, of the life and miracles of Christ (the earliest known narrative cycle of the life of Christ is that in Sant'Apollinare Nuovo) and the lives of the apostles. In the mausoleum of Galla Placidia Christ is depicted as the Good Shepherd. In contrast with contemporary mosaics in Rome (such as those in the church of Santa Maria Maggiore, built by a bishop with no particular allegiance to an emperor), the mosaics of Ravenna show a close link to royal or imperial power. Thus it was that Theodoric was originally represented beside his palace in Sant'Apollinare Nuovo (before he and his attendants were cut out by the agents of Justinian). The emperor Justinian and his empress Theodora are famously depicted in mosaic in San Vitale, in a style which harks back to the processional reliefs of Augustan Rome. Their presence underlines the allegiance to the Empire by the builders of the church after the Byzantine conquest of 540 and the emperor's approval of orthodox Christianity.

Ravenna is often described as a showcase of Byzantine art, and this is not simply because the design of San Vitale draws directly on a model in Constantinople. It is also because the link that is made between ruler and religion prefigures the theocratic world view of the Byzantine empire. One can go further, too, and note the different emphases in Western and Byzantine Christian art. Western Christianity increasingly stressed the need for redemption through the portrayal of the sufferings of Christ on the Cross (in ever more grotesque detail as the centuries progressed). Byzantine art concentrates on the salvation offered by Christ and He, or God the Father, is invariably represented as a protective figure looking down from above. In San Vitale the apse mosaics make explicit reference to the power of the Eucharist to transform.

The atmosphere of a Byzantine church was deliberately other-worldly: a contemporary described the dome of Hagia Sophia in Constantinople as if it were suspended from heaven. The chanting, the incense and the shimmering light on the mosaics were all designed to transcend the material world. Mosaics are composed of tesserae, cubes of coloured glass, stone and enamel set in a plaster bed (the pictorial design was sketched onto the wall beforehand; the original plan for the apse of Sant'Apollinare in Classe is in the Museo Nazionale). Blue was made by adding cobalt; green with copper oxide; and red with copper. Gold and silver were obtained by overlaying the tesserae with a thin layer of glazed metal, and in Ravenna the atmosphere of opulence was enriched by the use of mother-of-pearl as well as white and grey marble. Tesserae were often set into the plaster at different depths and angles, in order to catch as much light as possible and create a brilliant, sparkling glow.

IMPRESSIONS OF RAVENNA

Ravenna itself preserves perhaps more of the old Italian manners than any City in Italy—it is out of the way of travellers and armies—and thus they have retained more of their originality. They make love a good deal, and assassinate a little.

Lord Byron, letter to Lady Byron, 20 July 1819

Ravenna, where Robert positively wanted to go to live once, has itself put an end to all those yearnings. The churches are wonderful: holding an atmosphere of purple glory, and if one could just live in them, or in Dante's tomb—well, otherwise, keep me from Ravenna. The very antiquity of the houses is white-washed, and the marshes on all sides send up stenches new and old, till the hot air is sick with them.

Elizabeth Barrett Browning, letter, 1848

We ended in Ravenna and felt the splendour of Rome dying among barbarians in a way that I never felt again until I reached the ruins of the Levant.

Freya Stark, Traveller's Prelude, 1950

THE GREAT ECCLESIASTICAL BUILDINGS OF RAVENNA

No other city in the world has such wonderful mosaics dating from the 5th and 6th centuries. Those in the earlier buildings (the 'Mausoleum' of Galla Placidia, the baptisteries and Sant'Apollinare in Classe) have a naturalism inspired by Classical ideals while in the later churches (San Vitale and Sant'Apollinare Nuovo) the mosaics show a progressive movement towards the hieratic decorative quality of the purely Byzantine style. Visiting them all together, as proposed below, provides a fascinating glimpse of Byzantine culture.

Tickets and opening times

A combined ticket is available for San Vitale, the Mausoleum of Galla Placidia, Neonian Baptistery, Museo Arcivescovile (and Cappella di Sant'Andrea) and Sant'Apollinare Nuovo. Tickets can be purchased at the office and bookshop at Via Giuliano Argentario 22, close to the entrance to San Vitale (map Ravenna, 1). They are valid for 7 days. ravennamosaici.it.

The monuments are open Nov–Feb 10–5, March–Oct 9–7. Last entry is 15mins before closing for San Vitale, Mausoleum of Galla Placidia, Neonian Baptistery and Sant'Apollinare Nuovo. For the Museo Arcivescovile, last entry is 30mins before closing.

NB: Times are subject to change; check ravennamosaici.it for updates.

SAN VITALE &
THE MAUSOLEUM OF GALLA PLACIDIA

Map Ravenna, 1. This famous monument, together with the Mausoleum of Galla Palcidia, is surrounded by a peaceful garden entered through a 17th-century archway in Via San Vitale at the end of Via Fanti. In winter, conservation work on some of the mosaics is usually in progress.

This church is the most precious example of Byzantine art in Western Europe. A venerable 6th-century building, it has an exceptionally interesting octagonal plan surrounded by a double gallery, with an octagonal cupola. But it is above all famous for the wonderful mosaics and carved capitals which adorn its apsidal choir.

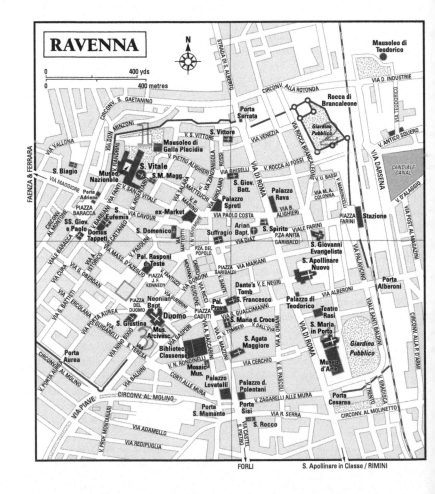

Building history of San Vitale

Theodoric allowed orthodox and Arian congregations to worship side by side in Ravenna, and in the 520s, around the time of Theodoric's death, the orthodox bishop Ecclesius, backed by funds from a wealthy banker, Julianus Argentarius, put in hand the building of a church to house the relics of San Vitale, martyred by tradition in the 3rd century. Ecclesius knew Constantinople well, and it was the church of Sts Sergius and Bacchus there which seems to have given him the Byzantine model for a centrally planned church, which provided a dramatic contrast to the simple basilican plan of the earlier Ravenna churches. Before the building was finished, however, the eastern emperor Justinian's troops invaded Italy in an attempt to win back the western empire. Ravenna fell in 540 and the as yet unfinished San Vitale was adorned with magnificent mosaics in honour of Justinian and his empress Theodora. San Vitale was eventually finished by the energetic orthodox bishop Maximian (*see p. 156*) in 547.

The original entrance was through the narthex, which stands oblique to the church, and which was formerly preceded by a quadrangular porch (but the narthex can now only be seen from the Museo Nazionale housed in the adjoining former Benedictine monastery, and the atrium was replaced by the Benedictines with a cloister during the 10th century).

Interior of San Vitale

The remarkable plan comprises two concentric octagons with seven exedrae or niches and an apsidal choir, or sanctuary. The eight pillars that support the dome are encased below in marble (largely renewed) and are separated by the exedrae with their triple arches in front of the matroneum, or women's gallery. It has been discovered that the dome was constructed from two rows of terracotta tubes laid horizontally in concentric rings and fitting into one another in order to ensure that the dome's weight would not compromise the stability of the building. The intended mosaic decoration of the dome was never executed. In the 18th century it received the (disappointing) painted decoration that we see today, which unfortunately detracts from the appreciation of the structure. The extremely interesting architecture of the interior recalls not only Roman buildings but also Byzantine monuments. The venerable pavement has inlay in precious marbles.

But the decoration of the sanctuary and apse, raised above two low steps, was carried out and survives intact and it is to this part of the church that the visitor is immediately drawn. Here every inch of the wall space is covered with exquisite mosaic, with incredibly varied colours (though green predominates). The mosaics include figurative representations as well as extraordinarily beautiful stylised friezes and borders. The intrados of the **entrance arch** has roundels, framed by pairs of green dolphins with their tails entwined, with busts of Christ and the Apostles together with St Gervasius and St Protasius, the sons of the patron saint (in the lowest two medallions).

The **sanctuary** has eight columns in two tiers, all of them with superb lace-work two-storied capitals (the combination of capital and impost block was used for the first time in Constantinople at this period, and so it is thought that these beautifully carved architectural elements may have been imported directly from the Eastern capital). Some of the impost blocks (at the top) bear the monogram of the patron Julianus Argentarius. Delicate stuccowork decorates the intradoses of the little arches between the lower (and larger) columns, while mosaic decoration decorates the intradoses of the arches between the upper (smaller) columns.

The lower columns support a mosaic lunette on either side: on the left are three scenes from the life of Abraham: in the centre three angels seated at a table in the shade of tree enjoying a meal served to them by Abraham in gratitude for their news that he is to bear a child. Behind him at the door of her house his elderly wife Sara is shown with a smile on her face having received the good news. On the right is the more familiar scene of the *Sacrifice of Isaac*, with the by now aged and more splendidly attired Abraham, stopped from killing his son by the Hand of God. In the spandrels above are *Jeremiah* and *Moses on the Mount Receiving the Tablets of the Law from the Hand of God*. The lunette on the right shows *Sacrificial Offerings of Abel and of Melchizedech* on either side of an altar with the symbols of the Eucharist. In the spandrels are more scenes from the life of Isaiah and Moses. On the upper walls, on either side of the columns, are four rectangular mosaic panels with the Evangelists and their symbols and exquisite decoration in the two lunettes.

The **vault** of the sanctuary is wonderfully decorated with vines and foliage including acanthus, amongst which can be seen peacocks and herons and other birds and animals. The four angels support the central roundel with the Paschal Lamb.

In the semi-dome of the **apse** is a splendid mosaic against a dazzling gold ground of the very young (beardless) Christ seated on an aquamarine sphere between two archangels who present St Vitalis and Bishop Ecclesius (holding a model of the church). There is more stylised decoration on the apse arch and in the spandrels above are representations of Jerusalem and Bethlehem, enclosed in bejewelled walls (symbolising the church of the Jews and the church of the Gentiles). The lower part of the apse walls beneath the windows is covered with marble inlay, reconstructed from traces of the original decoration.

On either side of the large windows are the two famous **processional friezes of the emperor Justinian and his empress Theodora**: they never came to Ravenna in person but their portraits here were an obvious reminder of the town's allegiance to them, and as they are shown bearing symbols of the Eucharist as gifts to the church, the emperor is clearly demonstrating his approval of orthodox Christianity. In the panel on the left, Justinian is shown with his train of officials, soldiers and clergy, among whom are Archbishop Maximian (who consecrated the church; named) and Julianus Argentarius (who paid for it)—although the latter may in fact be a likeness of Justinian's general, Belisarius. The emperor appears as the ruler elect of Christ (he is carrying a paten for the Eucharistic bread) and one of his attendants holds a shield with the *chi-rho* emblem). On the right is the splendidly attired Theodora in a jewelled head-dress with her attendants: the dark room beyond a doorway with a knotted hanging beside a fountain perhaps suggesting the hidden luxurious lifestyle of her court. (Note the figures of the Magi on the hem of Theodora's gown, in the same attitudes of proffering gifts as in the mosaic frieze of Sant'Apollinare Nuovo and on the reliquary urn in the Museo Arcivescovile.)

On the lower part of the intrados of the entrance arch, on either side, a miscellany of ancient sculptural fragments are preserved (framed in the 16th–18th centuries): they include four columns which once supported the ancient ciborium in the sanctuary (the first on the left is of rare green breccia from Egypt), and a fragment of a Roman frieze with putti and the empty throne of Neptune.

As in most of the other churches of Ravenna, some early Christian sarcophagi have been placed near the walls. Other parts of the building not accessible include an apsidal chamber preceding the Sancta Sanctorum, and staircase towers which ascend to the matroneum.

MAUSOLEUM OF GALLA PLACIDIA
Map Ravenna, 1. For opening times, see p. 147. Approached from the north side of the church, along a pathway across the lawn.

This very small cruciform building, its plain exterior decorated with blind arcades and pilasters, already stood here some hundred or so years before San Vitale was completed. It was erected towards the middle of the 5th century by the first great builder in Ravenna, the formidable Galla Placidia, half-sister of Honorius. She married the emperor Constantius II, and for ten years after his death in 421 she dominated the Western empire as regent to their son Valentinian III. A small oratory (once believed to be her mausoleum), it is the earliest surviving setting for mosaics in Ravenna and perhaps the loveliest, since it is entirely covered with them and they are in an excellent state of preservation (although they are restored periodically). Lit by alabaster windows, it has a memorable atmosphere.

Because of its small scale you are able to examine the mosaics, classical in character and predominantly blue in colour, in detail. The two barrel vaults are particularly beautiful, with their stylised mosaic roundels against a deep blue ground. The lunette with the scene of the martyrdom of St Lawrence shows the red hot flames below his gridiron next to a little cupboard with open doors showing the four books of the New Testament. The side lunettes have four very graceful stags quenching their thirst at the Holy Fount. The lunette over the little door has the dignified, calm figure of the Good Shepherd caressing his sheep. In the arches of the two shorter arms are four small figures of Apostles and above on the drum of the cupola, on either side of the little alabaster windows, the four lunettes have the other Apostles in pairs with doves drinking at a fountain between them. The dome has symbols of the Evangelists in the pendentives, and above everything is the Cross in a star-strewn sky. The stylised garlands of leaves and fruit, the green ribbon against a red ground, as well as the Greek key borders in *trompe l'oeil* and the little blocks of ultramarine decoration and the profuse use of gold, which even cover the ribs of the vaults and the window recesses, all add to the splendour and it is perhaps these elements and the depiction of animals and birds, rather than the human figures, which are the most striking part of the decoration.

The three huge empty sarcophagi are no longer considered to have held the remains of Galla Placidia, Constantius and Valentinian III, since only one of them is contemporary with the building. But their presence here adds to the feeling of solemn dignity and wonder.

SANTA MARIA MAGGIORE

The church (*approached along Via Galla Placidia, which skirts the railings which surround San Vitale; open 9–12; see turismo.ra.it for updates*) was founded in 525–32, but rebuilt 1671. It preserves Byzantine capitals above Greek marble columns, and a tiny cylindrical campanile (9th–10th century).

ARIAN BAPTISTERY

Map Ravenna, 2. In a quiet courtyard approached by Via degli Ariani, a lane which opens off Via Diaz. Open daily 9–dusk (see turismo.ra.it for updates). Tickets from the machine just outside the entrance.

This baptistery (Battistero degli Ariani) was the first building erected by Theodoric in Ravenna in the last years of the 5th first years of the 6th century. Like all Goths he was an Arian Christian: he believed that Christ was a later creation of God the Father, a view which had been declared heretical by the emperors in the 380s. But despite his faith he allowed orthodox and Arian congregations to worship side by side in the town. The tiny little octagonal building, now well below pavement level, is the surviving core of what was once a larger complex. It retains very well-preserved mosaics in its dome; the rest of the walls are bare but for a couple of tiny fragments of decoration.

The scene in the dome shows the *Baptism of Christ*, with Christ standing waist-high and naked in the Jordan (symbolised also by the elderly figure present) against a magnificent gold ground. Below is a circle of the twelve Apostles standing on emerald green grass, and all holding crowns, and also against a dazzling gold ground. Between them are stylised palm fronds shaped like cornucopia. But the most striking element in this frieze is the empty throne with its large purple cushion and above it a jewelled Cross with a cloth hanging on its arms. This symbolises the Arian belief in the physical nature of Christ and his future suffering on the Cross rather than his divine nature (which was fundamental to the orthodox church). On either side of the throne are St Peter with his key and St Paul with his scroll. The entire decoration has the familiar delicate borders in red and gold. The mosaics all date from Theodoric's time, except for some of the Apostles (those furthest from the throne), which were remade in the mid-6th century.

The ancient stoup has reliefs of birds enjoying bunches of grapes.

The Baptisery was reconsecrated in 561 as the orthodox church of Santa Maria in Cosmedin. Outside it, a wall has carved Byzantine crosses and reliefs in roundels.

The church of **Santo Spirito** (*map Ravenna, 2; only open for services*) was converted, like Sant'Apollinare, to the orthodox cult by Agnellus in the mid-6th century. It is now used by a Romanian Orthodox congregation. Fourteen columns and an ambo from the original church were retained after a rebuilding in 1543.

SANT'APOLLINARE NUOVO

On Via di Roma; map Ravenna, 4. Entrance through the bookshop and cloister (with its acanthus and palms) on the right of the façade. For combined ticket and opening times, see p. 147.

The façade with its portico, rebuilt in the 16th century, set back from the road, is flanked by a lovely round bell-tower dating from the 10th century. The church was built by Theodoric close to his palace in the early 6th century, and in its heyday was at the core of a Gothic quarter of the city which boasted at least six Arian churches, all of which competed in opulence with the well-endowed orthodox churches of the local Roman community. Dedicated originally to Jesus and later to St Martin, the church passed from the Arians to the orthodox Christians under Archbishop Agnellus in the mid-6th century, at the time of Justinian. The present dedication, the Ravenna's first bishop, dates from the 9th century. It takes the the name 'Nuovo' to distinguish it from the earlier church dedication to the same saint, at Sant'Apollinare in Classe (*see p. 165*).

The interior is one of the most beautiful in Ravenna: the nave walls bear two magnificent long mosaic friezes stretching from the west end all the way to the sanctuary. They show two processions: that on the north shows **22 virgin martyrs** leaving the port of Classe. These static majestic figures, all with slightly different expressions and stances, are headed by the three sprightly Magi (the iconography is copied on other works of art in town, notably the robe of Theodora in San Vitale and a reliquary casket in the Museo Arcivescovile) who offer gifts to the Infant Jesus seated on His mother's lap between four angels. On the south side a **procession of 26 martyrs**, all of them named and also of great dignity, set out from Theodoric's 'palatium' in Ravenna. Its portico used to have the figures of Theodoric astride a horse in the centre flanked by members of his court or the Arian church. These figures were removed by Bishop Agnellus when the church was reconsecrated in the orthodox faith and replaced simply with knotted curtains hanging in the arches against a dark ground (though disembodied hands remain on the columns). St Martin in his purple cloak heads the procession and is the first to arrive before Christ enthroned. The inclusion of illustrations of Ravenna itself is of great significance.

Above, on either side, between the windows, are **16 fathers of the Church**, or prophets; higher still and unfortunately really too high to see clearly with the naked eye, **13 scenes from the life of Christ** between coloured 'domes' with pairs of doves sitting on top of them, dating from the time of Theodoric. The scenes are of great iconographical interest, chosen to illustrate the role of Christ as a teacher on earth and include one of the very first representations of the *Last Supper*.

The 24 beautiful Greek marble columns, with stucco decoration on the intrados of the arches, provide the plan of this wonderful basilican interior, and the ambo in the nave also dates from Theodoric's time. The Baroque apse was poorly reconstructed in 1950, with a recomposed altar, transennae, four porphyry columns, and a marble Roman chair.

'Palazzo di Teodorico'

Map Ravenna, 4. Via Alberoni, corner of Via di Roma. Open 8.30–1.30.

Theodoric's name is associated with this building even though it is in fact the narthex of the ruined church of San Salvatore (8th–9th century), with an interesting old brick exterior with a few marble columns surrounded by a little garden. Theodoric's palace was close by, the site now hidden by later buildings, but some fine mosaic pavements and part of a marble intarsia floor found in the area in 1914 are thought to have belonged to it. They are exhibited on the walls and on an upper floor of the narthex, approached by a spiral stair, and some of them date from an earlier Roman building (1st century AD).

NEONIAN BAPTISTERY

Map Ravenna, 3. Entered from Via Rasponi, in a little garden beside the duomo. For combined ticket and opening times, see p. 147.

This octagonal baptistery was converted from a Roman bath-house in the early 5th century and was renovated in the mid-5th century, perhaps by Bishop Neon, hence its name. It is also known by the alternative name of Orthodox Baptistery, to distinguish it from the Arian Baptistery also in Ravenna (*see p. 152*). The plain exterior is decorated with vertical bands and small arches. The dome was constructed with the use of hollow tubes as in San Vitale, for structural purposes.

One of the most beautiful baptisteries to have survived anywhere, the venerable interior is entirely decorated with mosaics and sculptural details in marble and stucco that blend carefully with the architectural forms and are extraordinarily well preserved. The original floor is now more than 3m below the present surface.

Around the walls, eight corner columns support arches decorated with mosaics of prophets, each holding a scroll. In the niches and on the wall-spaces arranged alternately beneath the arches are mosaic inscriptions as well as marble inlaid designs from the original Roman baths. In the three niches are a beautiful pagan marble vase, a Byzantine altar and the 7th-century bronze Cross which used to crown the roof. The present font was installed here in the 12th–13th century.

Each arch of the upper arcade encloses three smaller arches; the 5th-century stucco decoration is very fine. In the centre of the dome is a mosaic of the *Baptism of Christ* (the old man with the reed represents the Jordan), represented in a way that is similar but subtly different (notably in the depiction of Christ himself) from that in the Arian Baptistery. Surrounding the central scene are the majestic standing figures of the (named) Apostles in togas, clearly influenced by Classical sculpture. The lowest band has a complicated decoration representing the city of Heaven, with *trompe l'oeil* niches occupied by four thrones, flanked by herb gardens behind transennae, and altars on which are the open Books of the Gospel flanked by empty chairs (waiting to receive the Elect), all remarkable for their contrasting colours.

DUOMO & MUSEO ARCIVESCOVILE

Founded early in the 5th century by Bishop Ursus and called the Basilica Ursiana, the **duomo** (*open 9–12 & 3–6*) retains very little atmosphere of its Byzantine days since it was rebuilt in 1733 after it had been almost totally destroyed in the same year. But the columns of the central arch of the portico and those on either side of the central door survive from the original church, and the round campanile, although many times restored, dates from the 10th century. In the nave the fascinating 6th-century ambo (pulpit) of St Agnellus, with its birds and beasts (and no human figures) was pieced together in 1913. The south transept chapel (*used for prayer*) contains two huge 6th-century sarcophagi with good high reliefs and a much-venerated 14th-century icon known as *Our Lady of Sweat* after an incident when it is said to have perspired blood after an impious attack. The north transept chapel has an altarpiece of *Moses*, dressed in red, in the desert by Guido Reni and frescoes by his school. In the corridor which leads to the museum (end of the north aisle) there is a good relief of St Mark enthroned with the lion below, and bookshelves on either side with books, some of them open. Set in a later frame, this is ascribed to the great Venetian sculptor Pietro Lombardo and dated 1492.

MUSEO ARCIVESCOVILE AND CAPPELLA DI SANT'ANDREA

Map Ravenna, 3. For combined ticket and opening times, see p. 147.

The museum, very well kept and well labelled also in English, contains some very precious works and incorporates the little Cappella di Sant'Andrea with its exquisite early 6th-century mosaics.

First floor
Beyond a lapidary collection, with sarcophagi, and transennae and other fragments from the original duomo and from San Vitale, and a headless 6th-century porphyry statue, thought to be Justinian, is the **Cappella di Sant'Andrea**, built by Bishop Peter II (494–519) during Theodoric's reign. It is preceded by an atrium with a barrel vault covered with a delightful mosaic of a great variety of birds. The lunette above the entrance shows, unusually, Christ as a warrior (the lower part is restored in fresco): he is dressed in armour, and crushes a lion and snake (symbols of evil) beneath his booted feet and he holds the Cross rather nonchalantly on his shoulder. The rectangular chapel itself contains more beautiful mosaics in the cross vault, with four angels holding up the simple monogram of Christ and the four symbols the Evangelists. There are portrait heads of apostles and saints in medallions on the intrados of the arches. The monogram of Bishop Peter (Petrus) is prominent in various places. The lower part of the walls is decorated in marble.

In the circular room close by is the famous ivory **Throne of Maximian**, an Alexandrine work of the 6th century, exquisitely carved with panels in relief and elaborately decorated friezes by four different masters. On the front are the standing figures of St John the Baptist flanked by the four Evangelists. On the sides are reliefs with the story of Joseph and his dreamcoat and on the back (both the inner and outer surfaces), stories of the life of Christ. This is recognised as the most magnificent work in ivory ever conceived. It was made for the great Archbishop Maximian (*see below*).

Other small rooms on this floor contain a reliquary urn dating from the 6th century with the *Adoration of the Magi* (in a similar pose to the mosaic in Sant'Apollinare Nuovo), a 6th-century Paschal calendar incised on marble, and carved Byzantine capitals and a marble pulpit with reliefs of birds, animals and fish (and just two human figures of St John and St Paul) from the church of Santi Giovanni e Paolo (596), very similar to the slightly earlier one in the duomo, with animals and birds in ranked order: fish, duck, peacock, stag, sheep.

ARCHBISHOP MAXIMIAN

Maximian, a friend of the emperor Justinian, was born in Istria and became a deacon in Pula, but towards the end of his life, in 546, Justinian sent him as Bishop to Ravenna where, after initial opposition from the local clergy, he came to be admired for his diplomacy and refined culture. In effect he contributed greatly towards the consolidation of Imperial Byzantine power in the west. In 551 he was appointed the first orthodox archbishop of the Western empire, and as such became a powerful figure in Ravenna and throughout his extensive diocese (he owned lands as far away as Sicily). He decided to transfer the relics of St Andrew from Constantinople to Ravenna. But he is remembered above all for having finished the building of San Vitale (in 548) and just a year later to have consecrated Sant'Apollinare in Classe. We can see his portrait from life in mosaic in San Vitale (the only figure in Justinian's train identified with an inscription), where he is memorably shown bald and holding a jewelled Cross. He is known to have commissioned the magnificent ivory throne preserved in the Museo Arcivescovile, and his name is also still associated with the altar in the centre of Sant'Apollinare in Classe, at which he is believed to have officiated. He built other churches in Ravenna which have not survived, before he died here in 556.

Second floor

The first room has paintings including a *Madonna Enthroned with Saints* and a *Pietà* in the lunette by Baldassarre Carrari, a little-known painter who was born in Forlì and died in Ravenna in 1516. Off it is a room with a very worn chasuble perhaps dating from the 12th century. A narrow passage leads to the circular room which has a splendid display of silver crosses, including the magnificent huge silver Cross of St Agnellus, probably dating from 556–69 (and restored in the 11th and 16th centuries). It has all four arms of equal length and heads in roundels in embossed silver. Another cross dates from 1366. The last room has fragmentary mosaics including heads of saints, and a very beautiful large *Virgin orans*, with both arms raised in prayer.

MUSEO NAZIONALE

Map Ravenna, 1. Open Tues–Sun 8.30am–7.30pm. Entrance at Via San Vitale 17, at the end of Via Fanti, through the garden in front of San Vitale. Shop.

Arranged in numerous rooms around the three cloisters of the huge former Benedictine monastery of San Vitale, this museum was founded after the monastery had been suppressed by Napoleon and the monastic collections were taken over by the municipality in 1804. In 1887 the museum became state-owned. In the 20th century, archaeological finds from the territory were brought here. It also contains the sinopia found beneath the apse mosaic of Sant'Apollonare in Classe, and the very beautiful frescoes by Pietro da Rimini recently detached from the church of Santa Chiara. Other objects of particular interest include Roman and Byzantine sculptural fragments, the coin collection, and the ivories. The museum has a slightly neglected air, but don't allow that to put you off: there are some lovely treasures here.

Ground floor

The **first cloister** with its well dates from the early 16th century and from it you can see the circular campanile and part of the exterior of San Vitale. Roman epigraphs and funerary stelae are arranged in the walks, including (at the end of the entrance walk) the funerary stele of a shipwright, showing him hard at work on a vessel and two fragments of a relief dating from AD 43 with a frieze of a sacrifice with Augustus (note the servant protecting the bull with his hand laid on its back). This was unearthed in the 16th century from under or near the Mausoleum of Galla Placidia. The two rooms off this cloister (entrance near the sacrifice reliefs) display architectural fragments including two huge rose windows from a Roman gate of the town (AD 43), carved capitals, and Roman portrait heads. The five copies of Greek herms dating from the 2nd century AD are known to have been purchased by Cardinal Ippolito II d'Este shortly after they had been unearthed in Rome, but when he shipped them to Ferrara in 1573 they sank in the sea near here and were only retrieved from the sea bed by chance, by fishermen in 1936.

The **second cloister**, with its Serlian arches, was built in 1560 by Andrea da Valle. Here, well below ground level, can be seen the narthex of San Vitale, which stands obliquely to the church and was formerly preceded by an atrium. In the refectory off this cloister, an entire **frescoed chapel from the ex-church of Santa Chiara** was reconstructed in 2005. The church, in Via Roma, was converted into the Teatro Rasi in the 19th century. The detached frescoes are extremely beautiful, if damaged, and were painted by Pietro da Rimini (clearly influenced by Giotto) some time around 1317. He worked for the Augustinians in Rimini and had an active *bottega* in Romagna. The scenes from the life of Christ have unusually large figures, and in the vault, which is better preserved, sit the Evangelists at their desks.

First floor

Between the two cloisters, a pretty curving staircase dating from 1791 leads up to a landing with Byzantine capitals and the sarcophagus of an archbishop. The former monastic rooms here house a rich collection including **small bronzes** and plaquettes, mostly Italian, but also earlier works from Germany; the 18th-century cupboards from a pharmacy in Ravenna; an **archaeological collection** from the territory, dating from the Palaeolithic era to Roman material found in the 1960s at Classe; **early Christian** stone lattice work and the huge bronze Cross made in the 6th century AD for the roof of San Vitale; architectural fragments dating from the time of Theodoric; **Egyptian works** (including two fragments of fabrics dating from the 7th or 8th centuries) and a splendid collection of **ivories**, including a relief of *Apollo and Daphne* (530 AD), a 6th-century diptych from Murano, and evangelistary covers.

Also here is a large **sinopia from Sant'Apollinare in Classe**, found beneath the current apse mosaic. It shows a design of peacocks which was never in fact executed (the apse mosaic has a procession of sheep instead). Beyond are two halls overlooking a garden which contain a huge collection of **icons** produced by the Cretan-Venetian school, from the 14th–17th centuries, arranged iconographically by type. An even larger hall (once part of the monastery dormitory) displays a collection of 16th–17th-century **armour** (note the rare round table top in leather made in Turkey in the 16th century and used to add grandeur to meals during military campaigns). Small rooms off this hall contain **ceramics** (Ravenna, Deruta, Faenza, Urbino, Castelli, etc.).

The route to the exit

Stairs lead down past a mezzanine floor with a splendid collection of **coins**, beautifully displayed in chronological order from the Roman period onwards. Back on the ground floor, a huge room once used as a storeroom for the monastery displays mosaic floors and a marble statue of Venice by Enrico Pazzi (1884), the first director of the museum. The hall parallel to this room has funerary stelae (1st century BC–1st century AD), many of them belonging to sailors, and finds (6th–5th centuries BC) from the necropolis of San Martino in Gattara including a large Greek krater.

Not on view at the time of writing was the fine collection of medieval fabrics with some precious examples from the tomb of St Julian at Rimini, and the so-called 'Veil of Classis', with embroideries of Veronese bishops of the 8th–9th centuries.

PIAZZA DEL POPOLO & DANTE'S TOMB

Piazza del Popolo (*map Ravenna, 3*) is at the centre of the town. It is surrounded by a medley of buildings, the most interesting of which is the lowest, the **Palazzetto Veneziano**, built in brick in 1444, with two-light windows restored in the 20th century. It has a lovely portico with granite columns supporting superb Byzantine capitals dating from the 6th century (some of them with the very worn monogram of Theodoric). Also in this corner of the piazza is the **Palazzo Comunale**, reconstructed from the 17th century onwards, but approached beneath an archway by an old staircase. In front of it are two columns erected by the Venetians in 1483, with elaborately carved bases by Pietro Lombardo with worn reliefs of rosettes, signs of the zodiac, putti and allegorical figures. In 1644 the two statues of St Apollonius and St Vitalis were placed on the top of the columns. At the other end of the piazza is a palace with a clock tower (and bell hanging above), erected by Camillo Morigia in 1785. Next to it across Via Diaz is the octagonal church of **Santa Maria del Suffragio**, which also dates from the 18th century.

DANTE'S TOMB AND THE MUSEO DANTESCO

When the great Tuscan poet died in Ravenna in 1321, his remains were interred in the old portico of San Francesco, and the friars jealously protected his bones in subsequent centuries. In 1483 the Venetian *podestà* Bernardo Bembo commissioned the great Venetian sculptor Pietro Lombardo to design a new monument in the same place (Pietro and his *bottega* were at work in the town on the bases of the columns in Piazza del Popolo and there is a relief by him now in the duomo). The relief made by Pietro of the poet in profile surrounded by his books is incorporated in the present gloomy little mausoleum (*map Ravenna, 4; open daily 9–7*), which was commissioned from the aristocratic local architect Camillo Morigia by Cardinal legate Luigi Gonzaga in 1780 to enshrine the older tomb. The epitaph beneath the relief, which records Dante's exile from his beloved 'mother', Florence, was composed by a disciple of the poet Bernardo Canaccio, who befriended him in Verona and then in Ravenna. The polychrome marble on the walls and floor in the interior were added in 1921, when the bronze doors by Lodovico Pogliaghi were installed. The two inscriptions on the right and left walls record Bernardo Bembo and Luigi Gonzaga. Since 1908 a votive lamp has remained permanently alight (the olive oil is donated annually in Sept by the city of Florence).

The little garden beside the mausoleum was also laid out just after the Great War, with its memorial bell-tower, and a restored open chapel built in 1480, which protects two huge early Christian sarcophagi, complete with their lids. The mound covered by ivy apparently protected Dante's bones during the Second World War.

The **Museo Dantesco**, entered through a restored 15th-century cloister at Via Dante Alighieri 4 (*open March–Oct 10–6, winter 10–4; closed Mon*), was first instituted in 1921 to celebrate the sixth centenary of the poet's death, with mementoes and material relating to various memorials to him. It includes a small room, intended as a homage to him by Italian emigrants 'exiled' in Uruguay, decorated by Ambrogio Annoni and artists influenced by the Arts and Crafts movement in England. The box in which the great poet's bones were preserved from 1677 to 1865 by the Franciscan friars is also displayed here. The three casts of 'masks of Dante' are considered those which bear the closest resemblance, and which may be modelled on the marble head of the poet made for the tomb in the 15th century. In 2013 the museum was expanded to other walks of the cloister with a didactic display designed with the help of school children and aimed at bringing the poet 'up-to-date'. There is an important library with works pertaining to Dante in the monastery.

DANTE ALIGHIERI (1265–1321)

Dante was the greatest of all the Italian poets. His famous *Divine Comedy* established Tuscan as the literary vernacular of Italy. In 1295 Dante entered Florentine politics and in 1300 served a two-month term as one of the six priors of the city. At this time the Guelph party split into two factions, the *Bianchi* (Whites) and the Neri (Blacks). Dante was sent to Rome as part of an official delegation to dissuade Pope Boniface VIII from his support of the *Neri* in Florence, but during his absence the *Neri* were able to take control of the city government and there followed a period of vindictive repression of the *Bianchi*. Dante was accused of fraud and corruption and when he failed to return in 1302 to defend himself he was sentenced to death and so went into exile. He never returned to Florence. He found refuge first at the court of Cangrande della Scala in Verona, and later, around 1317–20 with the Da Polenta family of Ravenna, and spent his last years with them here, finishing the *Divine Comedy* under their patronage. He died in the town on the night of 13–14 September 1321. The exact date of his arrival here is not known and the reason he chose Ravenna and Guido Novello da Polenta is also unclear. The beautiful Francesca da Rimini was a daughter of the Da Polenta family, married by proxy to the hunchbacked lord of Rimini, Gianciotto Malatesta. Gianciotto's brother Paolo became Francesca's lover; when Gianciotto discovered their secret, he killed them both. Dante used the story in his *Divine Comedy*. It seems clear that the mosaics of Ravenna also inspired Dante in some of his images of Paradise in the poem, including the jewelled cross in Sant'Apollinare in Classe, or the long processions of martyrs and saints in Sant'Apollinare Nuovo.

For centuries after Dante's death the Florentines contested their right to his remains, and came near to achieving their goal when the Medici pope Leo X ordered their transfer to Florence: but his delegation was unsuccessful since the Franciscan friars removed his bones from his tomb to their monastery.

SAN FRANCESCO & THE BASILICAS

Beside the two famous basilicas of Sant'Apollinare (Nuovo and in Classe), there are three other 5th-century churches in Ravenna (San Francesco, Sant'Agata Maggiore,and San Giovanni Evangelista) which retain their original marble columns and their basilican form which was to influence the ground plan of many other later churches in northern Italy, and came to be known as the 'Ravenna type' of palaeochristian architecture.

SAN FRANCESCO

Built by Bishop Neon in the 5th century and remodelled in the 10th, the church (*map Ravenna 3–4; open 8.30–12 & 3–6*) was almost entirely rebuilt in 1793. The piazza in front was redesigned in 1931 and today is a pleasant pedestrian area where markets are also held, and with two fine sarcophagi complete with their lids against the church façade. The 10th-century campanile was restored in 1921. Inside, the church preserves its lovely basilican interior which has 22 columns of Greek marble. Behind the fine 4th-century sarcophagus of St Liberius which serves as high altar, there is a little arched opening (*the coin operated light is essential*) covered with a grille and overlooking the 9th–10th-century **crypt** in the foundations of an earlier church with its mosaic pavement. It is permanently under water and so home to numerous decorative goldfish, who swim over to greet visitors. Built into the brick wall opposite the grille is a small sarcophagus marked 'Ossa Neonis', the bones of bishop Neon.

In the **north aisle** are three huge sarcophagi (including one with Christ and the Apostles in niches dating from the 5th century), and the pavement tombstone (set up on the wall) of Ostasio da Polenta, made out of red marble (except for his white death mask). This '*magnifico signore*', here appropriately dressed in the Franciscan habit, died in 1396 and was one of the last members of the distinguished family who had ruled the town since the 13th century (when they had given hospitality to Dante). The other pavement tomb set up on the wall here is that of a minister general of the Franciscan Order, the Blessed Enrico Alfieri, who died just a few years later (in 1405). The Numai funerary momument is by Tommaso Fiamberti (1509). The first chapel on the south side has carved pilasters by Tullio Lombardo (1525) . The last one has a statue of the Francsican friar Maximilian Kolbe, who perished in Auschwitz. At the west end are some fragments of Byzantine mosaic and carving.

SANT'AGATA MAGGIORE

This 5th-century basilican church (*map Ravenna, 4; open 9–12 & 4–6 except Sun afternoon*) has a squat round campanile completed in 1560, and sarcophagi on the lawn outside (and more inside). The basilican interior, similar to San Francesco, contains Roman and Byzantine capitals, a very unusual fluted 7th-century pulpit, reminiscent of a massive column, and an early-Christian sarcophagus with two birds used as a high altar. The altars at the end of the two aisles have Renaissance baldachins.

SAN GIOVANNI EVANGELISTA

The elaborately carved 14th-century marble doorway of this church (*map Ravenna 2–4; at the corner of Viale Farini; open 8am–7pm*) was reconstructed when the new wall was built to enclose the little garden in the church precinct. The church was built by Galla Placidia in fulfilment of a vow made in 424 during a storm at sea. It was well restored after serious damage in the Second World War: most of the façade and the first four bays were destroyed as well as the notable galleried apse. The 10th–14th-century campanile survives (leaning to the west); two of the bells date from 1208. In the basilican interior some columns, with their capitals and impost blocks, are original. Curious mosaics from the 13th-century floor, their naïve designs illustrating episodes from the Fourth Crusade, are displayed around the walls. Fresco fragments of the 14th-century Riminese school can be seen in a chapel off the north aisle. The chapel at the end of the south aisle has a little 8th-century carved altar.

The piazza outside the church is named after Garibaldi's wife Anita, who died from the hardships of her flight from the Austrians in the pine forest near the town, where Garibaldi himself had found a brief refuge. The grandiose monument here by Cesare Zocchi (1888), with its amusing lions, commemorates her and others who laid down their lives in the Risorgimento.

MUSEO D'ARTE DELLA CITTÀ DI RAVENNA (MAR)

Map Ravenna, 4. Via di Roma 13. Open Tues, Thur and Fri 9–1.30 & 3–6; Wed and Sat 9–1.30; Sun 3–6: closed Mon. museocitta.ra.it.

The museum is housed in the former monastery of the Canonici Lateranensi beside the church of Santa Maria in Porto, with a spacious grass lawn in front and facing an attractive row of houses of all different sizes and colours along the street. In the public gardens behind is the garden façade, with its lovely little early 16th-century double loggia, known as the Loggetta Lombardesca. There is a fountain on a lawn between trees, and the apse and crossing of the church of Santa Maria in Porto (*see below*) are well seen from here.

The Pinacoteca is spaciously arranged in well-lit rooms around a pretty cloister. It includes works by Lorenzo Monaco, Ludovico Brea, Antonio Vivarini, Gentile Bellini, Luca Longhi, Palma Giovane and Paris Bordone. The beautiful **effigy of Guidarello Guidarelli** is the work of Tullio Lombardo (1525). Guidarello was a soldier, troop captain to Cesare Borgia. He was killed at Imola in 1501 following a trifling quarrel at a masked ball. Legend says that any girl who kisses the effigy will marry the following year. There is also a painting of *St Romuald* by Guercino, and a *Pietà* by Vasari (1548). The 19th–20th-century section has works by Armando Spadini, Felice Carena, Giuseppe Abbati and Arturo Moradei. There are also galleries of later works and modern mosaics. Exhibitions are held here regularly.

Santa Maria in Porto

Well sited behind a pleasant green lawn (*map Ravenna, 4; open 7.30–12.30 & 3.30–7*), this is one of the few churches in the town which was begun *ex novo* in 1553. Its sumptuous façade, added in 1780 by the little-known architect Camillo Morigia, is reminiscent of the Roman Baroque and is in a style quite unlike all the other churches in the town. But even here Ravenna's Byzantine civilisation is recorded with a very fine marble relief of the *Virgin orans* (probably 11th century) over the altar in the north transept. Known appropriately as the *Madonna Greca*, this was once highly venerated as the ex-votos show. Visitors are not allowed into the choir to see the fine late 16th-century stalls by French craftsmen, but the scagliola side altars are all very pretty. Protected by glass in the nave is an ancient prophyry vase.

MOSAIC MUSEUM, CRIPTA RASPONI & DOMUS DEI TAPPETI DI PIETRA

These three museums can all be visited with one (combined) ticket. See ravennantica. it.

THE MOSAIC MUSEUM (TAMO)

Map Ravenna, 3. Entrance at Via Rondinelli 2. Open April–Oct 10–6.30 (in July and Aug Sun 10–2); other periods 10–5 and closed Mon. www.tamoravenna.it.

The huge late 15th-century church of San Niccolò, deconsecrated in the Napoleonic era, has, since 2011, provided a wonderful setting for this curiously-named museum, which is dedicated to the history of mosaic and much visited by school children. It explains the various techniques of mosaic, and has some original mosaic pavements (1st–6th centuries AD), as well as casts (many of them taken in the 1930s from ancient mosaics in the Vatican), and examples of all the different types of tesserae. With all the latest multi-media displays, it is well run. In the cloister there is a display of the 21 mosaics made in 1965 on various designs by artists of the day (including Domenico Purificato and Aligi Sassu) to illustrate episodes in Dante's *Divine Comedy*.

CRIPTA RASPONI

Map Ravenna, 3. Palazzo della Provincia, Piazza San Francesco. Open April and May Tues–Sun 10–6.30, June–Aug Tues–Sun 10–2, Sept and Oct weekends 10–6.30; closed at other times of the year.

In spring and summer the pretty garden is open and the neo-Gothic tower with an 18th-century crypt can be visited to see its 6th-century polychrome mosaic pavement. From the roof garden in the belvedere there is a good view. The former palace here was destroyed in 1922 and later in the same decade a new seat for the Province was built by Giulio Ulisse Arata.

DOMUS DEI TAPPETI DI PIETRA

Map Ravenna, 1. Via Barbiani. Entered through the church of Sant'Eufemia, which dates from 1747. Open March–Sept daily 10–6.30; Oct–Dec Mon–Fri 10–5, Sat, Sun and holidays 10–6. T: 0544, ravennantica.it.

During work on an underground car park at the end of the 20th century, remains of a Roman road and Byzantine edifices, as well as later medieval tombs, were found on this site. Today walkways are provided to view the geometric polychrome mosaic pavements of some 14 rooms of a house dating from the period of Theodoric (6th century AD) with a great variety of knot designs. This is the only private edifice of this date so far discovered in Ravenna. The two most interesting figurative mosaics are exhibited on the walls: the so-called *Good Shepherd* dates from the end of the 4th century, and the *Dance of the Four Seasons* from the end of the 6th century. The latter, with the four figures with joined hands dancing in a ring accompanied by a musician, is particularly unusual.

Further down Via Barbiani, on the corner of Via Massimo d'Azeglio, is the little church of **Santi Giovanni e Paolo**. The church itself was rebuilt in 1758 but it retains its cylindrical campanile of the Ottonian period (9th–10th century).

ISTITUZIONE BIBLIOTECA CLASSENSE

Map Ravenna, 3. Entrance in Via Baccarini. The Aula Magna, where important exhibitions are held, can be seen on request daily except Sun and Mon 10–12 & 3–6. classense.ra.it.

This huge 16th–17th-century former monastery building incorporates, on the second floor (off a long corridor with cells off either side), a very fine **Aula Magna**, designed by Giuseppe Antonio Soratini, with stuccoes and a frescoed ceiling and carved bookcases. Run by the municipality since 1803, this is still the most active and well-run library in Ravenna. Its name comes from the library of the monastery of Sant'Apollinare in Classe, founded in 1515 and augmented by Pietro Canneti (1659–1730) which forms the nucleus of the collection. Precious volumes include a 10th-century text of Aristophanes, illuminated manuscripts, choir books, and works relating to Dante. There is also a collection of **Byron's letters**: he lived in Ravenna in 1819 with the Count and Countess Guiccioli (the countess was his mistress) at their palace at no. 54 Via Cavour and there wrote the end of *Don Juan, Marino Faliero* and other poems.

The **Museo Risorgimento**, also in this building, in the former church of San Romualdo, is only open by appointment (*enquire at the library or T: 0544 482150*).

MAUSOLEUM OF THEODORIC

Map Ravenna, 2. Open 8.30–dusk. Approaches: beyond the rugged bastions of the Venetian Rocca di Brancaleone (which now enclose pleasant public gardens), it is a walk of c. 10–20mins (depending on where you start) along the busy Circonvallazione, across the railway line.

This remarkable two-storey tomb is unique in the history of architecture; its solid structure shows the influence of Syrian buildings as well as Roman models. Begun by the great Ostrogoth himself in c. 520, it was built of hewn Istrian stone without mortar and crowned by an unusual monolithic roof. It was never finished, and for a time, until 1719, it was used as a monastic church (Santa Maria al Faro).

The ten-sided lower storey has a deep recess on every side. The upper floor, which is decorated with unfinished arcading, was approached by two 18th-century staircases, which collapsed in 1921. The monolithic cupola of Istrian limestone from Pula has a diameter of 11m and weighs about 300 tons. It is possible to go into both the upper and lower chambers. The crack in the cupola, which is clearly visible inside the upper chamber, was probably the result of a harsh knock received during its installation. It is not known how the monolith was transported here. Also in the upper chamber is a porphyry bath which is thought to have been the original royal sarcophagus. It was replaced here in the early 20th century after being displaced several times. The tomb was raided in the Byzantine era and the fate of Theodoric's remains is unknown.

From the mausoleum, Via Teodorico leads down to the harbour area of Ravenna, still in use. The wide **Candiano Canal** links the inner harbour with the sea at Marina di Ravenna.

SANT'APOLLINARE IN CLASSE

Although about 5km south of the town (map C, B3), this church should not be missed as it is also of extreme interest for its mosaics. It can be reached by bus no. 4 (which runs from the railway station (Ravenna FS) about every 20–30mins and takes less than 20mins). The closest stop is the last one, behind the apse of the church.

Alternatively the church is a few steps from Classe railway station, served by slow regional trains on the Rimini and Pesaro lines (NB: Check they stop also at Classe—a 5-min journey—since many only stop at the following station, called Lido di Classe, which is on the sea and a long way from the church).

The basilica is open 8.30–7.30pm.

Eating and drinking near Sant'Apollinare in Classe

There are a few cafés and shops at the back of the church where the buses stop. On the other side, the Hotel Classense, unysmpathetically built onto the old monastic quarters, offers coffee, cake and other sustenance. There are also WCs.

Classe was the site of the Roman port of Ravenna, and so it was natural for this spot, on the Roman Via Caesarea, to be chosen for this great basilica when it was built for Bishop Ursicinus with funds donated by the banker Julianus Argentarius in 535–8, some ten years after he had spent some of his wealth on building San Vitale. It, too, was consecrated by the famous Archbishop Maximian (*see p. 156*), in 549, and dedicated to Ravenna's patron saint (and first bishop) St Apollonius (or Apollinaris), who was buried here. Although Classe is now just a small undistinguished (but peaceful) hamlet, some kilometres distant from Ravenna, the isolated site of the basilica has been largely preserved since a modern road has been provided which carries all through traffic well away from the church, which is also surrounded by a little garden. The magnificent late 10th-century campanile is the tallest and most beautiful of all the towers of Ravenna. The narthex which preceded the church was reconstructed in the first years of the 20th century (but the original quadriporticus no longer exists). The monks moved to Vallombrosa in Tuscany around 2000 and the church is now kept open by the state.

INTERIOR OF SANT'APOLLINARE IN CLASSE

The splendid basilican interior, extremely well lit by numerous uniform windows, has 24 magnificent Greek marble-veined columns with superb capitals decorated with acanthus leaves standing on low, square Byzantine bases. The two colonnades end at the east end with two large pilasters decorated with three rows of palmettes carved in relief (repeated in a frieze which is carried right round the apse). The eleven great sarcophagi, complete with lids, dating from the 5th–8th centuries and arranged all round the walls, give the church an especially sumptuous atmosphere. As in San Vitale, the mosaicists concentrated their attention at the east end in the raised sanctuary, where every inch of the surface is decorated with mosaic, including the niches of the windows. The patron saint Apollonius takes pride of place here, the first instance in Christian art where the Redeemer is no longer the central figure.

On the **triumphal arch** are five rows of mosaics, replete with early Christian symbolism (dating from the 6th century, but restored at intervals up to the 12th century). At the top is Christ in a roundel with the four symbols of the Evangelists set in a sky with scudding clouds coloured red and emerald green. In the spandrels are a procession of sheep (symbols of the Apostles), leaving the two cities of Jerusalem and Bethlehem and climbing a grassy mound. Two palm trees (representing the Tree of Life) fill the lower spandrels, and still lower are the two archangels Michael and Gabriel (6th century) with flowers at their feet, and at the bottom, two busts of Apostles (probably 12th century).

In the **apse** itself the mosaics date from the mid-6th century. The most striking feature is a jewelled Cross in a circular frame on a blue ground studded with gold and silver stars, against a golden sky with the Hand of God, the symbol of the Transfiguration, at the top. Also here are two half-figures of Moses and Elijah. The three sheep represent the apostles Peter, James and John who were also present at the Transfiguration. In the centre below stands St Apollonius, his arms raised in prayer, surrounded by sheep (representing the blessed in Paradise) in a field of lilies. The rocky landscape has little bushes inhabited by birds (symbols of light and life). Below again, between the windows, are Ravenna's first four bishop-saints: Ursicinus, Ursus, Severus and Ecclesius (6th century), standing in mosaic niches with the curtains drawn back. The two large scenes at the sides date from the late 7th century: they show (left) nine figures, including Constantine IV, granting privileges for the church of Ravenna to Archbishop Reparatus in the 7th century, and (right) a large altar at which Abel, Melchizedech and Abraham are sacrificing. The arches of the windows are also decorated with columns in mosaic, and all the scenes have lovely frames and borders, with geometric friezes, and wonderfully coloured patterns, typical of all Ravenna mosaics.

In the centre of the nave is the small **rectangular altar** at which Archbishop Maximian (*see p. 156*) probably officiated after the consecration of the church (it was restored in 1753). At the end of the north aisle is a delicate 9th-century ciborium (or baldachin) supported by four columns enclosing an altar with a 5th-century relief of eight apostles. Beneath it is an ancient carved tabernacle decorated with two sheep. The eight columns at the west end of the church used to support the two ciboria which belonged to the original church furnishings (and a fragment of its mosaic floor can also be seen here). The most interesting of the sarcophagi around the walls are the two at the west end: the carvings include sheep, palm trees and peacocks, and a niche with a knotted curtain.

RUINS OF THE PORT OF CLASSE

Via Marabina 7 (corner of Via Romea Sud). The ruins can be reached on foot along the cycle track which follows the Via Romea, past the west front of the basilica (and a copy of the famous statue of the emperor Augustus that was found at Prima Porta outside Rome; good view from here of the campanile). The walk takes about 40mins. Also accessible on bus nos 4 and 176 from Ravenna railway station (Ravenna FS). Ruins open mid-March–May daily 10–6.30; June–Aug 6pm–11pm; Sept–mid-Nov Sat and Sun 10–6. Hours are subject to change; see anticoportoravenna.it.

The name Classe comes from the Roman word *classis*, meaning a fleet. The Romans had two main naval bases: at Misenum near Naples and here at Classe, where the base was founded by Augustus in the 1st century BC. In the Roman era, Classe stood right on the seafront. Today, as a result of accumulations of silt brought downstream by the many-armed Po, the coast is a full 9km away. There are now only scant remains of the old harbour emplacements (mostly dating from much later than the Augustan period), but the site is well laid out and evocative, with good signage.

The harbour mouth would once have been protected by breakwaters and was guarded by an immense lighthouse. In the centre of the harbour was an island with buildings and walkways. The visit to the ruins begins at a modern bridge leading from the former island across to the main harbour area, where a section of deeply rutted paved road is visible. It is thought that in antiquity the island and main harbour were linked by ferry. Warehouses and loading stations giving onto the harbour channel had both a vehicular entrance and, on the further side, an opening onto porticoed wharves so that goods could be loaded from carts onto ships and vice versa. Traces of these warehouses can be seen, separated from each other by paths under which ran covered drainage channels. The port was in use from its foundation by Augustus to the end of the Byzantine era.

RAVENNA PRACTICAL TIPS

INFORMATION OFFICES

At three locations: Piazza San Francesco (*map Ravenna, 3*); Via delle Industrie (*map Ravenna, 2*) and at Classe, near the basilica of Sant'Apollinare. *T: 0544 35404 and 0544 35755, www.turismo.ravenna.it.*

GETTING AROUND

• **By rail:** Ravenna is not on a major rail line, but you can get there by commuter train (Diretti or Regionali) from Ferrara (1hr), Bologna (1hr 10mins) or Faenza (30mins). There is also one train a day direct from Florence on the spectacular branch line across the Apennines via the Mugello (in just over 2hrs); otherwise on this line from Florence you change at Faenza.

• **By bus:** Services are run by START (*startromagna.it*). Buses 4 and 176 run from the railway station (Ravenna FS; *map Ravenna, 2*) to the basilica of Sant'Apollinare in Classe (the stop on bus 4 is Classe Sant'Apollinare or Classe Piazza; bus 176 only stops at Classe Sant'Apollinare but both stops are close to the basilica). The same buses also go to the ruins of the ancient port (get off at Ponte Nuovo).

Country buses run from Piazzale Farini (opposite the railway station; *map Ravenna, 2*) to places of interest in the province, including Bagnacavallo and Lugo, and to the resorts on the coast. Faenza is best reached from Ravenna by train.

• **By bicycle:** Cycles can be rented in Ravenna from the Coop San Vitale, near the railway station at Piazza Farini 1 (*map Ravenna, 2*).

WHERE TO STAY

€€€ **Palazzo Bezzi**. A town house of little distinction has been transformed into a modern hotel with pleasant clean lines, and all the most up-to-date accessories. On Via di Roma which is open to cars but not particularly noisy. A few steps from the basilica of Sant'Apollinare Nuovo. *Via di Roma 45, T: 0544 36926, palazzobezzi.it. Map Ravenna, 4.*

€€ **Bisanzio**. Central and fairly elegant, with a nice garden. *Via Salara 30, T: 0544 217111, www.bisanziohotel. com. Map Ravenna, 1.*

€€ **M Club**. ■ Run by Michael Scapini Mantovani in his family home, this 'de luxe B&B' is beautifully appointed and comfortable, excellently situated in a peaceful square just inside Porta Adriana, a stone's throw from San Vitale. Friendly management, always helpful with advice and recommendations. Pleasant breakfast room. Parking available. *Piazza Baracca 26, T: 333 955 6446, www.m-club.it. Map Ravenna, 1.*

€ **Centrale Byron**. Warm and modern, in a well-renovated old town house. *Via IV (Quattro) Novembre 14, T: 0544 212225, www.hotelbyron.com. Map Ravenna, 3–1.*

€ **Ostello Galletti Abbiosi**. Very pleasant place near Sant'Apollinare Nuovo, with a garden. *Via di Roma 140, T: 0544 31313, galletti.ra.it. Map Ravenna, 4.*

RESTAURANTS

€€ Al 45. Opening onto the secluded little Piazza degli Ariani, with tables outside in good weather, right beside the Arian Baptistery. Specialities of the Romagna region and good pizza. *Via Paolo Costa 45/Piazza degli Ariani, T: 0544 212761, al45.it. Map Ravenna, 2.*

€€ Bella Venezia. Slightly more formal, old-fashioned place, serving lagoon specialities harking back to the days when Ravenna was part of the Venetian Republic. *Via IV Novembre 16, T: 0544 212746, bellavenezia.it. Map Ravenna, 1.*

€€ La Gardèla. Good restaurant specialising in regional grilled fish and meat. Excellent pasta with radicchio in season. Interesting wine selection. Just behind the old market building so very central. With outside seating in warm weather. Closed Thur. *Via Ponte Marino 3 (V.P. Marino), T: 0544 217147. Map Ravenna, 1.*

€€ Villa Antica. Elegant restaurant in a villa with park and outside seating in summer. Closed Sat lunch and all day Mon. *Via Faentina 136 (west of the centre, continuation of Via Maggiore), T: 0544 500522, villaantica.it. Beyond map Ravenna, 1.*

€ Ca' de' Vén. This large *osteria* situated in a beautiful old 16th-century palace, is a delightful place and has for long been a favourite place to eat in Ravenna. Just by Dante's tomb, it is well worth a visit. In the first room with a very high ceiling with charmingly painted vaults and lined with the shelves of a 19th-century shop which sold spices, you can sit and read and have a glass of wine (excellent selection including Trebbiano, Albana, Sangiovese, and Pagadebit). They quote Jacopino da Todi who observed in 1240 that only those who don't have wine should drink water. In the room beyond there are long tables where locals and visitors mingle for an excellent meal, very reasonably priced (there are also tables where you can sit separately). Professional friendly service. Closed Mon. *Via Ricci 24, T: 0544 30163, cadeven.it. Map Ravenna, 3.*

CAFÉS & BARS

Caffè Letterario. Appropriately close to two bookshops, it advertises 'coffee, food, books and chat'. A delightful busy place with books and newspapers and good things to eat and drink. Extremely popular. *Via Diaz 26. T: 0544 216461, caffeletterarioravenna.com. Map Ravenna, 2.*

Caffè Palumbo. Sicilian cakes and good coffee, and tables out under the arcades in this pleasant piazza. *Piazza San Francesco. Map Ravenna, 3.*

Caffè Roma in Piazza del Popolo (*map Ravenna, 3*) has tables outside, as do a number of other establishments on this lively, traffic-free square.

Fresco. A popular place to come for an early evening drink or after-dinner *digestivo*. Good tapas, inspired by Basque *pintxos*. *Via IV Novembre 51–53. Map Ravenna, 1.*

Pasticceria Nonna Iride. Good cakes, just on the corner of Piazza del Popolo. *Via Cairoli 1. Map Ravenna, 3.*

Sorbetteria degli Esarchi. Exceptional ice cream. The pistachio flavour is delicious, truly fit for an exarch. *Via IV Novembre 11. Map Ravenna, 1.*

RESTAURANTS OUTSIDE RAVENNA

€€ **Sorriso**. Family-run restaurant, specialising in traditional regional dishes and grilled meats. Closed Tues and one week in Nov. *Viale delle Nazioni 12, T: 0544 530462, Marina di Ravenna (map C, C2)*.

€€ **Taverna San Romualdo**. Nice restaurant a few kilometres north of Ravenna, on the SP1 just before the Lamone river, between Ravenna and Comacchio (*map C, B2*). Great wine selection, good regional food. Family atmosphere in the *osteria*, slightly more formal in the *ristorante*. Closed Tues evening. *Via Badarena 1 (corner of Via Sant'Alberto), T: 0544 483447, tavernasanromualdo.it*.

FESTIVALS & EVENTS

The Ravenna Festival of Classical music, June–July; Jazz festival, April. *Mosaico di Notte*, international organ music festival in Aug, with concerts every Mon evening in the basilica of San Vitale. Feast of Sant'Apollinare, 23 July. Dante is celebrated every Sept with a series of conferences and a medieval market.

LOCAL SPECIALITIES

Many places from holes in the wall to restaurants offer the traditional *piadina*, a round 'pancake' made with flour and lard which is a good snack when filled with cheese or ham. Ca' de Vén has a good selection of them on their menu. The tiny **Profumo di Piadina** shop sells nothing else, with a huge variety of fillings (*Via Cairoli 24, map Ravenna, 3*).

Pascucci has been in business since 1826, producing lovely hand-printed fabrics and linen, typical of Romagna. They run a pretty little shop, the Antica Bottega, at Via Mentana 12 (*map Ravenna, 3*).

Forlì

Forlì (*map C, B3*) has a spacious feel to it, with low buildings and numerous trees, and bicycles are the main means of transport. Mussolini was born nearby and many new buildings were erected here in the Fascist style, a style for long rejected outright as a product of a discredited regime, but in recent years re-evaluated for its clean, Rationalist lines. Forlì has now become one of the most important places for the study of Italian urban architecture of the 1920s and 1930s.

HISTORY OF FORLÌ

Forlì takes its name from the Roman *Forum Livii*, a station on the Via Emilia, which, as is also the case in neighbouring Faenza, runs straight through the town. Caterina Sforza, countess of Forlì, was besieged here by Cesare Borgia in 1499–1500, since she had refused to allow her son to marry Cesare's sister Lucrezia. In revenge their father, Pope Alexander VI, had given Caterina's lands to Cesare.

Forlì today is an agricultural centre: there are extensive plantations of fruit trees between here and Faenza. The idea of 'renewing' the town, proposed in 1927 by a number of local aristocratic industrialists, was soon taken up and imposed by the Fascist government. The architects included Cesare Bazzani, Cesare Valle, and Gustavo Giovannoni and examples of their work from the 1930s can be seen on the walk from the railway station (by Ezio Bianchi, 1925) along Viale della Libertà to Piazzale della Vittoria, with its First World War memorial column and twin palaces at the entrance to Corso della Repubblica, all by Bazzani.

EXPLORING FORLÌ

Corso della Repubblica leads straight to the pleasant central **Piazza Aurelio Saffi**, with its monument to Saffi, a hero of the Risorgimento, and decorative lamp-posts. Here the impressive Palazzo del Municipio, with its clock-tower, was first built in 1459, but its present appearance dates from 1826. On Corso Mazzini (which leads out of the piazza) are two public buildings by Cesare Bazzani (1930s).

San Mercuriale (12th–13th centuries but altered later), dedicated to the first bishop of Forlì, is the most interesting church in the town. It has a fine contemporary campanile, 76m high, a high relief of the school of Antelami above the west door, and a graceful cloister. In the red-brick interior are paintings by Marco Palmezzano, born in Forlì in 1460, and the tomb of Barbara Manfredi (d. 1466), wife of Pino II Ordelaffi. Beneath the apse are remains of the 11th-century church and the crypt of 1176.

MUSEI SAN DOMENICO

Piazza Guido da Montefeltro. Reached from Piazza Saffi by Corso Diaz, then (right) Via Missirini, and Via Caterina Sforza. Open Tues–Fri 9.30–7, weekends 9.30–8. www.cultura.comune.forli.fc.it.

The huge former convent of San Domenico now houses the very well displayed **Pinacoteca Civica** (founded in 1846), and important exhibitions are held here. The church is being restored also as an exhibition space. The arrangement is strictly chronological. In Room 1 is a triptych by the Maestro di Forlì, who was at work in the town between 1280 and 1310. In Room 4 is a druggist's street sign, the *pestapepe*, painted around 1475 by an unknown master and showing the influence of Francesco del Cossa. The Tuscan works in this room include a diptych by Fra' Angelico and a beautiful portrait of a lady by Lorenzo di Credi. In Room 5 is the sarcophagus of the Blessed Marcolino Amanni by Antonio Rossellino (1458). In the Long Gallery (Room 6) is a detached fresco of the *Crucifixion* by Marco Palmezzano, Forlì's most famous painter (1459–1539), and more good paintings by him can be seen on the other side of the stairs in Rooms 8 and 9. In Room 11 there is a *Holy Family* by Francia (*see p. 11*) and in Room 13, works by Livio Agresti, born in Forlì around 1508. In the last wing are 16th- and 17th-century paintings, mostly by local artists.

Displayed on its own in a little oval room is a beautiful statue of Hebe, commissioned from Canova in 1816 by a countess of Forlì and purchased by the *Comune* from her heirs in 1887. It is the last of four versions of this statue (the others are at Chatsworth in England, in the Nationalgalerie, Berlin, and the Hermitage).

The 19th- and 20th-century collection was opened in 2014 in **Palazzo Romagnoli** (*close by at Via Albincini 12*). The ceramics collection and Archaeological Museum were still closed at the time of writing.

CORSO GARIBALDI

This street has some grand mansions including **Palazzo Gaddi**, which contains a Risorgimento Museum and Theatre Museum (*both only open by appointment; T: 0543 712627, musei@comune.forli.fc.it*). It leads to the **cathedral**, mainly an elaborate reconstruction of 1841 but preserving a huge tempera painting of the *Assumption*, the masterpiece of Carlo Cignani, an artist of the Bolognese school who died in Forlì in 1706. The campanile, in Piazza Ordelaffi, was formerly the watchtower of the Orgogliosi, a rival family to the Ordelaffi, who ruled the town from 1315 to 1500.

FORLÌ PRACTICAL TIPS

INFORMATION OFFICE

Piazzetta della Misura 5. *T: 0543 712435; turismoforlivese.it.*

GETTING AROUND

The nearest **airport** is at Bologna. Trains from Bologna to Forlì in 1hr 20mins (Forlì is on the mail **railway line** between Rimini and Bologna). There are also buses: journey time is shorter but services are infrequent. In Forlì itself, there is an excellent small electric **bus service** runs from the railway station to Piazza Saffi. There is a **car park** in Piazza Guido da Montefeltro in front of the Musei San Domenico.

WHERE TO STAY

€€€ **Hotel della Città**. In a 20th-century building by Gio Ponti with a restaurant. *Corso della Repubblica 117, T: 0543 28297.*
€€€ **Hotel Masini**. In a central position, but a little dated. *Corso Garibaldi 28, T: 0543 28072, masinihotel.it.*

RESTAURANTS

€€ **La Casa Rusticale dei Cavalieri Templari**. In an ancient house of the Knights Templar, offering good meat and seafood dishes, interesting desserts and wines. Closed Sun–Mon. *Viale Bologna 275, T: 0543 701888, www.osteriadeitemplari.it.*
€€ **La Monda**. Family-run *trattoria*, serving regional dishes and grilled meats. Closed Wed, Thur and Sun. *Via Monda 72, T: 0543 86372.*

Rimini

Rimini (*map C, C4*) was first visited for its bathing beaches in 1843; by the 1950s it was the largest seaside resort on the Adriatic. Its beaches extend along the shore in either direction; some 16 million tourists visit this coast every year (there are over 2,000 hotels in the province). In the mid-to-late-20th

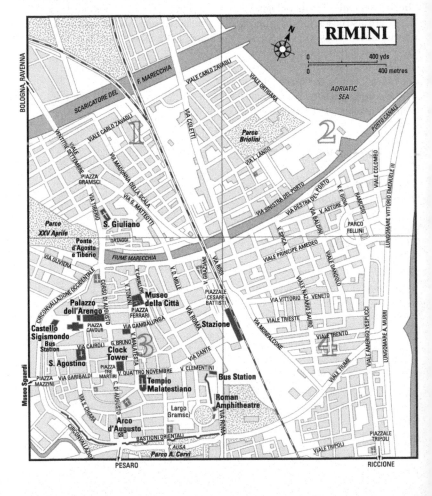

century Rimini became famous throughout Europe as a meeting-place for young (and not so young) singles.

The old town is over a kilometre from the sea front, and separated from it by the railway, and although somewhat characterless, it contains the famous Tempio Malatestiano, one of the most important Renaissance buildings in Italy. It also has a good local museum, and it preserves a splendid Roman arch and bridge.

HISTORY OF RIMINI

Rimini occupies the site of the Umbrian city of *Ariminum*, which became a Roman colony c. 268 BC and was favoured by Julius Caesar and Augustus. In the 8th century it became a papal possession and it was contended between the papal and imperial parties in the 12th–13th centuries. Malatesta di Verucchio (1212–1312), Dante's 'old mastiff', was the founder of a powerful dynasty of Guelph overlords, the most famous of whom was Sigismondo (1417–68), a man of violent character but an enthusiastic protector of art and learning. Malatesta's son, Giovanni the Lame, was the husband of the beautiful Francesca da Rimini (d. 1258), whose love for her brother-in-law Paolo inspired one of the tenderest passages in Dante's *Inferno* ('we read no more that day'). Pandolfo (d. 1534) surrendered the town to Venice, but after the battle of Ravenna (1512) it fell again into papal hands. In the Second World War Rimini, bombarded from sea or air nearly 400 times, was the scene of heavy fighting between the Germans and the Eighth Army and was captured by Canadians in September 1944. In the Coriano ridge War Cemetery, 10km south of the town, 1885 soldiers are buried. The film director Federico Fellini (1920–93) was a native of Rimini, and some of his films were inspired by the town.

THE TEMPIO MALATESTIANO

Via IV Novembre. Map Rimini, 3. Open Mon–Fri 8.30–12 & 3.30–6.30, Sat 8.30–12.30 & 3.30–7, Sun 9–12.30 & 3.30–6.30.

This building is famous both for its architecture and for the wonderful sculptural reliefs which decorate the interior. It was designed by the most famous architect and theorist of the Renaissance, Leon Battista Alberti. The church of San Francesco, built by the Franciscans in the late 13th century (on the site of a 9th-century church), had already been used by the Malatesta family in the 14th century for their family tombs. But in 1447–8 Sigismondo Malatesta transformed the church into a personal monument, as his own burial place, and so it became known as the Tempio Malatestiano. Sigismondo commissioned Leon Battista Alberti to redesign it (with the help of Matteo de' Pasti in the interior) and had Agostino di Duccio decorate it with exquisite sculptural reliefs. Sadly the decline of Sigismondo's fortunes caused the suspension of the work in 1460, and it was left to the Franciscans to complete the building.

Exterior of the Tempio

The façade in Istrian stone, on a high basement or stylobate, is inspired by the form of the Roman triumphal arch (and in particular by the classical Arch of Augustus nearby). One of the masterpieces of Alberti, who was greatly influenced by the buildings of ancient Rome, it was to have a lasting effect on 16th- and 17th-century church architecture in Italy. The upper part is clearly incomplete. The two sides of the building have wide round-headed niches surmounting the stylobate, beneath which (on the south side) are seven plain Classical sarcophagi containing the ashes of eminent humanists who belonged to Sigismondo's court. Latin and Greek inscriptions record Sigismondo and his victories.

Interior of the Tempio

The interior has been beautifully restored. The spacious nave is flanked by a series of deep side chapels connected by remarkably fine sculptural decoration by Agostino di Duccio, and closed by fine balustrades in red-and-white veined marble. The walls are covered with beautiful sculptural details (including the vaults and window frames): no other Renaissance church in Italy is more richly decorated. On the right of the entrance is the tomb of Sigismondo, whose armorial bearings (the elephant and rose) and initials (SI) recur throughout the church.

In the first chapel on the south side is a seated statue of St Sigismund supported by elephants' heads, and very low reliefs of angels, all elegant works of Agostino di Duccio. In the niches are statues of the Virtues and armour-bearers. The little sacristy (formerly the Chapel of the Relics) preserves its original doors surrounded by marble reliefs, including two putti on dolphins. Inside is a damaged fresco (above the door) by Piero della Francesca (1451), representing Sigismondo kneeling before his patron, St Sigismund of Burgundy, and relics found in Sigismondo's tomb. The third chapel has a frieze of putti at play on the entrance arch and (over the altar), *St Michael* by Agostino. Here is the tomb of Isotta degli Atti, Sigismondo's mistress and later his third wife. The crucifix was painted for the church by Giotto before 1312. The fourth chapel has more superb decoration representing the planetary symbols and signs of the zodiac, also by Agostino.

The fourth chapel on the north side is the masterpiece of Agostino, with reliefs representing the Arts and Sciences. The third chapel has particularly charming putti. In the first chapel (of the Ancestors) are figures of prophets and sibyls, a tiny *Pietà* (15th-century, French), above the altar, and the Tomb of the Ancestors, with more splendid reliefs by Agostino.

The end chapels and presbytery do not belong to the original Malatesta building: Alberti's design is thought to have incorporated a dome at the east end. It was completed by the Franciscans (and rebuilt in the 18th century and again after damage in the Second World War). The temple has served as the cathedral of Rimini since 1809.

ROMAN REMAINS IN RIMINI

Corso d'Augusto links the two most interesting buildings which survive from the Roman city of Rimini: the ancient bridge to the north and the gate to the south, both associated with Augustus. The **Ponte d'Augusto e Tiberio** (*map Rimini, 3*) is a five-arched bridge across the Marecchia river begun by Augustus in the last year of his life and finished by Tiberius (21 AD). It is remarkably well-preserved (and used by cars and pedestrians). Its handsome dedicatory inscriptions are still in place in the centre of the bridge. The north arch was rebuilt after the Goths destroyed it in order to cut Narses off from Rome in 552.

At the opposite (south) end of the Corso is the **Arco d'Augusto** (*map Rimini, 3*), a Roman archway (c. 27 BC; restored) with composite capitals, which marked the junction of the Via Emilia with the Via Flaminia. It was later inserted into the medieval walls. To the east, at the end of a stretch of the walls, are the ruins of the **Roman amphitheatre** (*map Rimini, 3*); only two brick arches remain above the foundations.

MUSEO DELLA CITTÀ & DOMUS DEL CHIRURGO

Via Tonini 1. Map Rimini, 3. Open winter Tues–Sat 9.30–1 & 4–7, Sun and holidays 10–7; summer (from mid-June) Tues–Sat 10–7, Sun and holidays 10–1 & 4–7. Open 9pm–11pm on Wed in July and Aug. museicomunalirimini.it.

The Museo della Città is housed in the large ex-Jesuit college built by Alfonso Torreggiani in 1746–55. It has an extensive collection. In the garden courtyard is a **lapidary collection** with numerous Roman insciptions. In a small room are exhibited two **sketchbooks used by Fellini** from 1960–90. In the upper floor **Pinacoteca**, the two masterpieces are Giovanni Bellini's *Dead Christ with Four Angels*, commissioned by Sigismondo Pandolfo Malatesta c. 1460, and Domenico Ghirlandaio's *Pala of St Vincent Ferrer*, commissioned by Pandolfo IV, with portraits of the Malatesta family. Also interesting are the works by Riminese artists, including a fine Crucifix by Giovanni da Rimini (14th century), and 17th-century works. There are also three works by Guercino and a painting by Guido Reni. The archaeological collection includes the surgeon's instruments found in the Domus del Chirurgo.

DOMUS DEL CHIRURGO

Outside in Piazza Ferrari, a Roman house, the Domus del Chirurgo (*for admission ask at the Museo della Città*), was discovered in the late 1980s and opened to the public in 2007. This was the house and operating theatre of a Greek surgeon: some 150 surgeon's instruments were found here (the largest find of this kind known anywhere). There are mosaic floors and the finds include medicine jars and a glass panel with three fish.

PIAZZA TRE MARTIRI & PIAZZZA CAVOUR

In the arcaded central Piazza Tre Martiri (*map Rimini, 3*), the little **Oratory of St Anthony** marks the spot where the saint's mule is supposed miraculously to have knelt in adoration of the Sacrament.

Piazza Cavour (*map Rimini, 3*) has a fountain of 1543 incorporating Roman reliefs and a seated 17th-century statue of Paul V. Here are two restored Gothic buildings: the battlemented Palazzo dell'Arengo (1204), now used for exhibitions, and the 14th-century Palazzo del Podestà, the Town Hall. At the end is the Neoclassical façade of the theatre, built in 1857 by Poletti, which hides the foyer (used for exhibitions): the theatre itself was bombed in the Second World War and is only now being slowly reconstructed. The **Castel Sismondo** dates from 1446. The interior is used for exhibitions.

The **Cinema Folgor**, on Corso d'Augusto, built in the 1920s, was often visited by Fellini as a child.

In Via Sigismondo the Romanesque church of **Sant'Agostino** (*map Rimini, 3*) has a fine campanile, damaged 14th-century frescoes by local artists (including Giovanni da Rimini) and a huge painted 14th-century crucifix.

ACROSS THE RIVER & TOWARDS THE SEA

The church of **San Giuliano** (*map Rimini, 1*), in the suburb beyond the bridge, contains a fine *Martyrdom of St Julian* by Paolo Veronese. The pleasant Parco XXX Aprile occupies the former bed of the River Marecchia (now channelled to the north).

TOWARDS THE SEA

Viale Principe Amadeo (*map Rimini, 4*) was laid out in the 19th century to connect the old town with the sea. It is lined with pretty Art Nouveau villas with their gardens. By the railway line is the only skyscraper in the city.

The sandy beaches along the coast northwest and southeast of Rimini, ruined by uncontrolled new building which began in the 1950s, attract millions of holidaymakers every year from all over Europe. There is a continuous line of resorts, including Riccione, with numerous hotels.

THE MUSEO DEGLI SGUARDI

On the hill of Covignano, 4km outside the town (beyond map Rimini, 3; bus 15 from the station). It can be visited by appointment. T: 0541 704421 or 704426 office hours Mon–Fri or T: 0541 793851.

This remarkable ethnological collection has been housed in the Villa Alvarado built in 1721 since 2005. Founded by Delfino Dinz Rialto (1920–79) in 1972 it covers Oceania, pre-Columbian America and Africa.

RIMINI PRACTICAL TIPS

INFORMATION OFFICE

Piazzale Cesare Battisti 1 (by the railway station; *map Rimini, 3*). *T: 0541 51331; riminireservation.it, riminiturismo.it.*

GETTING AROUND

• **By air:** Rimini's Federico Fellini Airport (at Miramare, c. 6km south of the city) has low-cost flights from all over Europe.

• **By rail:** Italy's main Adriatic rail line closely follows the Via Emilia from Bologna to Rimini (journey time 1hr 20mins). Most fast trains stop at Rimini bus station (*map Rimini, 4*). Commuter trains (Regionali and Interregionali) connect Rimini with Ravenna and Ferrara.

• **By bus:** In Rimini buses and trolley-buses depart from the bus station (*map Rimini, 4*) to Piazza Tre Martiri and the shore. For country buses to places in the region, including Cesena and Ravenna, see *startromagna.it*. For buses along the shore to Riccione, see *adriabus.eu*.

WHERE TO STAY

€€€ **Grand**. A huge *belle-époque* affair, first opened on the seafront in 1908 and truly grand in elegance and service. *1 Viale Ramusio, Parco Fellini 2, T: 0541 56000, www.grandhotelrimini.com. Map Rimini, 2.*

€€€ **Duomo**. In a renovated building in the centre of the old town, a 'design hotel' with ultra modern décor. *Via Giordano Bruno 28, T: 0541 24215, duomohotel.com. Map Rimini, 3.*

RESTAURANTS

The best fish restaurants are in the fishing enclave of Borgo San Giuliano. *Map Rimini, 3.*

FESTIVALS & MARKETS

Sagra Musicale Malatestiana, Classical music festival, usually in early Sept (*see www.sagramusicalemalatestiana.it*). Market around the castle, Wed and Sat.

The Smaller Towns of Romagna

The region of Romagna has many interesting towns. The largest—Ravenna, Faenza, Forlì, and Rimini—have been given chapters of their own. But there are also numerous smaller towns situated in green and gently rolling countryside where farming is still the primary activity, as well as the wild and craggy Montefeltro with its precariously perched castles. Seven of its small towns voted to join Emilia Romagna in 2009.

BAGNACAVALLO

This small town (*map C, B2*) has a delightful theatre (1855) in its central piazza. In Via Garibaldi, next to a 13th-century tower, is the **convent of San Giovanni** where Allegra, daughter of Byron and Claire Clairmont, died in 1821 at the age of five (plaque). Another former convent, Le Cappuccine, the orchard of which is now a pretty public garden, houses a **pinacoteca** (*open Tues–Sun 10–12 & 3–6 or 4–7; centrolecappuccine.it*) with paintings by Bartolomeo Ramenghi (1484–1542), called Il Bagnacavallo after his native town. Also under the same roof are a local ethnographic museum, a library and a natural history museum. The Collegiata and Carmine also have paintings by Bagnacavallo. San Francesco, next to its huge convent, has a small Flemish painting and a tombstone (of a certain Tiberio Brandolini) with a relief of him in armour mounted on a horse charging up a hillside, thought to date from the 15th century. Piazza Nuova is a charming little 18th-century oval cobbled marketplace surrounded by porticoes.

The church of **San Pietro in Silvis** (*usually open on Fri and weekends; for info, T: 0545 280898*), just a kilometre outside the town (in the direction of Lugo and Fusignano), has a lovely basilican interior of the Ravenna type, probably dating from the early 7th century, with a raised presbytery above the crypt. It has frescoes in the apse by Pietro da Rimini (c. 1323).

At **Villanova**, on the river Lamone, is an interesting local museum (*T: 0545 47122, erbepalustri.it; closed Mon*) illustrating life on the wetlands in the district, with handicrafts made from the reeds which grow in the marshes.

LUGO

This pleasant little town (*map C, A2–B2*) has interesting 18th-century architecture. The **Teatro Rossini** was begun in 1757–9 by Francesco Petrocchi, and Antonio

Bibiena designed the boxes, stage and three backcloths in 1761. It is built entirely of wood (with excellent acoustics) and the stage is the same size as the auditorium, which seats 500. The town was already known by 1598 for the excellence of its musical performances, and important opera productions were given in the theatre in the 18th century, and concerts are now held in spring. The huge Neoclassical **Pavaglione** was built at the end of the 18th century on the site of a marketplace in use since 1437; the arcading on one side dates from the early 16th century. Beneath the porticoes are attractive shops with uniform fronts, and a weekly market is held here on Wed.

The colossal incongruous **monument to Francesco Baracca**, aviator and First World War hero, was inaugurated here in 1936 by Mussolini (though originally intended for another site). The **Rocca Estense**, the town hall (*open daily except Sun and holidays*) dates in its present form from the 15th–16th centuries. In the well-restored courtyard is a 15th-century well-head. Upstairs, the Salotto Rossini has a portrait (1828) of the composer, who lived in the town as a child in 1802–4. The hanging garden is now a public park.

The church of the Carmine preserves an organ by Gaetano Callido (1797) used by Rossini. At Via Baracca 65 is the **Museo Francesco Baracca** (*open Tues–Sun 10–12 & 4–6; museobaracca.it*) with mementoes of the pioneer aviator (1888–1918), born in Lugo, including the plane he used in the First World War. There was an important Jewish community in the town from the 15th century onwards and their cemetery survives just outside the centre of town, in Via di Giù (towards San Potito on the Bagnacavallo road). It was moved here in 1877 (but has earlier tombstones). Not open regularly (*for information, ask at the Tourist Office*).

IMOLA

Imola (*map C, A3*) was the Roman *Forum Cornelii*, founded by L. Cornelius Sulla in 82 BC on the Via Emilia, and it still preserves the main outlines of its Roman plan. The cathedral was entirely rebuilt in the 18th century. The early 14th-century castle was rebuilt by Gian Galeazzo Sforza, whose daughter Caterina married Girolamo Riario, lord of Imola, and held the fortress after his death until her defeat by Cesare Borgia (1500). It contains a collection of arms and armour (*only open at weekends*). In the pinacoteca in the former convent of San Domenico (*open Tues–Fri 9–1, Sat 3–7, Sun 10–1 & 3–7; museiciviciimola.it*) is a painting by Innocenzo Francucci (known as Innocenzo da Imola; c. 1494–c. 1550). It was here that Cesare Borgia's dashing captain Guidarello Guidarelli (*see p. 162*) was stabbed to death as the result of a personal squabble.

Imola is well-known to motor racing enthusiasts for its **race track** opened by Enzo Ferrari in 1950. Since 1963 it has hosted Formula One world championships, including the first Grand Prix in 1981.

BRISIGHELLA

Brisighella (*map C, A3*) is a charming little town in the foothills of the Apennines above Faenza. It lies in a lovely valley beneath three conical hills, all reached by pretty paths. One is crowned by a clock-tower of 1290 (rebuilt in 1850), and another by a 14th-century Manfredi castle with two drum towers (restored by the Venetians in the 16th century), which has a local ethnographic museum, the **Museo del Lavoro Contadino** (*open at weekends 10–12.30 & 3–7*). On the top of the third hill is a 17th-century sanctuary. Excellent olive oil is produced in the vicinity.

Above the main street runs the **Strada degli Asini**, a very picturesque covered lane with a wooden vault and arches. The **Museo Civico G. Ugonia** (*see brisighella. org for opening times*) contains an interesting collection, beautifully displayed, of lithographs and watercolours by Giuseppe Ugonia (1880–1944). The church of the **Osservanza** is decorated with fine stuccowork of 1634 and a painting by Marco Palmezzano (d. 1539), a native of Forlì.

Just outside the town is the 16th-century **Villa Spada** (with an 18th-century façade), surrounded by a large garden. A little beyond stands the **Pieve del Tho** (*only open Sun afternoons; see brisighella.org*). This ancient church, first mentioned in 909, has primitive columns and capitals, on one of which is an inscription mentioning four late Roman emperors. The name 'Tho' is thought to come from *ottavo*, referring to the eighth mile on the Roman road from the Adriatic: there are Roman remains beneath the church.

PREDAPPIO AND CASTROCARO TERME

The town of **Predappio** (*map C, B3–B4*), south of Forlì, is notorious as the birthplace of Benito Mussolini (1883–1945). The village, originally a hamlet called Dovia in the commune of Predappio Alta, received communal rank in 1925, and many new public buildings were erected by Florestano Di Fausto. In Piazza Sant'Antonio is the **Casa del Fascio** by Arnaldo Fuzzi and the **church of Sant'Antonio** by Cesare Bazzani, both built in the 1930s. In the cemetery are Mussolini's remains, finally interred here in 1957 (he had been executed in 1945), and those of his wife 'Donna Rachele' (Rachele Guidi), buried there in 1979. Predappio was taken from the Germans by Poles of the Eighth Army in October 1944. There is a British military cemetery at Meldola 11km east, on the river Ronco.

Castrocaro Terme (*map C, B3*), on the river Montone with a park, is a spa which was purchased by the Fascist Regime in 1936 and new thermal buildings were erected and decorated by Tito Chini, with paintings and ceramics.

CESENA

Cesena (*map C, B3*) now lacks distinction, although it enjoyed a period of brilliance under the Malatesta family (1379–1465), and their famous library together with its contents survives here—a perfectly preserved 15th-century library. The **Biblioteca Malatestiana** (*open Mon 2–7, Tues–Sat 9–7, Sun 3–7*) is approached through a handsome doorway, with a relief of the Malatesta heraldic elephant. It is a beautiful aisled basilica built in 1447–52 by Matteo Nuti for Domenico Malatesta Novello, and some precious old books, in their original presses, are still kept chained to the reading desks. The opaque windows look onto the cloister. Two Roman silver plates (early 5th-century AD), with banquet scenes in gold and niello, are displayed in the vestibule. Another room contains a display of some of the library's most valuable holdings, which include illuminated manuscripts and incunabula.

Near the 15th-century Palazzo del Ridotto (rebuilt in 1782) is the church of the Suffragio, with a late Baroque interior and a high altarpiece by Corrado Giaquinto (1752). The **cathedral**, begun in 1385, contains late 15th- and early 16th-century sculpture. The theatre was opened in 1846.

The central Piazza del Popolo has a pretty fountain of 1583, opposite which steps lead up to the public gardens surrounding the 15th-century **Rocca Malatestiana** (*open from 10am daily except Mon; roccamalatestianadicesena.it*), which was a prison until 1969 and has been heavily restored. It contains 17th-century tournament armour and a Garibaldi collection. From the battlements are views of the coast, including the tower of Cesenatico, and inland to the Apennines. One of the towers houses a local ethnographic museum.

From Piazza del Popolo, Viale Mazzoni leads round the foot of the castle hill to San Domenico with 17th-century paintings. In Via Aldini is the **Pinacoteca Comunale**, with works by Sassoferrato, Antonio Aleotti and Giovanni Battista Piazzetta.

Outside the town is the **Madonna del Monte**, a Benedictine abbey rebuilt in the 15th–16th centuries, with a collection of ex-votos and a *Presentation in the Temple* by Bolognese master Francesco Francia. A British military cemetery northeast of Cesena recalls the heavy fighting in this area by the Eighth Army in October 1944.

Cesenatico (*map C, C3*) was the port of Cesena (designed in 1502 by Leonardo da Vinci for Cesare Borgia) from which Garibaldi and his wife Anita set sail on their flight towards Venice in August 1849. It is now the biggest of the seaside resorts here, which stretch for some 30km south to Rimini and Pesaro. It has a marine musuem.

Near Gatteo a Mare (*map C, C3*) is the mouth of the **Rubicone river**, the fateful Rubicon which Caesar crossed in defiance of Pompey in 49 BC. A Roman bridge (c. 186 BC) survives over the river inland at **Savignano sul Rubicone**.

SANTARCANGELO DI ROMAGNA

Santarcangelo (*map C, C4*) is a pleasant small town close to Rimini. The **Sferisterio**, below the walls in the lower town, was built for ball games (and is now used for the game of *tamburello*). In Via Cesare Battisti are the fish market of 1829 and the Collegiata. Also in this street is an old family-run shop where fabrics are still printed by hand (the wheel dates from the 17th century); all the old books of samples have been preserved.

Uphill, Piazza delle Monache, in the 17th-century Palazzo Cenci is the **Museo Storico Archeologico** (*opening times vary; see museisantarcangelo.it*) with paintings (including a Venetian polyptych dated 1385, formerly in the collegiata) and an archaeological collection. Also in the piazza is the entrance to a grotto (*opened on request at the information office; T: 0541 624270*), used as a wine cellar since the 16th century. A passageway leads to a remarkable circular underground room with an ambulatory and niches carved in the sandstone rock, possibly a pagan temple. There are many other similar grottoes beneath the town, for information see above.

Further uphill is the picturesque old *borgo*, with three long straight streets of low houses leading from the Gothic-revival clock-tower to the 14th–15th-century **Rocca** (still privately owned by the Colonna family) which can be visited by appointment (*T: 0541 620832*). The **Museo Etnografico**, in Via Montevecchi (*for opening times, see museisantarcangelo.it*), has collections documenting the popular traditions (symbolism, social life, work, ritual aspects, arts) of southern Romagna.

THE MONTEFELTRO & MARECCHIA VALLEY

In the pleasant Marecchia valley, with hilly outcrops, is **Villa Verucchio** (*map C, C4*), with an early medieval Franciscan convent. The church contains a 14th-century Riminese fresco. **Verucchio** is an attractive hill-town from which the Malatesta clan set out to conquer Rimini. Its site, on a low hill where the river Marecchia emerges into the plain, has been of strategic importance since earliest times, and an Etruscan centre flourished here in the 7th century BC. An ancient *pieve* lies at the foot of the hill. From the pretty Parco dei Nove Martiri an old walled mule track leads up to the Rocca. A lane descends to the former convent of Sant'Agostino, the handsome seat of the Museo Civico Archeologico (*usually open daily April–Sept, weekends only at other times; T: 0541 670222 or ask at the Tourist Office*), with finds from an important Etruscan and Villanovan necropolis (9th–7th centuries BC) at the foot of the hill. Particularly beautiful is the amber and gold jewellery. The Rocca (*open as the museum*) has a splendid view of the Adriatic coast (Rimini and Cesenatico marked by their two skyscrapers) and inland. The Collegiata has a 14th-century Riminese painted cross, and an early 15th-century cross attributed to Nicolò di Pietro in the north transept.

Montebello (*map C, C4*) is a delightful little hamlet with just one street. Steps lead up to the entrance to the Castello dei Guidi di Romagna, still privately owned by the Guidi (*castellodimontebello.com*). There are fine views over the beautiful river valley and the former estate (now a nature reserve), which includes the castle of Saiano (reached by a path) with a church perched on an outcrop of rock. San Marino is also prominent. The courtyard is partly 12th–century (with a tower built onto the rock), and part-Renaissance. The interior, interesting for its architecture, has particularly good furniture in the Renaissance wing. A pretty corner room in the medieval part of the castle has an interesting collection of *cassoni* (marriage chests), including three dating from the 13th and 14th centuries, an old oven, and a painted Islamic panel thought to date from the 11th century. The family still owns a private archive dating from 980. There is a small garden inhabited by peacocks inside the walls. The castle was used for a time as German headquarters in the Second World War, and during a battle here 386 Gurkhas (part of the British Eighth Army) lost their lives; their military cemetery is on the San Marino road south of Rimini.

SAN LEO
San Leo (*map C, C4*) stands on a limestone crag, almost inaccessible, with a castle perched on the top. The wild character of the Montefeltro area has made it historically a place of refuge and strong defence. San Leo was chosen as a place of

refuge by the runaway Christian Dalmatian slave St Leo in the late 3rd century. The impregnable rock also made it an important military base; in 962 Berengarius II even declared it the capital of the Kingdom of Italy, and it was consequently besieged for months by Emperor Otto I. Later it became a key position during the struggles between Guelphs and Ghibellines. Famous visitors include Dante (who commented on the stiff climb up) and St Francis of Assisi. In fact, in 1213 St Francis received here, as a gift from Count Orlando of Chiusi, the mountain of Verna, where he would build his convent.

Entering the town through the south gate—the only access—you reach Piazza Dante. On the left is Palazzo Municipale (16th century), once the residence of the Montefeltro counts, and next to it the ancient and beautiful **Pieve di Santa Maria Assunta**. Inside are some columns and capitals from Imperial Roman temples. In the presbytery, which is raised over the crypt, is a 9th-century ciborium supported by slender columns with medieval capitals. At the beginning of the south aisle is a narrow stair leading to an underground chamber, said to be the church founded here by St Leo.

Outside in the lovely, peaceful little square is an octagonal fountain where birds swoop down to drink. A little further along, on the right, is **Palazzo Nardini**, where St Francis of Assisi stayed in 1213. On the same square is the Palazzo Mediceo (1521), housing the **Museo d'Arte Sacra** (*open daily 9.30–6.30 but T: 0541 926967 for updates*), with a *Madonna and Child with Sts Leo and Marinus* by Luca Frosino (1487) and a *Deposition* by Guercino.

The duomo

The duomo is in the highest part of the town, built of mellow sandstone with graceful apses decorated with little blind arches and lancet windows. The interior is solemn, with a nave and two aisles divided by pilasters, with the date 1173 carved on the fourth south one. There are also two Roman columns with 3rd-century capitals. The presbytery is particularly interesting, quite high, and curving to form the three apses. In the central apse is a 13th-century Crucifix. Underneath is the crypt, with the lid of St Leo's sarcophagus. Behind the duomo is the 12th-century bell-tower.

The Fortezza

The fort of San Leo or Rocca (*open 9.30–6.45, last entry 6*), considered by some to be the most beautiful castle in Italy, owes its present aspect to Francesco di Giorgio Martini, who devised the immense cylindrical towers and the triangular fortification at one end, like the prow of a ship, ideal protection against powerful cannons. In the castle is the Museo della Fortezza, with a collection of arms and armour. The Fortezza was for many years notorious as a prison. Among its inmates was Giuseppe Balsamo, count of Cagliostro. Born in 1743 in Palermo, the city from which he fled after being accused of theft, he went to Rome, but soon became restless, and went to London. Setting himself up as an alchemist, he was soon much in demand among the European aristocracy for his skill as a healer. He founded a Masonic lodge, inspired by the cult of the goddess Isis, appointing himself as its head. Sentenced to death for heresy by the Inquisition in 1791, his life was spared by Pope Pius VI, who condemned him to spend the rest of his days in solitary confinement. Cagliostro was sent to San Leo, where he died four years later, in a tiny, dank dungeon (into which he had been thrown from above; his food and water arrived the same way); all he could see through the barred window was a church, and all he could hear was the sound of church bells—a terrible sentence indeed for a man who valued his freedom above all else and who was an avowed atheist.

A pleasant walk leads c. 2km north of San Leo to the **convent of Sant'Igne**, founded by St Francis in 1213 and with a lovely Gothic cloister; 'Igne' derives from *ignis*, fire, because of the comforting blaze which miraculously sprang up on this spot to light and warm the saint during a storm.

TALAMELLO

Talamello (*map C, C4*) stands opposite San Leo, on the other side of the Marecchia river, on a crest of Mt Aquilone. The name of this delightful little town derives from *thalamos*, Greek for 'secluded chamber', a reference to the numerous caves carved into the limestone tufa. In the central Piazza Garibaldi, with its lovely fountain, is the church of **San Lorenzo**, with a Giottesque painted Crucifix attributed to Giovanni da Rimini. It attracts many pilgrims, especially on Whit Monday, when it is carried through the streets.

At Via Saffi 341 is the **Museo Gualtieri** (*for opening times, T: 0541 920036 or 0541 922893, www.gualtierimuseum.it*), with a collection of paintings by the Paris-based artist Fernando Gualtieri (b. 1919), whose family was from Talamello. His oeuvre includes still-lifes, naïf city scenes, Japanese landscapes and portraits.

At the town cemetery is the '**Cella'** (*normally open, or T: 0541 922893*), a small chamber entirely frescoed by Antonio Alberti in 1437, with charming pictures of saints, angels, the *Nativity* and the *Resurrection*.

NOVAFELTRIA AND MAIOLO

Novafeltria (*map C, B4–C4*) is one of the most important towns of the Montefeltro, famous for its summer fairs, which once attracted merchants from all Italy. The central Piazza Vittorio Emanuele, with an elegant 19th-century fountain, has been the market place for over 1,000 years, and the weekly market still takes place every Monday.

East of Novafeltria is the steep conical hill of Maiolo (624m), with the ruins of a castle poised dramatically on the pointed top and the houses of the village of Serra di Maioletto on the hillside. The town of Maiolo on the northern slope was carried away by a landslide in 1700, and now the town centre is at nearby Serra di Maiolo, known as Capoluogo. For centuries Maiolo was a rival to San Leo and was bitterly contested by the Malatesta and the Montefeltro. It is famous for its bread, made with a particular type of wheat. Old wood-fired stone ovens are still in use for the baking.

SANT'AGATA FELTRIA

Under the looming Monte Ercole, is Sant'Agata Feltria (*map C, B4*) is instantly recognisable by its picturesque castle. It was an important medieval fortress belonging to the Malatesta and the Montefeltro families, and finally seat of the Fregoso, an aristocratic family from Genoa, who claimed it through marriage.

Just south of the town is the convent church of **San Girolamo** (1568), with a lovely *Madonna with Sts Jerome and Christina* by Pietro da Cortona (1640) over the main altar. In the central Piazza Garibaldi is the cherry-pink Palazzone with a little portico, built by the Fregoso family in 1605 and now the Town Hall. It encloses one of the oldest opera houses in Italy, **Teatro Mariani** (1723; *www.teatromariani. it*), built of wood and exquisitely decorated with *trompe l'oeil* lace curtains in front of the boxes. Continuing up the steep Via Vittorio Emanuele, you reach the **Rocca Fregoso** (Francesco di Giorgio Martini) high on the rock and with an inaccessible tower (*request visit at the Tourist Office, T: 0 541 848022*). Inside is the civic museum with manuscripts of the 15th–19th centuries, antique furniture, 16th-century detached frescoes and displays on alchemy and tailoring.

PENNABILLI

Pennabilli (*map C, B4*), richly colourful and peaceful, was formed in 1330 by the union of two fortified villages, Penna and Billi. After belonging first to the Medici, then the Malatesta and then to the Montefeltro, in the 16th century it became the seat of the bishop of San Leo and was declared a city. It lies between two peaks, Roccione (once Penna; the castle has disappeared) and Rupe (once Billi; a few ruined walls and a Crucifix are still there).

Via Roma leads up under the impressive, decrepit 16th-century monastery of the Suore Agostiniane on the left—once the castle of the Lucis family and donated by them to a cloistered order of nuns (who still live there)—to the central **Piazza Vittorio Emanuele**, with the 15th-century Palazzo della Ragione and the Loggia dei Mercanti built by the Medici, and the 16th-century cathedral; in the centre is the Fontana della Pace, the fountain erected in 1350 to celebrate the peace between Penna and Billi. The ancient Via Carboni leads up to the Roccione, through the oldest part of the city, passing through two gates, Porta Carboni (1474) and Porta Malatesta (13th century).

On the right is the side of the church of Sant'Agostino, or **Santuario della Madonna delle Grazie**, housing a museum of objects relating to the cult of the Virgin Mary. The church was built in two parts, one in the 15th century and the other in the 17th. The organ is signed and dated 1587. Over the north altar is the much-venerated 14th-century fresco of the Madonna. Close by, in the old Palazzo Bocchi, is the magnificent **Museo Diocesano A. Bergamaschi** (*open Thur 9.30– 12.30, Fri and Sun 3–6.30, Sat 9.30–12.30 & 3–6.30; T: 0541 913750*), with paintings (including works by Giovanni Francesco Guerrieri and Carlo Cignani), vases from Casteldurante, furniture and Church items.

Pennabilli attracts many artists, some of whom become permanent residents; one of these, Tonino Guerra (Fellini's favourite screenwriter; d. 2012), created a series of *Luoghi dell'Anima* (*those inside buildings can be visited daily 9–7; T: 0541 928578*), best described as places for reflection that awaken emotions. For example, in the centre of Pennabilli, in Piazza San Filippo, is the **Orto dei Frutti Dimenticati**, or 'Orchard of Forgotten Fruits', once the kitchen garden of a convent, with a mulberry planted by the Dalai Lama in 1994 and an orchard with about 80 fruit trees: rare varieties of plums, cherries, apples and pears once frequently grown in the Apennines but without the intervention of Tonino, destined to disappear from the face of the earth. Along the streets you will see many different sundials, inspired by famous works of art; here and there, Tonino's verses give new significance to commonplace things.

At no. 1 Piazza Garibaldi, at the foot of the Roccione hill, is the fascinating science museum, **Mateureka** (*for opening times, see www.mateureka.it*), with hundreds of objects illustrating the history of calculus and mathematics, from the earliest times to the present day—the 4,500-year-old Sumerian nail to the latest robotics.

Viale dei Tigli joins Roccione to Rupe, or Penna to Billi. At no. 5/a is the **Museo Naturalistico** (*www.parcosimone.it*), dedicated to local flora and the fauna.

THE SMALLER TOWNS PRACTICAL TIPS

INFORMATION OFFICES

Brisighella: *Via Naldi 2, T: 0546 81166, brisighella.org*. Branch offices are open in summer at Santarcangelo di Romagna (*Via Cesare Battisti 5*) and at Verucchio (*Piazza Malatesta 15*). There is a tourist office in Bagnacavallo (Piazza della Libertà 4) which also serves Lugo (*T: 0545 280898, romagnadeste.it*). Imola and Cesena also have information offices (*T: 0542 602207, iat@comune.imola.bo.it and turismo.comune.cesena.fe.it*). In San Leo the information office is in Palazzo Mediceo on Piazza Dante (*T: 0541 916306*). Pennabilli's tourist office is on Piazza Garibaldi (*pennabilliturismo.it*).

GETTING AROUND

• **By air:** Miramare Airport (c. 6km south of Rimini).
• **By rail:** Bagnacavallo and Lugo are on a branch line reached by frequent services from Ravenna in 20–30mins.

Imola is on the main Adriatic railway line between Bologna and Rimini (services from Bologna in under half an hour). Brisighella is on the pretty single-track branch line across the Apennines from Florence, with its station just a few minutes from Faenza. Cesena is on the main Adriatic line (reached in 50mins from Bologna and 1hr 10mins from Rimini), and also Sant'Archangelo di Romagna has a station on this line (slow trains only), just before Rimini.
• **By bus:** Verucchio is served by bus from Sant'Arcangelo di Romagna, and there are buses to Cesena from Rimini (*see startromagna.it*). START Romagna also connects Rimini to Novafeltria, Pennabilli, San Leo and Sant'Agata Feltria.

WHERE TO STAY

BAGNACAVALLO (*map C, B2*)
€€ **Palazzo Baldini**. A pleasant *agriturismo* in a former 16th-century

hunting lodge built at the end of the 15th century, with just five bedrooms and a restaurant. A short way outside the town. *Via Boncellino 170, T: 345 716 3615 or 0545 61610, palazzobaldini.it.*

BRISIGHELLA (*map C, A3*)
€ **La Meridiana**. Calm and quiet, with a shady garden on the river. Closed Nov–March. *Viale delle Terme 19, T: 0546 81590, lameridianahotel.it.*

NOVAFELTRIA (*map C, B4–C4*)
€€ **Corte del Sasso**. Situated in a quiet village, with four beautiful rooms, B&B with dinner on request. *Via Cà Gianessi 47, T: 0541 921742, cortedelsasso.it.*
€€ **B&B Pietra Salara**. Country location, beautiful villa with garden, 3 comfortable rooms, pool; help offered for trekking and gathering medicinal herbs. Closed winter. *Via Pietra Salara, Secchiano 20, T: 0541 912344, pietrasalara.com.*

PENNABILLI (*map C, B4*)
€€€€ **Duca del Montefeltro**. A new hotel, much nicer inside than out, with 42 ample, comfortable rooms and suites, parquet floors, fitness centre with small pool, restaurant and garage. *Via Aldo Moro 12, T: 0541 161 3400, hotelducamontefeltro.it.*

SAN LEO (*map C, C4*)
€€ **Castello**. ■ Small family-run hotel in ancient building next to the Pieve. 14 rooms, restaurant, car park, bus stop close by. *Piazza Dante Alighieri 11/12, T: 0541 916214, hotelristorantecastellosanleo.com.*
€€ **Locanda San Leone**. B&B in a 13th-century water-mill, set in an old stone-built village close to Sant'Igne, with 7 beautiful rooms, garden, pool

and car park. *Via Sant'Antimo 102, T: 0541 912194, locandasanleone.it.*

RESTAURANTS

BAGNACAVALLO (*map C, B2*)
€ **Celti Centurioni**. An organic farm just over 1 kilometre from Bagnacavallo which prepares food to order (it is necessary to book in advance). *Via Crocetta 10, T: 0545 937382, celticenturioni.it.*

BRISIGHELLA (*map C, A3*)
€€ **Cantina del Bonsignore**. Very nice restaurant in the basement of a historic building; good selection of regional wines associated with regional and creative food. Closed Wed and midday. *Via Recuperati 4a, T: 0546 81889.*
€€ **Infinito**. Elegant restaurant with garden and terrace, specialising in regional and creative cooking. Closed Mon and mid-day from Tue to Fri. *Via del Trebbio 12/14, T: 0546 80437.*
€ **La Grotta**. Very good regional cuisine at excellent prices. Closed Wed in winter. *Via Metelli 1, T: 0546 81488, ristorante-lagrotta.it.*
€ **Trattoria di Strada Casale**. Good country restaurant outside the village, offering good service, great wine and excellent regional food. Closed Wed and midday (except Sat and Sun). *Via Statale 22, T: 0546 88054.*

CASTROCARO TERME (*map C, B3*)
€€ **Trattoria Bolognesi**. Historic establishment (formerly La Frasca) recently moved to this fine old building in the town centre. Award-winning cuisine, excellent interpretations of regional recipes. CLosed Mon. *Piazzetta San Nicolò 2, T: 0543 769119, trattoriabolognesi.it.*

CESENA (map C, B3)

€ **Cerina**. *Trattoria* specialising in traditional regional dishes. Closed Mon evening, Tues and Aug. *Via San Vittore 936, T: 0547 661115.*

€€ **Micheletta**. The oldest *osteria* in town: excellent traditional dishes, with organic ingredients. Closed Sun. *Via Strinati 41, T: 0547 24691, osteriamicheletta.com.*

CESENATICO (map C, C3)

€€€ **Vittorio**. One of the best fish restaurants on the Costa Romagnola. Closed lunchtime Tues and Wed. *Via Andrea Doria 3, Onda Marina harbour, T: 0547 672588, vittorioristorante.it.*

NOVAFELTRIA (map C, B4–C4)

€€ **Da Marchesi**. In a hamlet along the road from Novafeltria to Perticara, a simple restaurant specialising in pasta dishes and meat, with fungi and truffles in season. Also comfortable rooms. Closed Tues. *Via Cà Gianessi 7, T: 0541 920148.*

€ **Trattoria Da Checco**. Old tavern serving excellent gnocchi, ravioli and lasagne; try the rich *crema catalana* for dessert, and drink the local Sangiovese. Closed Thur; July–Aug open every day. *Piazza Roma 3, T: 0541 921642.*

PENNABILLI (map C, B4)

€€€ **Il Piastrino**. Elegant restaurant in the Begni park, where Riccardo and Claudia prepare exquisite and original dishes; good wine list. Closed Tues and Wed. *Parco Begni 9, T: 0541 928106, piastrino.it.*

SAN LEO (map C, C4)

€€€ **La Corte di Berengario II**. Bright tavern serving excellent local cuisine with good house wines. Closed Tues. *Via Michele Rosa 74, T: 0541 916145, osterialacorte.it.*

€ **Il Bettolino**. ■ Friendly coffee bar downstairs, *trattoria* upstairs (pizza in the evenings); try the delicious *ravioli con formaggio di fossa* (with pit-matured cheese) followed by *tagliata con lardo di Colonnata*, sliced steak dressed with pit-matured lard (scrumptious). They also make their own mascarpone. Closed Wed. *Via Montefeltro 6, T: 0541 916265.*

SANT'AGATA FELTRIA (map C, B4)

€€ **Trattoria Bossari**. Charming old-fashioned *trattoria* where pensioners spend the afternoon playing cards. Wonderful pasta; try also the *lombo al vapore*, steamed pork, served with fungi and truffles. Closed Mon. *Via San Girolamo 2, T: 0541 929697.*

TALAMELLO (map C, C4)

€ **Da Tapir**. Very simple bar-*trattoria*, no menu, order what you see everybody else eating; perhaps a platter of ham and cheese with hot flatbread, or a huge bowl of steamed green beans, to dress with oil and balsamic vinegar. Local wine. Closed Thur evening. *Piazza Garibaldi 30, T: 0541 920430.*

FESTIVALS & EVENTS

A delightful medieval pageant is held by candlelight in June and July in the little town of **Brisighella**.

The racetrack at **Imola** hosts numerous motoring events throughout the year including Formula One championships.

In **Novafeltria** the *Notte dei Cento Catini*, celebrations for the feast of St John and the summer solstice, include the positioning of bowls of flower petals along the streets, a witches' dance, and impromptu open-air entertainment, 23–24 June.

Buskers from all over the world congregate in **Pennabilli** for *Artisti in Piazza*. They perform in the streets and squares and thousands of spectators flock here each year, June (*www. artistiinpiazza.com*). Antique Market, well-known open-air exhibition and sale, July (*www.pennabilliantiquariato. net*).

Sant'Agata Feltria holds a white truffle fair every Sun in Oct and a Christmas Market, every Sun in Dec.

In Talamello the *Festa del Crocifisso* sees the town's famous Crucifix take to the streets on Whit Monday. *Fiera del Formaggio di Fossa*, festival of the famous pit-matured cheese (*see below*) a, when the pits are ceremonially opened, first two Sundays in Nov.

LOCAL SPECIALITIES

Brisighella is known for the quality of its olive oil. The inhabitants of Sant'Agata are skilled at finding white fungi, called *trifole*, in the surrounding woods; the season is Oct–early Nov. Talamello is famous for its cheese nd Sant'Agata Feltria for its saffron.

AMBRA DI TALAMELLO

Among the delicious local cheeses is *formaggio di fossa*, pit-matured cheese from Talamello, made with a mixture of cow's and sheep's milk, rightly described as 'amber' and protected by the *Denominazione d'Origine Protetta* label. In early August the cheeses are wrapped in cloths and buried in straw-lined pits or caves, carved into the limestone, and the entrances are cemented over. In November the pits are opened and the cheeses are recovered and cleaned, simply by scraping with a spoon. The results are rather deformed in shape, but with superb consistency and flavour, having lost all excess liquid. This tradition developed with the necessity of hiding various foodstuffs from the surprise attacks of bandits; now it provides a true gastronomic delight.

Practical Information

PLANNING YOUR TRIP

WHEN TO GO
The best time to visit Emilia Romagna is May–June or September–October. The earlier spring and later autumn months are often wet and chilly, with strong northerly winds. The height of the summer is unpleasantly hot, especially in the Po Valley and the larger towns. Seaside resorts are crowded from mid-June to early September; before and after this season many hotels are closed and the beaches are practically deserted.

DISABLED TRAVELLERS
All new public buildings are obliged to provide facilities for the disabled. Historic buildings are more difficult to convert, and access difficulties still exist. Hotels that cater for the disabled are indicated in tourist board lists. Airports and railway stations provide assistance, and certain trains are equipped to transport wheelchairs. Access to town centres is allowed for cars with disabled drivers or passengers, and special parking places are reserved for them. For further information, contact the tourist board in the city of interest.

GETTING AROUND

BY CAR
The easiest way to tour northern Italy is by car. Regardless of whether you are driving your own car or a hired vehicle, Italian law requires you to carry a valid driving licence. You must also keep a red triangle in the car (you can hire one from ACI for a minimal charge and returned it at the border).

As 80 percent of goods transported travel by road, lorries pose a constant hazard, and the degree of congestion in even the smallest towns defies imagination.

Certain customs differ radically from those of Britain or America. Pedestrians have the right of way at zebra crossings, although you're taking your life in your hands if you step into the street without looking. Unless otherwise indicated, cars entering a road from the right are given precedence. Trams and trains always have right of way. If an oncoming driver flashes his headlights, it means he is proceeding and not giving you precedence. In towns, Italian drivers frequently change lanes without warning. They also tend to ignore pedestrian crossings.

ROADS IN ITALY

Italy's motorways (*autostrade*) are indicated by green signs or, near the entrance ramps, by large boards of overhead lights. All are toll-roads. At the entrance to motorways, the two directions are indicated by the name of the most important town (and not by the nearest town), which can be momentarily confusing. Dual-carriageways are called *superstrade* (also indicated by green signs). Italy has an excellent network of secondary highways (*strade statali, regionali* or *provinciali*, indicated by blue signs marked SS, SR or SP; on maps simply by a number).

PARKING

Many cities have closed their centres to traffic (except for residents). Access is allowed to hotels and for the disabled. It is always advisable to leave your car in a guarded car park, though with a bit of effort it is almost always possible to find a place to park free of charge, away from the town centre. However, to do so overnight is not advisable. Always lock your car when parked, and never leave anything of value inside it. Many car parks operate the '*disco orario*' system, which allows you to park free for 2hrs. You indicate the time that you parked on the adjustable disc. Hire cars are usually fitted with a disc in their windscreens. They are also available at petrol stations and tobacconists. Many hotels allow special access for customers' cars to restricted central streets.

BY TRAIN

Information on rail links is given in individual chapters. The Italian Railways (Trenitalia) have good, cheap services and an excellent website: *trenitalia.com*. Tickets must be validated before travel at the machines on the platforms.

BY BUS

Information on regional bus services is given in each individual section. Services can be infrequent, sometimes only in the early morning or later afternoon, but most places are served by their regional networks.

TAXIS

These are hired from ranks or by telephone; there are no cruising cabs. Before engaging a taxi, it is advisable to make sure it has a meter in working order. Fares vary from city to city but are generally cheaper than London taxis, though considerably more expensive than New York taxis. No tip is expected. Supplements are charged for late-night journeys and for luggage. There is a heavy surcharge when the destination is outside the town limits (ask roughly how much the fare is likely to be).

ACCOMMODATION

HOTELS

A selection of hotels, chosen on the basis of character or location, is given at the end of each chapter. They are classified as follows: €€€€ (€900 or over), €€€ (€350–900), €€ (€150–300) or € (€150 or under). It is advisable to book well in advance, especially between May and October; if you cancel the booking with at least 72 hours' notice you can claim back part or all of your deposit. Service charges are included in the rates. By law breakfast is an optional extra, although a lot of hotels will include it in the room price. When booking, always specify if you want breakfast or not. If you are staying in a hotel in a town, it is often more fun to go round the corner to the nearest café for breakfast.

FARM STAYS—*AGRITURISMO*

The short-term rental of space in villas and farmhouses (*agriturismo*) is an alternative form of accommodation. Terms vary greatly, from bed-and-breakfast to self-contained flats. For travellers with their own transport, or for families, this as an excellent (and usually cheap) way of visiting the Italian countryside. Some farms require a minimum stay. Cultural or recreational activities, such as horse-riding, are sometimes also provided. Information is supplied by local tourist offices, or visit the official Emilia Romagna *agriturismo* website (*agriturismo.emilia-romagna.it*).

RELIGIOUS INSTITUTIONS

Religious institutions sometimes offer simple but comfortable accommodation at reasonable prices. Monastery Stays (*http://www.monasterystays.com/*) is a good website through which to make bookings.

BLUE GUIDES RECOMMENDED

Hotels, restaurants and *osterie* that are particularly good choices in their category—in terms of excellence, location, charm, value for money or the quality of the experience they provide—carry the Blue Guides Recommended sign: ▬. All these establishments have been visited and selected by our authors, editors or contributors as places they have particularly enjoyed and would be happy to recommend to others. To keep our entries up-to-date, reader feedback is essential: please do not hesitate to contact us (*blueguides. com*) with any views, corrections or suggestions.

LANGUAGE

Even a few words of Italian are a great advantage in Italy, where any attempt to speak the language is appreciated. Local dialects vary greatly, but even where dialect is universally used, nearly everybody can speak and understand standard Italian.

Double consonants call for special care as each must be sounded. Consonants are pronounced roughly as in English with the following exceptions:

c and **cc**	before e and i have the sound of **ch** in chess
ch	before e and i has the sound of **k**
g and **gg**	before e and i are always soft, like **j** in jelly
gh	always hard, like **g** in get
gl	nearly always like **lli** in million (there are a few exceptions, for example, *negligere,* where it is pronounced as in English)
gn	like **ny** in lanyard
gu and **qu**	always like **gw** and **kw**
j	like **y** in you
s	voiceless like **s** in six, except when it occurs between two vowels, when it is pronounced like the English **z** or the s in rose
sc	before e and i is pronounced like **sh** in ship
ss	always voiceless
z and **zz**	usually pronounced like **ts**, but occasionally have the sound of **dz** before a long vowel

ADDITIONAL INFORMATION

CRIME AND PERSONAL SECURITY

Pickpocketing is a widespread problem in towns all over Italy: it is always advisable not to carry valuables, and be particularly careful on public transport. Crime should be reported at once to the police or the local *carabinieri* office (found in every town and small village). A statement has to be given in order to get a document confirming loss or damage (essential for insurance claims). Interpreters are provided. For all emergencies, T: 113. The switchboard will co-ordinate the help you need. For medical assistance: T: 118.

OPENING TIMES

The opening times of museums and monuments are given in the text, though they often change without warning. National museums and monuments are usually closed on Mondays. Archaeological sites generally open at 9 and close at dusk.

Some museums are closed on the main public holidays: 1 January, Easter, 1 May, 15 August and 25 December. Smaller museums have have suspended regular hours altogether and are now open by appointment only. Their telephone numbers are included in the text. Entrance fees vary. EU citizens under 18 and over 65 are entitled to free admission to national museums and monuments but you need to provide ID.

Churches open early in the morning (often for 6 o'clock Mass), and most are closed during the middle of the day (12–3, 4 or 5), although cathedrals and larger churches may be open throughout daylight hours. Smaller churches and oratories are often open only in the early morning, but the key can usually be found by inquiring locally. The sacristan will also show closed chapels and crypts, and a small tip should be given. Some churches now ask that sightseers do not enter during a service, but normally visitors may do so, provided they are silent and do not approach the altar in use. At all times they are expected to cover their legs and arms, and generally dress with decorum. An entrance fee is often charged for admission to treasuries, cloisters, bell-towers and so on. Lights (operated by coins) have been installed in many churches to illuminate frescoes and altarpieces. In Holy Week most of the images are covered and are on no account shown.

Shops generally open Mon–Sat 8.30/9–1 and 3.30/4–7.30/8, although larger stores and shops is bigger towns do not close for lunch.

PHARMACIES

Pharmacies (*farmacie*) are usually open Mon–Fri 9–1 & 4–7.30 or 8. A few are open also on Saturdays, Sundays and holidays (listed on the door of every pharmacy). In all towns there is also at least one pharmacy open at night (also shown on the door of every pharmacy).

PUBLIC HOLIDAYS

Italian national holidays are as follows:

1 January	15 August (Assumption)
Easter Sunday and Easter Monday	1 November (All Saints' Day)
25 April (Liberation Day)	8 December (Immaculate Conception)
1 May (Labour Day)	25 December (Christmas Day)
2 June (Festa della Repubblica)	26 December (St Stephen)

Each town keeps its patron saint's day as a holiday.

TELEPHONES

For all calls in Italy, dial the city code (for instance, 51 for Bologna), then the telephone number. For international and intercontinental calls, dial 00 before the telephone number. The country code for Italy is +39.

TIPPING

Service charges are normally included and tipping in Italy is not routinely expected. It is normal to round up the bill and leave a few coins in appreciation.

FOOD & DRINK

Italian food is usually good and inexpensive. Generally speaking, the least pretentious *ristorante* (restaurant), *trattoria* (small restaurant) or *osteria* (inn or tavern) provides the best value. A selection of restaurants is given at the end of each chapter. Prices are categorised as follows: €€€€ (€80 or more per head), €€€ (€60–80), €€ (€40–50) and € (€30 or under). Many places are considerably cheaper at midday. It is always a good idea to reserve.

Prices on the menu do not include a cover charge (shown separately, usually at the bottom of the page), which is added to the bill. The service charge (*servizio*) is now almost always automatically added at the end of the bill; tipping is therefore not strictly necessary, but a few euro are appreciated. Note that many simpler establishments do not offer a written menu.

BARS AND CAFÉS

Bars and cafés are open from early morning to late at night and serve numerous varieties of excellent refreshments that are usually taken standing up. As a rule, you must pay the cashier first, then present your receipt to the barman in order to get served. It is customary to leave a small tip for the barman. If you sit at a table the charge is usually higher, and you will be given waiter service (so don't pay first). However, some simple bars have a few tables that can be used with no extra charge, and it is always best to ask, before ordering, whether there is waiter service or not.

COFFEE

Italy is considered to have the best coffee in Europe. *Caffè* or *espresso* (black coffee) can be ordered *alto* or *lungo* (diluted), *corretto* (with a liquor), or *macchiato* (with a dash of hot milk). A *cappuccino* is an *espresso* with more hot milk than a *caffè macchiato* and is generally considered a breakfast drink. A glass of hot milk with a dash of coffee in it, called *latte macchiato* is another early-morning favourite. In summer, many drink *caffè freddo* (iced coffee). The city of Trieste is particularly known for its coffee and many historic importers have or have had their warehouses there.

SNACKS

Gelato (ice cream) is always best from a *gelateria* where it is made on the spot. *Panini* (sandwiches) are made with a variety of cold meats, fish, cheeses, or vegetables, particularly *melanzane* (aubergines) or *zucchine* (courgettes) fried in vegetable oil; vegetarians may also ask for a simple sandwich of *insalata e pomodoro* (lettuce and tomato). *Pizze* (a popular and cheap food throughout Italy), *arancini* (rice croquettes with cheese or meat inside), and other snacks are served in a *pizzeria*, *rosticceria* and *tavola calda*. A *vinaio* often sells wine by the glass and simple food for very reasonable prices. Sandwiches are made up on request at *pizzicherie* and *alimentari* (grocery shops), and *fornai* (bakeries) often sell individual pizzas, focaccias, *schiacciate* (bread with oil and salt) and cakes.

PASTA

Pasta is an essential part of most meals throughout Italy. A distinction is drawn between *pasta comune* (spaghetti, rigatoni and so on) produced industrially and made of a simple flour and water paste, and *pasta all'uovo* (tortellini, ravioli and so on), made with egg.

Pasta comes in countless forms. An ordinary Italian supermarket usually stocks about 50 different varieties, but some experts estimate that there are more than 600 shapes in all. The differences of shape translate into differences of flavour, even when the pasta is made from the same dough, or by the same manufacturer. The reason for this is that the relation between the surface area and the weight of the pasta varies from one shape to another, causing the sauce to adhere in different ways and to different degrees. Even without a sauce, experts claim to perceive considerable differences in flavour, because the different shapes cook in different ways. Northern Italy is home to *pasta fresca*, usually home-made, from a dough composed of flour, eggs, and just a little water.

REGIONAL CUISINE

Emilia Romagna stands on the border between the 'land of butter' and the 'land of olive oil'—between the European tradition of the north and the Mediterranean culture of the south. Ostensibly one region, Emilia Romagna is in reality two entities with very different characters, histories and traditions. There is an 'inland' part— Emilia—comprising the five provinces of Bologna, Modena, Reggio Emilia, Parma and Piacenza, and an Adriatic seaboard—Romagna—with the provinces of Ferrara, Ravenna, Forlì and Rimini. *Emiliani* and *romagnoli* are different by temperament and these character differences reappear at the table. Emilian cuisine, which glides along softly and persuasively on flavours tempered in the amalgam of delicious butter and delicate sauces, becomes increasingly sharp and aggressive as one crosses the invisible border of Romagna.

A sampling of appetisers might include *belecott* (boiled ground pork spiced with cinnamon, cloves and nutmeg, from the area around Ravenna), *erbazzone* or *scarpazzone* (a simple country dish popular throughout the region, made with boiled spinach sautéed with spiced lard, mixed with parmesan cheese and egg, then baked in a crust) and the famous *piada* or *piadina* of Romagna (which bears a tell-tale resemblance to the unleavened breads of Greece and the Middle East: made with flour, water and lard, it is often stuffed to make a fold-round sandwich).

First courses not to be missed include *anolini di parma* (fresh egg pasta stuffed with braised beef sauce, breadcrumbs, parmesan cheese, egg and other ingredients, usually served in broth), *brodetto alla romagnola* (a rich fish-and-tomato soup), *lasagne alla bolognese* (the classic dish of oven-baked pasta squares, meat sauce, white sauce and parmesan cheese) and *pasticcio alla ferrarese* (a sumptuous legacy of the Este court: macaroni or other short pasta in a pie crust with meat sauce, white sauce and mushrooms). *Tortellini in brodo* is a very popular dish: fresh stuffed pasta floating in meat broth.

Characteristic sweets are *buricchi* (an invention of the Emilian Jewish community: little square pastries filled with almonds and sugar), *erbazzone dolce* (an interesting twist on the classic *erbazzone* described above: the beet greens are mixed with ricotta cheese, sugar, almonds and other ingredients) and *torta nera* (a rich Modenese cake made with almonds, sugar, butter, chunks of chocolate, cocoa, eggs, coffee and sometimes rum).

WINE

Most Italian wines take their names from the geographical area in which they are produced, the blend of grapes of which they are made, and the estate on which the grapes were grown. The best come in numbered bottles and are marked

DOC (*di origine controllata*). This is Italy's *appellation controlée*, which specifies maximum yields per vine, geographical boundaries within which grapes must be grown, permitted grape varieties and production techniques. Superior even to DOC is the DOCG (*di origine controllata e garantita*), where the denomination is also guaranteed. This is not to say that DOCG wines are automatically superior to any other. The plethora of regulation inevitably runs the risk of sclerosis, and winemakers wanting to experiment with alternative grape varieties or vinification techniques found themselves barred from the DOC or DOCG classifications, and had to label their vintages IGT (*vino da tavola con indicazione geografica tipica*). IGT denotes a vin de pays, a wine of special regional character. This does not necessarily mean that an IGT wine is of lesser quality than a DOC. Indeed, in some cases it may be particularly interesting and many producers, frustrated by the inflexibility of the rules, have chosen to exit the DOC system. Simple *vino da tavola* is table wine. It can be excellent, but the quality is not guaranteed.

ORDERING WINES

Red wines are *vini rossi* on the wine list; white wines, *vini bianchi*; rosés, *chiaretti* or *rosati*. Dry wines are *secchi*; sweet wines, *amabili* or *dolci*. *Vino novello* is new wine. *Moscato* and *passito* is wine made from grapes that have been left on the vine or dried before pressing.

When ordering, remember also that many DOC wines come in versions labelled *spumante, liquoroso, recioto* and *amarone*. Spumante is the Italian equivalent of champagne and uses some of the same methods to obtain its foamy (*spumante*) effervescence. It is much bubblier than sparkling whites such as Prosecco, which is popular both before meals and as a light dinner wine. *Liquoroso* means 'liqueur-like' and usually refers to dessert wines. The term *recioto* is applied to wines made from grapes that have been dried like raisins; *amarone* is the dry, mellow version of *recioto*.

Emilia Romagna is traditionally considered the homeland of sparkling wines, where quantity triumphs over quality. This judgement is not altogether fair, for the vast and varied market offers, if not great wines, excellent quality/price ratios. For a light and refreshing aperitif, it is difficult to do better than sparkling Pignoletto (*Pignoletto frizzante*), fruity and crisp.

The only DOCG is Albana di Romagna, a white made in the provinces of Ravenna, Forlì and Bologna. It is vinified *secco, amabile, dolce* and *passito*. Albana secco is dry and somewhat tannic, warm and harmonic, good with fish, soups and egg dishes. Albana amabile has a characteristic fragrant nose and is good with cakes and fruit.

The DOC Colli Bolognesi, which also appears on labels as Monte San Pietro or Castelli Medioevali, covers seven or eight kinds of grape, and is often subdivided by territory.

The best-known wine of Emilia is Lambrusco, a fresh, fruity, dry or sparkling red best with heavy meat sauces and pork dishes. For a non-sparkling everyday red, Sangiovese is popular and widely available. Umberto Cesari (*www.umbertocesari.it*) is a reliable producer.

Index

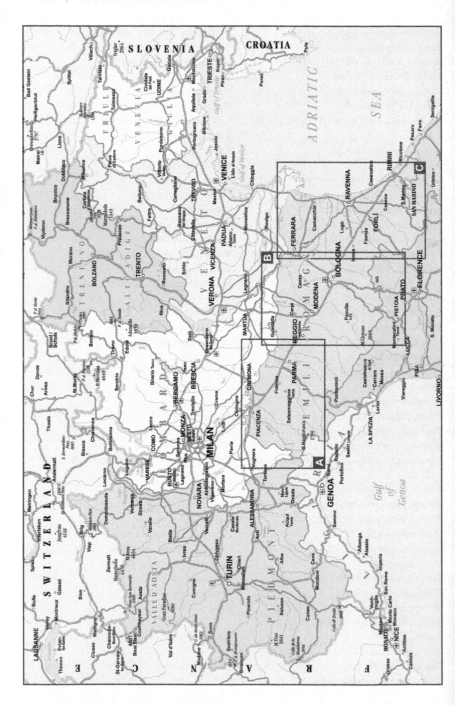

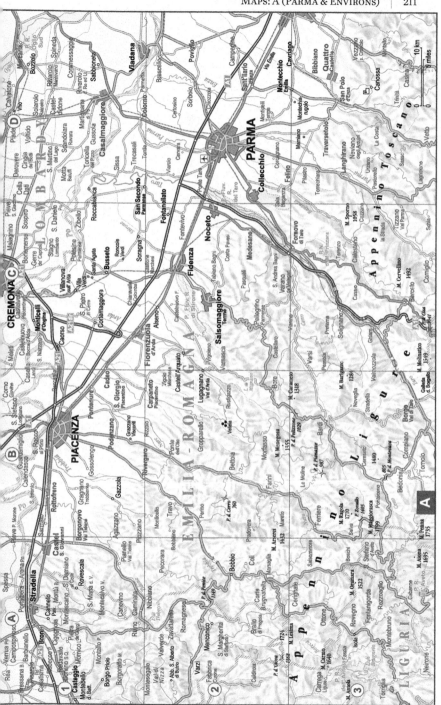

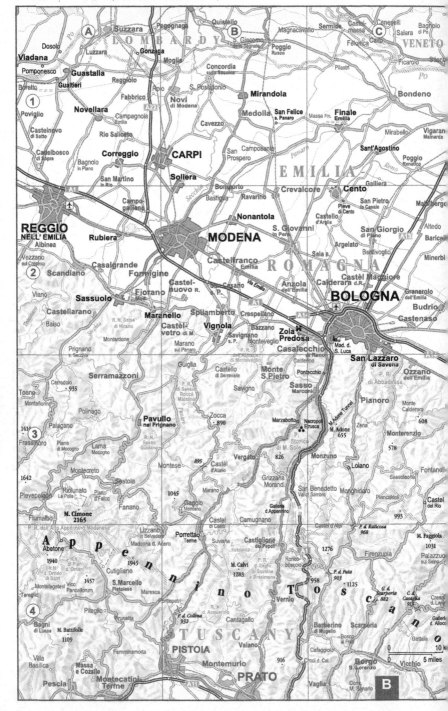